Lawyer storytelling: a sacred craft.

Miller, Nelson P., ed.

Published by:

Crown Management LLC – August 2017

1527 Pineridge Drive
Grand Haven, MI 49417
USA

ISBN: 978-0-9980601-7-0

Lawyer Storytelling:

A Sacred Craft

Nelson P. Miller, ed.

In tribute to the passions of those whom the law attracts and fascinates.

Table of Contents

Editor's Introduction

The minds of those whom the law attracts are fertile zones. For proof, consider former criminal-defense lawyer and state representative John Grisham, whose fiction works including *The Firm* have sold over 250 million copies worldwide while spawning both films and television series. While Grisham is definitely the current dean of lawyer fiction writers, we shouldn't so quickly forget former Assistant U.S. Attorney Scott Turow, also recently a partner at the world's largest law firm Dentons. Law students still today buy thousands of copies of Turow's autobiographical *One L*, although we know Turow just as well for his acclaimed fiction works including *Presumed Innocent* and *Personal Injuries*.

Also consider the not-a-household-name Erle Stanley Gardner who wrote no fewer than eighty-two novels featuring the definitely household-name Los Angeles defense attorney Perry Mason. Oh, by the way, actor Raymond Burr who famously played Perry Mason in the television series, and also Ironsides in that television series, was *not* a lawyer, even though he played lawyers. Burr did, however, fund and dedicate a student scholarship at Western Michigan University Law School where I teach and administer. We give the award at Honors Convocations every term, each time briefly recounting Burr's famous-but-fading roles and generous personal character.

Many other current or former lawyers do quite well as fiction writers. Notable among them is Lisa Scottoline, best known for the novels *Everywhere that Mary Went* and *Final Appeal*, and who has written many other novels including a series about an all-female law firm. Consider also Meg Gardiner, at one time a Los Angeles lawyer

1

and writing instructor to law students, whose *Evan Delaney* thrillers earned her the highest praise of no less than Stephen King. Former town attorney David Drake has earned a substantial following as a fantasy and science-fiction writer. One-time lawyer Marjorie Liu has written the *Dirk & Steele* paranormal romances and, as if that were not enough, nearly two-dozen issues of Marvel's *Astonishing X-Men* comics. Natural-resources lawyer Robert Buettner pens the *Jason Wander* science-fiction series in which the hero battles aliens from Ganymede. The list of distinguished lawyer fiction writers goes on.

A personal favorite, though, is Michigan Supreme Court Justice John D. Voelker who under the pen name Robert Traver wrote *Anatomy of a Murder.* Voelker based the best-selling novel, a crime-and-courtroom drama today better known for its film adaptation of the same name, on a murder case that he defended while in law practice a few years before the novel's publication. The 1959 film was Hollywood's first mainstream effort exploring sexual assault, in that respect foreshadowing the even-better-known 1962 film *To Kill a Mockingbird* based on the 1960 Atticus Finch novel by non-lawyer Harper Lee. Pick your favorite fictional lawyer: Jimmy Stewart in *Anatomy of a Murder* or Gregory Peck in *To Kill a Mockingbird?*

Lawyers make good fiction writers in part because of their writing training and practice—or in spite of it, depending on whom you ask. Law school teaches law students to write properly, concisely, clearly and analytically, all skills that help fiction writers. At WMU Law School, for instance, students must complete the three-credit Research & Writing and three-credit Advanced Writing. Many more also take the two-credit Scholarly Writing and then serve as editors on the two-credit Law Review or Law Journal (sometimes both). Students must also complete a three-credit skills course like Pre-Trial Skills involving written court papers, Trial Skills involving oral advocacy based on written scripts, or, among many other choices, Alternative Dispute Resolution involving written case summaries. Students must also complete at least three credits of a clinical experience that involves additional substantial writing.

Law students also learn to write rigorous analyses, *essays* we call them, on instant demand. Essay exams, in both finals and interim exams, quickly get students past any kind of writing block. As a result, law professors generally see vast improvement in student writing. Some students bring little writing skill. Every student leaves writing-proficient. Other students enter law school with decent writing skills but vastly improve because of the frequency and rigor of their writing challenges, and the writing instruction's quality. Some of those students become masterful technical writers. Still other students, though, bring special writing skill and experience to law school. Through law school, they both hone those skills while also vastly increasing their knowledge of human behavior in all its endeavors.

So, aspiring writers: consider law school. You will not only get substantial and skilled writing instruction, write often across a wide variety of entirely human subjects, and write on strict time demand. You will also learn a ton about human character and motivation. Beyond being a fully fascinating and fabulous intellectual challenge, law school is the greatest and most-satisfying exploration of human endeavors that one will find anywhere on the planet. You want to learn about human character, covenant, commitment, care, motivation, design, intrigue, crime, corruption, and depravity, in every familial, social, commercial, and political endeavor? Law school's your answer. Every casebook, every text, is a study in all of those things, both our greatest aspirations and greatest failures, all rolled up in one grand tortilla, which is why law school sets on fire students' passions for life.

Indeed, lawyers make good fiction writers for another reason beyond that they all completed law school. The best art imitates life. Law practice lifts decorum's curtain not only on our mundane affairs but also on the bizarre and profound. Lawyers have the richest possible fodder for fiction because they see *everything*. Try looking through a homicide file. Or an autopsy report, photographs and all. Or an engineering study on a man-made disaster. Or a probate court caseworker's abuse-and-neglect file. Or an NTSA air-crash report. Or an arson investigator's file. Or a psychological evaluation of a suspected mass murderer. Or a personal-injury client's pain journal. Or the transcript of the license-revocation hearing for a medical professional suspected of serial patient sexual assault. Or a federal agency report on conditions of sex-slave minors trafficked across international borders. You get the picture. These sorts of rich materials are the routine stuff of law practice.

What law students and lawyers must alter, modify, reform, or drop when going from legal writing to writing fiction is an open question. Much of legal writing is descriptive. Case briefs, for one example, begin with a concise statement of the facts. So may a myriad of other legal writings such as legal-research memoranda, opinion letters, case-evaluation summaries, and even contracts. Those summaries are not literary, certainly not imaginary. To the contrary, lawyers must assert only evidence-supported facts. Yet lawyers should and generally do well craft the fact section of any legal writing. Some lawyers are especially good at writing compelling, again not *fanciful* but captivating and persuasive, fact statements. Advocacy's value is often in precisely that degree of craft. Indeed, call it *literature* or *art* if you like, even if the lawyer author must cite to the trial transcript of every asserted fact.

So now you may have a better idea of why law students and lawyers can make particularly good fiction writers. Why, though, do lawyers and law students write fiction? Website biographies and autobiographies of successful lawyer authors suggest different motives. Some apparently write fiction out of need for income, such as when bearing or caring for a child, or caring for a spouse or elderly parent, suddenly keeps them at home, away from fruitful office work. We should suspect different motives, though, given the very difficult market for generating any such income from fiction. Some seem to write out of challenge, trying to prove to themselves or others that they can publish and, beyond publication, maybe amuse or entertain. Of course, some probably write out of pride, like *look at me, see how inventive I am*. Others, though, write to examine themselves, perhaps even to heal themselves, while exploring, examining, informing, and perhaps even healing the world. One suspects that these latter writers are the better ones, those whom we read with such pleasure.

If you are a law student or lawyer and haven't yet written fiction, then consider for a moment why you might do so. Writing is intensely self-reflective. You cannot write, especially write *fiction*, without deeply questioning yourself. Every fiction writer stops frequently to ask, *why am I doing this?* Because almost by definition it has no obvious, instrumental purpose, fiction has to prove its intrinsic value to the writer over and over again, with every sentence. Some of us live, at least some of the time, to create. Writing fiction is creating. Yet beyond its value simply as a time-occupying and mind-satisfying activity, writing fiction can also accomplish instrumental purposes, like helping the author recall, organize, shape, order, interpret, and understand experiences. Fiction can heal almost all by itself (although one suspects from some of Stephen King's experience that fiction can also threaten or harm nearly all by itself—watch out what demons you loose). Given the drama that lawyers encounter in law practice, lawyers may need and appreciate, more than other professionals do, fiction's healing effect.

Why, though, do readers read lawyer fiction? One reason is that courtrooms are utterly fascinating arenas, where real-life dramas get constantly played out. Trials present the perfect dramatic climax in that they are by design both a significant event unto themselves while also a deliberate look back to prior critical events. After all, courtroom look-back drama is what made so strikingly powerful the filmed novels *Anatomy of a Murder* and *To Kill a Mockingbird.* Another reason why readers love lawyer fiction is that crimes, bankruptcies, environmental spills, air crashes, other manmade disasters, and even certain divorces and paternity or custody disputes, and other things with which lawyers regularly deal, make for great stories. If confidentiality rules did not constrain them, then lawyers would have a lot of good *real-life* stories to tell. Instead, they write good, readable, fast-moving, entertaining, titillating, and lurid fiction. These real-life experiences probably inform even the fantasy and science fiction that lawyers write, as they have mine.

What makes good lawyer fiction? Good fiction of any kind involves sound character development, clear plot, compelling context, believable dialogue, emotional tension, and responsible pace, on top of the full toolbox of vocabulary, grammar, sentence and paragraph structure, punctuation, and other good-writing basics. Good *lawyer* fiction, though, involves reflecting a lawyer's technical, strategic, analytic, ethical, political, and other professional insight. Lawyers know what a preliminary examination is, why law requires it, and how lawyers strategically employ or waive such prelims. They know First Amendment and Fourth Amendment rights, why the Constitution grants those rights, and how and why government officials threaten and violate those rights. They know conflicts of interest, the motives out of which conflicts arise, and the deceptions in which the conflicted engage to conceal their interests. Lawyer fiction often involves that special knowledge. Even when it does not, as in the case of a lot of fantasy, romance, or science fiction, the special knowledge may still be at work behind the character's circumstances and reactions.

So, maybe we are doing the right thing as lawyers and law students when writing reflectively out of our law interests, commitments, and experiences. Readers seem to tell us so by reading what we write. The fiction market is always looking for the next Turow or Grisham. And lawyer authors seldom seem to regret their fiction-writing experiences, whether they garner readers or not. Lawyers and law students spur their professional development when writing fiction. Meet an especially thoughtful, engaging, and effective lawyer, and chances are that the lawyer has at least contemplated, if not attempted and completed, writing a work of fiction.

Hence, this book collecting law student, law professor, and lawyer short stories. I wanted to encourage my professional community with an opportunity to write and read more lawyer fiction. The contributors to this collection are students, graduates, and professors of Western Michigan University Thomas M. Cooley Law School. Several had already published fiction works, some of us frequently. Others of us have now done so for the first time. All of us doubtless spent abundant hours in earnest thought and effort writing these entertaining, amusing, profound, in instances surprisingly practical, and in other instances (my contribution particularly) simply baffling stories. Several did so in a special course at the law school, one enticement of which was a chance at publishing here in this book the resulting fiction. I thank the contributors deeply for their effort and for the generosity that they have shown in sharing their innermost thoughts and outermost talents. I also thank you for your interest. Please now enjoy the rich writing of some passionate lawyers and law students.

—*Nelson P. Miller, ed.*

The Smile

Mark Cooney

Here, a law professor with both substantial experience in personal-injury cases and many fiction and non-fiction publications uses a client-intake setting to illustrate the extraordinary imagination and sensitivities of the best practitioners.

She got on tiptoe to inspect his face, absently twining a mousy lock.

"That's Nick Lidstrom," I said. "Best d-man ever."

"Her daddy likes hockey," said her mother.

"Do you like hockey?" I asked. But the knick-knacked shelves wouldn't share her attention.

"Be polite, baby," said her mother.

"Oh, she's fine," I said. "That stuff mesmerized me, too, at her age."

"Looks like it still does."

We watched, anticipating. Sure enough, her curiosity won out, and her unsure fingertips stammered down until she touched the top, barely, as if afraid of getting burned. A slight movement registered. She tapped again, now with purpose. Nick Lidstrom's ceramic head began to quiver and shake.

She hopped and shook her hands, yet her face betrayed no delight, her profile like a coin's dour president.

"Be careful with that, baby."

"Impressive bobble," I said.

Her mother smiled.

"Will she be comfortable listening?"

"Oh, yeah. Nobody talks about anything but."

"Can you give me a sense of what happened?"

"Pretty much, it was a dog. She wanted to pet it."

"Your neighbor's?"

"Right next door. Never had any trouble."

"Did you see?"

"No. I heard Ellie shouting, and she brought Beck straight over. Crying. Both crying."

I nodded.

"She felt horrible. Ellie, I mean."

"What about Becky?"

"Some blood, but not a ton. I didn't know if it was bad at first, you know?"

I nodded and turned to look at her again. She was still entranced by the shelf dwellers, having shifted to Charlie Brown—a gift from my own daughter, not much older.

"My daughter thinks I look like Charlie Brown. What do you think?"

She jumped and hopped again, with a quick little clap. But her face kept its sour curl.

"We got her in the car and drove over to Munson. Don't know why we didn't call an ambulance. We just went. Got going and kept going."

"Where exactly is it? The worst, I mean."

"You see it there? Sort of pokes there, with a jagged little line?"

"On this side?"

8

"Yes, facing us."

"So those puncture marks?"

"Yes."

"Anything on the other side?"

"Nope. Just this. That's what happened. Mostly punctures. He didn't tear at her so much. But the bigger teeth got deep enough."

I watched.

"You don't think it looks bad?"

"Well, I've seen a lot in this line of work. It's significant, certainly."

"But the scar isn't the thing."

"Nerves, you said?"

"See it?"

"I haven't, but we've been talking."

She picked up Nick Lidstrom and began shaking him with some violence.

"Careful with poor Nick," I said, with all the good nature I could muster. "He's more of a finesse guy."

She turned to face me now, beaming, and I felt a sharp blow to my stomach.

"See?"

I sat up. "Yes," I said, with more breath than voice.

"The doctor said people think you can just fix it up like rewiring a radio. Not so," she said, clearing her throat. Then she lifted her chin and smiled a mother's smile.

Nick Lidstrom was back on the shelf and steady, but Charlie Brown was now bushwhacking through a flower-put jungle. "Haha!"

I saw again, felt it hit me.

"She won't be able to smile on that side. Her lips and cheek sort of stay where they are. Droop a little. You really only notice when she smiles. It's like someone combined those happy and sad theater masks into one, split right down the middle. That's what my father said. He likes the theater."

"Yes." I nodded slightly.

"Maybe she should just stay unhappy her whole life," said her mother, weakly.

She hopped in a circle now, lost in weightless thoughts. Three now. Almost four. But she began to age before me. I saw her in kindergarten, laughing with classmates. Then in middle school. Life less carefree. Children not so childlike. Then high school. A football game. A dance. So many new faces now—faces new to hers. So many first reactions, unspoken words.

Unhappy, yes. Don't let slip a smile.

"I said are you there? Still home?"

"Oh, yes, I beg your pardon."

"What else do you need today?"

"Some photos, please. For the insurer."

"I e-mailed them to you, like Jan asked."

"Ah, right. Let me pull those up."

I clicked until she was looking at me through the screen—her face in two dimensions. Smiles cut in half. A dozen or so. And then more in my mind's eye. Arcade photos beside a true friend. Yearbook photos. Senior photos. Engagement photos. Wedding photos. I saw photos of her with her own daughter. A thousand photos now, and my own daughter in each.

A small figure brushed my elbow, and I glanced over to catch her first peek at the monitor. "Me!" she burst, thrilling at her on-screen persona.

Full joy. Full love of life.

She turned and smiled up at me.

I smiled back.

The Accessory

Kris Johnson

Here, a law student with substantial publishing experience gives an insightful account of an unfortunate crime representing a divided town, as crimes so often do represent the communities in which they arise.

"A fight!" shrieked a red-haired boy, sticking his head into the Quick-N-Go Mini Mart. Answering the call, two other middle school-aged boys darted from the store to stake out a prime view amid the crowd gathering in the park nearby.

Inside, seventeen-year-old Doreen slid a box of Sour Patch Kids into the pocket of her dull blue smock before slipping to the door; arranging the rest of the candy display could wait. Her suspicions were confirmed when she saw Brandon's red sports car hastily left along the park's edge: Dennis and Brandon were at it again. Tension had been rising all spring, making a fight inevitable. Brandon was bigger and stronger, a Ridge Park High varsity running back and starting point guard. But Dennis had a knife. Doreen edged out the door to get a better look, the bells on the door belying her efforts to quietly sneak away.

For weeks, Dennis and his boys had been padlocking the south basketball court gate to keep out Brandon and his West Side friends. Word had spread that Brandon planned to "take care of the situation" after school today. Sure enough, Dennis stood next to the padlock with arms crossed. Brandon wielded a bolt cutter.

A casual observer might dismiss this confrontation as a teenage squabble, but anyone who lived in Ridge Park could tell you it was a

11

bellwether of local unrest. The town carried its name for a steep ridge of rock running north and south, dividing the town down the center. The municipal park, with a playground and basketball court located at both the north and the south ends, stood astride the divide. As the town grew, Ridge Park East collected gas stations, strip malls, and renters. Ridge Park West featured posh boutiques, trendy cafes, and large family homes. Residents of each side were suspicious of the other.

The East Siders generally played ball at the gravelly south end of the park and the West Siders at the groomed north. However, last fall the town council rehabbed the south park, and the basketball court was now resurfaced, fenced, and lit. For once, the East Siders had something worth envying. Thus, Brandon and his friends ventured into Dennis's territory, though not without resistance. A few weeks ago, Doreen overheard Dennis saying to the neighbors, "They just take everything. We finally get something nice, and they want that, too. Over my dead body!" Now, Brandon would test Dennis's words.

"Step aside," Brandon directed, bolt cutters in hand.

"Get out of my face," Dennis growled.

Doreen swallowed hard.

What happened next, Doreen couldn't be sure. But when the dust settled, the padlock had been cut, Brandon's front left tire had been slashed, a small amount of blood was on the sidewalk, and the police were arriving at the scene.

"Doreen, get yourself back in here!" her supervisor snapped through the Mini Mart's open door. "The candy cases are blocking the aisle. Get it cleaned up and take over for Tami at the register while she's on break."

Doreen hustled back into the store, heart pounding. The register panicked Doreen, and a line of customers had formed. The numbers on the register seemed to dance, and counting change was impossible. Doreen had repeated the second grade for a reason. Impatient customers regularly complained about her ineptitude. She hated her job, yet she still took every shift she could get. Fortunately, the customers in line had straightforward credit-card transactions. Thankfully no change to count!

The last customer in line was Glenn Field, a county police officer. Glenn used to date Doreen's mother years ago, before she drank her whisky straight. Glenn was one of the few warm people in Doreen's life. He once told her that *good things come to those who work hard.* She was still waiting for those good things.

"I suppose you saw what was going on out there, Doreen," began Glenn. "Don't get mixed up with those guys. They're all bad news. You're still in school, right?"

"Yes, sir." She didn't add, "hanging on by a thread."

She watched Glenn walk out the store and down the street. The crowd across the street had dispersed, although Brandon was still there changing his tire. His friends stood around reliving the action. Brandon had been Doreen's best friend since they were four years old, two mischievous hellions devising endless exploits and expeditions while their single mothers gossiped and sipped beer. Tucked in the frame of her bedroom mirror was an old photo of the two of them, both wearing baggy bathing suits and pirate smiles, sitting in a kiddie pool with plastic buckets on their heads, handles tucked beneath their chins.

When Brandon and Doreen were in elementary school, Brandon's mom hit the books while Doreen's mom hit the bottle. Eventually, Brandon's mom earned her associate's degree and married a Ridge Park West two-story with solarium and country club membership. A bland husband came with the deal. That's when Brandon found a new set of friends. Doreen's mom barely got herself to work most days but somehow managed to birth a brother for Doreen twelve years her junior. Little Tommy, now five, was a strain on Doreen's Mini Mart paycheck but also the light of her life. Tommy reminded her of a young Brandon.

Tami soon returned from her break, and Doreen again slipped outside and crossed the street.

"You alright?" Doreen asked as she approached Brandon, now standing and wiping his hands.

Brandon nodded, his wide, white smile chomping a piece of gum as though nothing had happened. Aimee Birch stroked his arm. Aimee was a shiny West Side girl with options. Brandon and Aimee stood like catalog models: confident, fashionable, with friends and want-to-be friends orbiting them like satellites. They could have anything they wanted. Doreen was keenly aware how fundamentally unfair life had played out. Brandon was once an East Sider like her. They had been tight. Underneath his polished, tan exterior and outside his fancy sports car, wasn't he still that same boy in the kiddie-pool photo?

"You know her?" asked Aimee as she examined Doreen. She formed the word "her" with the slightest curl of her lip, imperceptible to anyone but an overworked seventeen-year-old girl with greasy hair, wearing a stained smock and Converse knock-offs. Aimee probably never noticed plain flunkies like Doreen.

"Yeah," Brandon chuckled. "We used to be friends."

Brandon noticed Doreen flinch at the "used to," so he added a casual, "Relax, Dory, we're still friends, alright? And since you're a friend, I'll let you in on a little secret. Tonight, we're going over to Dennis's house to straighten this out once and for all."

"And Brandon's got a gun!" piped his friend.

"Shut it!" Brandon warned. Then to Doreen, "But, yeah, we're going to scare the crap out of him so that he never pulls a stunt like this again. And Aimee is going to be our driver, right Aimee?"

"I don't know.... I...."

"Aw, come on, Aimesy," Brandon sang. "I promise you won't get in trouble. You won't tarnish your gold star." And then he gently dropped his forehead down to hers and whispered through a cheesy grin, "Come on, come on, come on, come on."

She closed her eyes, slowly shook her head, and laughed. "Okay, fine."

And then he winked at Aimee.

Pangs of jealousy overtook Doreen. Was it validation Doreen so deeply craved? Maybe because she didn't have a father or a boyfriend? Maybe because she wasn't good at Any. Single. Thing. in this entire world. She had loved Brandon first; he used to belong to her. What she wouldn't give for him to wink at her like that.

Brandon's plan was to wait until Dennis's father left for his third-shift job at the foundry, and then he and his buddies would threaten

Dennis to stay away from the south ball courts. The gun was just a scare tactic, not to be used. That way Dennis wouldn't consider pulling his knife.

Doreen should have finished her shift at 10 p.m., but it took her three tries to total her drawer correctly. By this time of night, her mother had been passed out for hours. Doreen couldn't afford driver's training courses, so she'd have to wait until she was eighteen to take her test and begin driving herself in her mother's car. Walking home in the dark always frightened her a bit, and she jogged the last few blocks.

She was ravenous for whatever dinner she could scrounge in the kitchen, but first she climbed the stairs to Tommy's room. Her sweet Tommy. She pushed aside his stuffed dog named Pinkerton, after the book series that she had bought him last Christmas. She crawled into bed with Tommy, and felt his small hands on her face. "Dory," he mumbled. He immediately fell back to sleep in her arms, and she kissed his forehead. Doreen wondered whether anyone had ever kissed her in her sleep.

"Dor-een! Getcher butt down here!" She must have woken her mother when she came in. She looked back at Tommy, kissed him again and decided, no, probably no one had ever done the same for her. She carefully placed the box of Sour Patch Kids on Tommy's bedside table. He would squeal with delight in the morning. Doreen smiled at the thought.

She descended the stairs to attend to her mother, who had fallen back asleep on the living-room couch. The house stank of rotting kitchen garbage, cigarettes, and whisky. Doreen stepped outside and sat on the porch steps to clear her head.

Just then, she heard the deep purr of Brandon's car. He stopped the car, strolled up the porch stair, and sat by Doreen. His friends remained in the car.

"Say, Doreen. Whatcha been doing?"

She squinted and cocked her head. "I just got home from the Quick-N-Go," she said incredulously.

"Well, don't you know how to live it up on Friday night?!"

15

"I'm just going to eat something and go to bed. I have to work again in the morning."

"Why don't you come out for a drive?"

"Sorry, what?" Was he asking her out?

"Okay, so Aimee got scared and flaked out on me. I need you to be my driver. It's no big deal. Just sit in the car while me and my guys have a chat with Dennis. I just don't want to leave my car running in a crappy neighborhood like this."

"This is where I live," Doreen shot back. Not only had he not asked her out, he had insulted her.

Brandon rolled his eyes. "You know what I mean. Nothing personal. But we might have to move fast."

"I don't even have a license."

"So what? You'll literally just be driving around the neighborhood, right back to your house."

Then Brandon dropped his forehead down to Doreen's. Time stopped. He smelled amazing. He smelled like money. And he was asking her to drive his car. What could it hurt? Driving without a license can't be too bad of a crime. Brandon whispered with a smile, "Come on, come on, come on, come on." Then he looked her straight in the eye with a pout. He had stoked her desperate longing to be wanted.

"Okay, yes, fine, I'll drive," Doreen said with a shake of her head and a chuckle. "You'll have to show me how."

With a bit of laughter and after several stops and starts, Doreen was driving! Driving a beautiful car next to a beautiful boy whose hands kept grazing hers as he helped her steer. It was absolute heaven.

As they stopped at Dennis's house, Brandon told Doreen to wait with the engine on and explained how to make a quick escape. The boys piled out of the car and approached Dennis's dark house. They pounded on the door, barking Dennis's name. The porch light flickered on and the door began to open. Dennis, clearly caught off guard, tried to pull the door closed again, but Brandon's gang forced it open. Doreen saw what she thought was the glint of a gun. Within seconds a shot rang out, and the boys rushed to the car, leaving Dennis's front door wide open.

"Go, go, go!" they all screamed. Doreen was overcome by the chaos and Brandon's cursing at her to speed away. Flustered, she put the car in neutral rather than drive. When Brandon stomped his foot over hers to hit the accelerator, the roar sent Doreen into panicked tears. Brandon cursed her again and grabbed the gear shift, pinching her fingers in his haste. She screamed as the car lurched forward, "I want out!" As they flew down the street, Doreen jerked the steering wheel in an attempt to pull over, resulting in a spectacular collision with a parked car.

An explosion of glass, air-bag dust, seemingly a thousand lights. Police cars, ambulances, even a firetruck. After what may have been minutes or hours passed, Doreen came to with Glenn by her side. His concern turned to horror as she related what happened.

"Don't look at me like that, Glenn. I didn't do anything but drive."

"Oh, Doreen. I told you not to get mixed up in this."

"I didn't do anything. Brandon was just going to scare Dennis with his gun."

"Dennis is dead."

"What?" Doreen struggled to process this.

"Doreen," Glenn said, his voice full of disappointment. "If you knew Brandon was going to scare Dennis with a gun, you were a co-conspirator and are an accessory to the murder."

"A conspirator? An accessory?" Doreen couldn't breathe. "Murder?"

"Yes, scaring someone with a gun is called 'assault with a deadly weapon.' Doreen, that's a felony. Because you were the driver and you knew about the plan, you are an accessory to the crime. Even though you didn't pull the trigger, an accessory can be found guilty of whatever happens that is directly related to the crime. I have to take you in."

"That can't be true. I didn't shoot anyone!"

"It is true. It's called Pinkerton liability."

Pinkerton? Like Tommy's dog? Oh, sweet Tommy! Doreen sobbed uncontrollably. What had she done?

On the heels of this revelation, Brandon passed by, handcuffed. "Hang in there, Dory." And then he winked at her. Doreen turned her head and vomited.

Gratitude

Curt Benson

Here, a law professor with substantial practice experience gives the reader a glimpse into the inner workings of defending those charged with common but serious crimes.

Merrill, wearing a smart grey suit and holding a brown briefcase, walked across the jailhouse lobby. He walked briskly, his shoulders back and his free hand swinging loosely by his side, his black Oxford shoes clicking on the terrazzo floor. Merrill is 61. He's tall, thin and reasonably fit, though he does suffer, as do nearly all men of a certain age, from a soft, rounded midsection that protruded slightly from his tailored white dress shirt. His brown and silver hair was still thick, a blessing Merrill never took for granted.

The jail's lobby was large and round. Merrill passed two long, narrow, empty inmate visiting rooms to his left. Visiting hours were over for the day. To his right was a small memorial to fallen law enforcement officers. Directly across from the entrance was a raised semi-circled visitor's desk topped with bulletproof glass. On the cadet-grey tile wall, behind the desk, was a picture of the County Sheriff just below an improbably large wooden county seal. On the floor, just below the picture and county seal, stood two tall staffs, one bearing the United States flag, the other the flag of Michigan. Both were fringed in gold. Next to the Michigan flag was a windowless steel security door.

Behind the glass sat a deputy about Merrill's age. He too was fit, but much bigger and stockier than Merrill. Merrill guessed that the deputy was ex-military, given that the deputy had what Merrill's father used to call "command presence" even while sitting down. The deputy wore a light brown uniform, a color that marked him a corrections officer. The rest of the department wore the traditional dark brown of the County Sheriff.

Earlier, in his car, Merrill had removed his driver's license and bar card from his wallet and placed them in his shirt pocket. Now he slid them to the deputy though the little rectangle opening in the glass. The deputy took them without glancing at Merrill. After the deputy duly typed the information into the computer, he spun in his chair away from Merrill and faced a wooden rack behind him. Into a little cubby hole the deputy placed Merrill's driver's license and bar card. Out of the same hole he took a badge marked PROFESSIONAL VISITOR. He slid the badge to Merrill, looking at the lawyer for the first time.

"Mr. Lindsey," is all he said.

The Deputy reached below the glass and pushed a button. Merrill heard the heavy metal door click resoundingly. Merrill pulled the door open and entered a large corridor. Immediately past the door were a metal detector and a simple metal table. Merrill put his briefcase on the table and waited for the deputy to come out from around the visitor's desk. The deputy appeared and took hold of Merrill's briefcase. He slid the little brass opener until he heard a loud click.

Inside the briefcase was a paper thin brown file, nothing more. The deputy looked up at Merrill.

"You've been at this a while," he said, not smiling.

Merrill looked deep into the man's eyes. He sensed no malevolence. Merrill softened his look and smiled. "Why? Do I look tired?"

"Your briefcase," the deputy said. "Very old school. Most of the lawyers who come here nowadays carry shoulder bags with laptops."

Merrill regarded his briefcase. It was a law school graduation gift from his very proud mom and dad some 35 years ago. He had maltreated it over the years, often overstuffing it, throwing it in trunks of cars, dropping it on courtroom floors and cement parking

20

lots. It was even lost for a few years. It was scuffed, scraped and scratched. The gold embossed "Merrill Lindsey" had long ago faded away. Merrill had never given his briefcase a moment's thought.

"Well I guess so," Merrill said. "I guess so."

Merrill grabbed the briefcase off the table and began walking down the corridor towards the elevator. On either side of him, Merrill glanced at the art on the walls, cheap-looking floral scenes hung to momentarily distract the "professional visitor" from the actuality of the place. Nope, thought Merrill. It's still jail, no matter how lovely the brown-eyed Susans.

In the elevator, Merrill read the sign for the thousandth time: "If the inmate you're visiting seems depressed, or if you have just delivered sad news, please inform a corrections officer." When have I ever not delivered sad news? Merrill thought, for the thousandth time.

Just off the elevator, on the second floor, Merrill encountered another windowless security door. On the wall next to it was a red intercom button with a grey speaker.

"Yes?" Merrill heard a voice through the speaker after he pushed the button.

"I'm here to see Inmate Ryan Blunt. I'm his lawyer."

Merrill heard a bell ring. Then he heard a muffled clanging as the door shook a little and began to slide open. Merrill stared indifferently forward as another grey security door slowly came into view. As the moving door stopped, a bell rang, and Merrill stepped into a grey, empty room, not more than 10 feet square. Merrill stood passively as the door behind him slowly rumbled back into place. When it finally slammed shut the room was silent and Merrill felt the claustrophobia rise in his throat. Then the bell rang again and the door in front of him began its muffled clanging as it began sliding open. Merrill stared ahead as the inmate housing area slowly came into view.

The housing area was large and round, like the lobby. Dead center was the Command Center, an elevated pod encased in security glass. Inside the pod, two deputies sat before a dozen or so monitors, each displaying different areas of the jail. The light inside the pod was dim, almost dark, so the deputies could better see the monitors, as well as the brightly lit jail cells laid out before them. The jail cells were large common rooms. Directly in front of the Command Center was a twenty-man cell, with its bunks lined up across the back of the cell. Three metal picnic tables with built-in benches, bolted to the floor, were arranged before the deputies in the pod. There were no bars; cadet-grey tile walls and a thick plastic window confined the men.

Two inmates were playing chess. A half dozen or more were playing cards. Several sat alone just looking ahead. At least six were under covers in their bunks at three in the afternoon. A table in the cell held a dozen magazines. Merrill noticed that none of the men were reading.

A young deputy, ("was he old enough to shave?" wondered Merrill,) leaned into a microphone.

"Conference room three, please."

Merrill knew the location of conference room three and walked there straight away. The door was unlocked, and Merrill walked inside. The room was a plain rectangle shape without anything on the walls. It had a plastic conference table with four chairs. Merrill took the chair closest to the door but positioned it so the door was in front of him. He put his briefcase on the desk, removed the file and began to read it. The file was nothing more than a three-page police report that the court had sent when it assigned him the case. There wasn't much to it: suspect pulled over for taking a wide turn, bloodshot eyes, slurred speech, smell of intoxicants, failed the horizontal-gaze test. Suspect refused breathalyzer at the jail, search warrant obtained, blood drawn, .22 BAC. Suspect charged with OUIL 3rd, driving on suspended license and violating the implied consent law.

Merrill put down the report and wondered. There must be a million police reports reading exactly like this one. He glanced at the date of birth and did a quick calculation. Client is forty-three years old. He turned to the last page to look at his client's criminal history: two convictions for "minor in possession" back in the eighties, a 1996 misdemeanor-trespassing conviction, and four drunk driving convictions spread out over twenty years. Yes sir, Merrill thought, there are a million police reports reading exactly like this one.

The conference room door opened up slowly, and in walked Ryan Blunt. He was tall and gangly in his blaze-orange jail-issued cotton shirt and pajama-type pants, the orange dulled after years of wear and laundry. He wore jail-issued clear plastic flip flops with white socks. His dirty-blonde hair was pulled back in a frowzy ponytail. His eyes were heavy, almost sleepy and dark.

A scaly, white crusty patch of skin spread out along the hairline of his scalp. He was itching it as he sat down without looking at Merrill's eyes. He just stared blankly in Merrill's direction.

"Mr. Blunt," Merrill said. He did not offer his hand. "I'm Merrill Lindsey. I'll be representing you in this matter."

Blunt nodded vaguely and looked at the table top. "What kind of time am I looking at?"

Merrill did not hesitate. "If you're convicted, it'll be drunk driving number five for you, plus your blood-alcohol level was really high. What did you get for your fourth conviction?"

"A year in the County. I got out in eight and a half months."

"Where was that?"

"Up north."

"Honestly, Ryan, that's pretty light. You've drawn Judge Steadman. He can be tough." Merrill paused to let his comment sink in, before continuing, "Realistically, I could easily see you doing three years for this." Merrill quickly added, "if convicted."

Blunt spoke quietly, again refusing to look Merrill in the eyes. "My dad is really pissed," he said slowly.

Merrill was surprised by the remark, coming as it did from a forty-three-year-old man. Merrill knew enough not to say anything. If a client has something he wants to say, he'll say it. No point in asking.

"My mom died a couple of weeks ago."

"I'm sorry."

"I was on my way to her funeral when I was arrested."

Merrill looked down at the police report on the table top. He never did look at the time of the arrest – 10:45 AM.

"Damn, Ryan. That's tough."

"You know, I hadn't had a drink in a couple of months. But then my mom died. I went over to a friend's house and he took out some whiskey. We kind of lost track of time." Blunt leaned back in his chair and looked at the ceiling. "After a while, it didn't make much sense to go to bed, so we just stayed up drinking. I was driving to my dad's house to take a shower and change my clothes and I got pulled over right in front of the house. My dad and my sisters were coming out of the house, all dressed up and going to the church. They stood there and watched me get arrested, get handcuffed, get put in the police car." Blunt's eyes were turning red and he put his head on his arms on the table. "My dad is really pissed."

"Jesus, Ryan. I am sorry you had to go through that."

Blunt suddenly snapped his head up and for the first time looked Merrill in the eyes.

"Hey. Can you get me a Bible?"

"Sure, I can get you a Bible. What version do you want?"

Blunt stared at Merrill uncomprehendingly.

Merrill leaned forward, "You a religious man?"

"Yes."

"For very long?"

"No."

"You Catholic?"

"No."

"I'll get you the King James version."

"It's a regular Bible, right?"

"Yeah, Ryan. It's a regular Bible."

"I started reading the Bible two drunk drivings ago." Blunt sat up and stared intently at Merrill. "I was driving down M-47 at about 3 AM, drunk as a skunk, and big semi pulled out of a gas station. I was messing with a cigarette and didn't see it. My car hit and went right under the trailer. It tore the top of the car right off. I got pulled out of the car and ended up in the street. I was clinically dead."

"You died?" Merrill said.

"I was clinically dead," Blunt repeated.

"Who said you were clinically dead?" Merrill asked.

"The doctors, the nurses, everyone said I was clinically dead." Blunt leaned back looking at Merrill a little suspiciously. He's told this story a dozen times. No one has ever questioned that he was clinically dead.

"What does that mean? Clinically dead? I've never really understood that phrase."

Blunt raised his voice slightly, "It means I was dead, alright? Right there on the highway. Right on M-47. Even the ambulance drivers said I was dead."

Merrill sensed that he was flustering his client, so he decided to relax his tone. Merrill smiled, "Did you see a tunnel with the light at the end, and feel all peaceful, like everyone says happens to you when you're—," Merrill held up his arms and used air quotes, "'—clinically dead.'"

Blunt stared hard at Merrill. He spoke slowly, in a gravelly whisper, like he was the voiceover for a movie trailer. "No. I was going to the other place." He leaned forward. "I left my body. I was up in the air. I was watching the ambulance guys working on my dead body."

Blunt's voice was getting louder. "Then I felt, like, hands or something grabbing my legs and pulling me down. My feet started getting really hot. I started screaming NO! NO! God NO!"

Blunt began waving his arms. "I started begging God to let me live. I promised him I'd change. I'd live a good life. I'd be a good man. God answered my prayers. I woke up in the ambulance. The ambulance guys couldn't believe it. They thought I was dead. I scared the hell out of them. And ever since then, I've read the Bible and led a Christian life."

Merrill nodded thoughtfully. "And here we are... in jail."

Blunt raised his chin indignantly, leaned back in his chair and folded his arms across his chest. "I have a drinking problem."

The conference lasted another half hour or so. Merrill spoke with authority. He promised to subpoena the blood test results and examine the qualifications of the nurse who drew the blood and the technician who analyzed it. He'll question the legality of the stop. He'll even challenge the underlying scientific theory of the "horizontal gaze test," a test Merrill referred to as "little better than voodoo."

But both men were, in their different ways, experts on drunk driving and both men knew that Blunt's fifth conviction was likely drawing near. Drunk driving cases are simple prosecutions. And simple cases are the worst to defend. Merrill had little to work with, and Blunt knew it.

Nonetheless, Merrill did everything he promised to do, and over the next few months visited Blunt regularly, much more often than the usual court-appointed lawyer. In each visit, Merrill found himself delivering, to quote the elevator sign, "sad news."

The first concerned the prosecuting attorney. In one visit, Merrill said, "She's not offering any plea deals. Nothing. Plead straight up guilty, or go to trial. That's what she said."

Blunt, sitting at the plastic table in conference room number three, barely moved, and displayed no emotion.

"Nothing?" He was barely audible.

"Nothing." Merrill closed his briefcase. "Sometimes, when I have a really tough case, I'll ask the prosecutor that if, hypothetically, my client pleads guilty as charged, will she at least agree to take no position at sentencing. She won't even do that. She says once you're convicted, and she doesn't care how, by jury verdict, guilty plea, or whatever, she's going to argue you deserve the full five years."

Again, Blunt did not move, but when Merrill said, "five years," his eyes focused on Merrill's eyes.

"Five years? For a simple drunk driving? No accident, no nothing? Just drunk driving?"

Merrill lowered his eyes and looked at the top of the table and spoke softly. "It'll be your fifth conviction, Ryan."

Merrill looked up into Blunts eyes and resumed his normal authoritative tone. "Listen, Ryan. I've known this prosecuting attorney for years. We're good friends. She can be a real hard ass sometimes. But the fact is, she benefits nothing by giving you a break. It can only hurt her. Think about it. If God forbid one day you kill or injure someone while driving drunk, and the media and the victim find out she gave you a break on your fifth conviction, there'll be hell to pay."

And that is how the meetings went as the two men approached the trial date. In one meeting, Merrill told Blunt that he confirmed that the nurse who drew his blood in the jail was a properly licensed phlebotomist. The jail's nurse's quarters had just passed a state inspection for hygiene, and the needles were properly sterilized and were the proper gauge. In another meeting, Merrill told Blunt that the technician who analyzed the blood sample was also properly certified and had an unimpeachable record. Plus, there was no problem with the chain of custody between the time the blood was drawn and the time the results were deposited in the prosecutor's file.

In every meeting, Blunt sat still and asked no questions. Finally, one day, Merrill switched topics. "How's your dad?"

Blunt looked up and stared for a long time before speaking. "I don't know."

"Has he been here to see you?"

"No."

"Any of your sisters?"

"No."

"Has anyone?"

"Just you."

Finally, a month before trial, Merrill decided it was time to explain a more elusive side of the criminal-justice system.

"Listen, Ryan." Merrill and Blunt were once again in conference room number three.

Blunt appeared phlegmatic as usual. Merrill continued.

"I know guys are suspicious of court-appointed attorneys. They think that court-appointed lawyers just want to cop to any kind of a plea to avoid the hassle of trial. We don't make money trying cases. We only make money if we plead them out quickly. People think that we're not really fighting for our clients. I just want you to know that I am prepared to try this case. I am ready to, and I want to. We both know it's a tough case, but this is what I do for a living."

Blunt, for the first time in months, moved his shoulders around and looked at Merrill with genuine interest.

"I think you're fighting for me," Blunt said simply.

Merrill stopped talking and paused. "Thank you, Ryan."

The two men stared at each other for just a moment before Merrill continued.

"There is something you should know. It's hard to explain, but it affects you and you need to know it. We lawyers believe there is something called a trial penalty."

Blunt repeated Merrill's words. "Something called a trial penalty."

"Well, see, technically, it does not exist. It would be unconstitutional. But we all think it exists."

"A trial penalty," Blunt rolled the words out slowly.

"Here's the thing. It does not matter whether a judge thinks a guy is guilty or not. If a guy has a shot at winning a trial, the judge figures, go for it. But if a judge thinks a guy is guilty and the judge thinks the guy has absolutely no defense and no way of winning a trial, but the guy goes to trial anyway, well that's different. You're tying up his docket for no reason. You're inconveniencing the cops and witnesses and jurors, and, well...." Merrill paused. "It seems like maybe the judge's sentence is a little harsher than if the guy just pled guilty."

Blunt frowned as he processed this information. Merrill continued, "Look, you have an absolute right to a jury trial. And if a judge penalized you for exercising that right, well, it would be an illegal sentence. But no judge is stupid enough to announce it from the bench."

Blunt asked, "So what are you getting at?"

"Just this," Merrill said. "If you plead guilty as charged, you'll likely get about three years. If we try the case and lose, I would not be surprised if you get the full five years. I'm just being realistic, Ryan."

Two weeks later, Merrill sat at his desk in his office. He wore blue suit trousers, a blue shirt, and no tie. His stocking feet were folded at the ankles and up on the traditional seven-drawer mahogany desk with tarnished brass fittings. Papers and file folders were strewn about the desk's surface. A closed laptop was set on top like a jumbo paperweight. A small radio on a matching credenza softly played classical music.

Merrill had a copy of a handwritten letter on his lap, sent to him by Judge Steadman's clerk with a simple note reading, "Enclosed please find correspondence received by the Court today."

Merrill read the letter. It was written in pencil. The letters were written in a childish block form:

"Dear Judge Steadman. I want to fire my lawyer Mr. Merrill Lindsey. I do not believe he has my best interests at heart." Merrill noted that "interests" was spelled wrong. "He's friends with the prosecutor and I think he is really working for her. He says you'll violate my constitutional rights unless I plead guilty to a crime I did not commit." Merrill noted that "constitutional" was spelled with an "sh."

"I have heard that you are a wise and good Christian man, your Honor." The letter continued, "I am a Christian. I am innocent. Please give me another lawyer. I do not feel Mr. Lindsey is doing a good job. Plus, he lied to me. He said he would get me a Bible and he didn't."

The letter was signed, "Very truly yours, Ryan Blunt."

Merrill rolled his eyes upward. Damn, he thought. I forgot the Bible. Why didn't Blunt remind me during one of my dozen or so visits? Merrill smiled at his own naivety.

29

"Jennifer!" Merrill called his secretary. Jennifer, a diminutive soul with a strangely loud voice, came into the office.

"Is Blunt going to get a new lawyer?" she asked as she entered. She had already read the letter, Merrill realized.

"Ha!" Merrill said without mirth, dropping the letter on the desk. "Do you know what would happen to the legal system if judges removed lawyers from cases every time an inmate sent a letter, especially two weeks before trial? No, Jennifer. Mr. Blunt is stuck with me." Merrill took his feet off his desk and hunted around for his shoes with his toes. "And I with him."

"He's a jerk. Does he have any idea how much time you have spent on this case? Does he know what this is costing you?" Jennifer was also Merrill's bookkeeper. "One or two more of these cases and we're bankrupt."

"Listen Jennifer, I'm leaving. It's Katie's birthday and I have to buy her a present."

"Well, give my regards to Mrs. Lindsey." Jennifer was returning to her desk when she heard Merrill shout, "and find me a Bible! A King James version!"

Jennifer shouted back, "Is there any other version?"

A pause ensued before Merrill shouted back, "Not to you Protestants."

Merrill walked towards the mall's anchor store with the enthusiasm of a POW walking to a jungle prison camp. The department store was crowded with teenagers and women. There were very few men. Merrill walked alone, head down, lost in thought, tinged with self-pity. He was losing lots of money on the Blunt case. He hated the mall. And he hated shopping for Katie. He loved Katie. But he hated shopping for her. "What more could this woman possibly need?" Merrill wondered, nearly out loud.

"Mr. Lindsey?" Merrill heard the soft feminine inquiry come from behind. He turned and found a fairly small but very pretty woman before him. Merrill judged her as rather young, perhaps his own daughter's age, not quite 30 years old. She had thick blond hair pulled back into a tight pony tail. Her eyes were a rich blue, her skin nearly flawless, her makeup very light.

She wore cutoff blue jeans, leather sandals and a simple white buttoned blouse. On her left ring finger was a modest diamond engagement ring and wedding band. She smiled broadly as she spoke.

"Mr. Lindsey, it is you!" She made two little hops and clapped her hands twice. "I've always meant to call you to thank you. I'm so happy to see you!"

Merrill studied the woman's face, her body, her clothes, looking for something, anything, familiar. There was nothing. Who is this woman? A friend of his daughter? The daughter of a colleague? A former client perhaps? It was no use. This woman was a stranger to him, at least for the moment.

"I always meant to call you," the woman repeated. "I really feel bad that I never called you."

"No need to feel bad," Merrill stammered somewhat, wondering if his confusion was obvious. "We're here now."

"I wanted to thank you for the advice. I followed your advice and it's made all the difference."

Merrill nodded. "Of course, of course," he took a deep breath. "You're welcome."

The young woman continued. "I went to school. I got a nursing degree. I met this really great guy and we got married. And, and...." The woman paused for dramatic effect. "I have a little girl. She's three and beautiful. I'm so happy."

Merrill again looked the woman over. I gave her advice, he thought. She must be a former client.

"My husband is going to freak when I tell him I ran into you. I tell him all of the time that if it wasn't for Mr. Lindsey, we'd never have gotten married. He wants to meet you."

Merrill still had no idea who she was, but he decided that she was a former client, which relaxed him considerably. He spoke now with confidence, with the familiar authority.

"Well that's wonderful. I'm very proud of you."

"It's because of your advice."

31

Merrill looked into her eyes. This is the third time she mentioned "advice," both times with emphasis. Merrill wondered, could he tell her that he could not remember the advice without disclosing that he could not remember her?

"Listen," Merrill tightened his lips, tilted his head, and shrugged just a tiny bit. "What advice did I give? I can't remember."

The young woman raised her eyebrows and lifted her chin.

"Oh," she said.

"I'm sorry."

"It's okay." The young woman looked right and left and lowered her voice. She leaned closer to Merrill's chest. "The first time we met I was crying so hard you could barely talk to me."

"I remember that," Merrill lied.

"My boyfriend was still in jail. He told me not to talk to anyone, even you, until he got out. He said court appointed lawyers just sell you down the river and I'd be a fool to trust you. I was so scared I couldn't stop blubbering. The next time we met, well – that is when you told me you had it all arranged." The young woman dropped her voice to a whisper. She looked around again, and leaned even closer.

"I'd plead guilty and get probation. If I finished probation without getting into trouble, they'd drop the charges. I'd have no criminal record. I could go to school, get a nurse's license and everything else 'cause I'd have no criminal record."

Merrill nodded. It sounded like pretty standard stuff for a young, first time offender, depending of course on the crime. Who is she? What was her crime? Merrill's mind almost yelled at itself.

"I was leaving your office, and you said, 'Come back here, Trish.' You said you had something else to discuss with me.

"So I sat down. Do you remember what you said?"

Merrill thought "Trish," Her name is Trish. Still no recollection. He shrugged.

"You told me to dump my boyfriend. You said that I was a real smart girl. I remember you said it just like that, 'a real smart girl.' You said that I deserved a great guy and that my boyfriend was a loser and a criminal and he'd drag me down with him. And you know what, Mr. Lindsey? He's in prison."

Trish paused and patted her chest with her fist.

"And I'm a nurse!"

Merrill laughed out loud. He grabbed her lightly by the arm and said, "Trish, I am really proud of you." And he laughed again. A few shoppers glanced at him as they walked by.

The conversation lingered on for a few moments. Trish made Merrill promise that he'd talk to Katie about coming over for dinner and meeting her husband and daughter. Merrill knew it would never happen, but he promised anyway. He took her phone number. Merrill again said how proud of her he was. The two hugged lightly, and Trish walked off. Merrill watched her walk away. He stood staring for a while until he accepted the fact that it was no use: he just could not remember her. Maybe Jennifer will remember a young client named Trish.

Merrill turned and headed towards the jewelry section. Whenever he could not decide what to buy Katie, he headed to the jewelry section.

Proper Instincts

Shelley Stein

Here, a practitioner shares divorce-case insights, in a study of highly strategic clients in a peculiar family and life crisis.

She sat at her office desk momentarily transfixed, trying to make sense of what had happened that afternoon, trying also to connect with something deep in her soul or psyche. The late-day sun slanted through the half-drawn blinds, making a pattern on the desktop that shifted with each rustle outside of the treetop branches and their leaves. She could just barely hear the pleasant street noise below her second-floor corner-office windows, one of those subtle features that eased her law-practice labors.

And this new matter needed some of that tonic ease. She had met earlier that afternoon with a great-looking couple, husband and wife. He was tall, tanned, lean, and magazine-model handsome. She, a petite natural blond, seemed so perfectly formed as to have stepped out of Disney. As they entered her office and took their seats across the desk, he had doted after her, charmingly warm and solicitous. She had returned his favor. Indeed, the love that they so theatrically shared was what made the matter that they brought so disconcerting.

He, the husband, was the first and only one to raise their issue. His petite wife had sat silently throughout the consult, simply nodding in polite agreement to whatever he had said. He, the husband, was to be her client in ... a divorce. They needed her help to ensure that she, the wife, had everything that she needed in their divorce. He had heard how competent and collaborative she could be, and so he was sure that she was just the lawyer to help them.

Hold on, she had said at her first decent opportunity. *While I may be sensible, civil, and accommodating, I don't practice collaborative law.* To make her point even clearer, she had added her standard response that *conflicts rules permit me to represent only one side or the other in any divorce, no matter how congenial.*

In saying so, she knew that she wasn't just satisfying rules, though. Despite that she was a divorce lawyer, she hated to see couples divorce. Oh, she knew the economic and social value of helping to make two productive households out of one broken one, which, other than the sustaining fees and steady income, was largely why she continued in family-law practice. But in most of her divorces, she had sensed that the marriage wasn't so broken as was each individual party. She was so often frustrated at client insensibility—the oddly irrational, even corrupt nature of every soul—that she often wanted to try to just *shake* some sense into them.

Yet here, neither husband nor wife had shown any hesitation in response to her rebuke. Instead, the husband had promptly continued that, *oh yes, they had already seen and retained scumbag to represent her in their divorce.* Of course, they hadn't said *scumbag* but had instead named the local lawyer whom every wife who wanted to strangle her cheating husband tended to hire in this town. The lawyer carefully stoked among his often-wealthy and routinely female clients a reputation for beating up on deadbeat and desperado husbands.

She, though, like all the other divorce lawyers in the area, knew that scumbag's reputation was bogus. He did no more, and often did less, for his clients than any other lawyer in the area. The law is the law. While the quality of representation can make a difference in the outcome, fisticuffs of the lawyer seldom do. Indeed, they more-often backfire, ultimately working against the naïve client's interest. She had seen it proven repeatedly: the clients pay more for the fisticuffs but get less in the outcome.

The funny thing was that she would never have thought of her opposing counsel as *scumbag* except that his own law partner once referred to him as such in one of their several contested cases. She had been having her usual unpleasant tussles with the lawyer over nothing of any consequence, him just making things harder for both

35

parties and for her, making a morass of the case while drawing it out interminably. Then, at a motion hearing in the case, she had met his law partner for the first time when the lawyer had briefly taken ill.

She had girded for battle, thinking that the partner would be just like the fisticuffs lawyer. But no, when the partner walked into the back of the courtroom for the hearing, he had motioned her into the hallway and then amiably asked her to follow him up the stairs onto the courthouse roof, where he had proceeded to fire up a cigarette and smoke. As he did so, he vented to her about how his law partner embarrassed him taking exorbitant fees from naïve clients, only to make such a mess of things that he, the partner, had to bail him out. The partner had ended his mini-tirade using the *scumbag* appellation, as he stubbed his half-smoked cigarette out on the roof's railing preparing to return to the courtroom. On the way down the stairs, the partner had agreed to resolve amicably the disputed motion.

Her attention returned to the earnest husband whose largesse had hired scumbag to represent his wife. She asked the wife to excuse herself to the waiting area, which the wife politely did. She then began to explain her fee agreement and the process that she envisioned for fair resolution of the divorce. But the husband politely interrupted her, saying that he was familiar with how things should proceed. And he had brought a substantial retainer, several times her usual fee, in cash. He apologized for the cash as he withdrew several bundles of twenty-dollar bills from the brown leather soft case he had carried in and held on his lap. He explained that he had a fruit-trading and distribution business that required him to travel to growers' orchards and processing plants to pay and receive payment in cash.

Drug money, her mind instantly told her. She scolded herself silently to give her client a decent chance. She had twice before represented grower clients who indeed seemed at times to deal on the fly if not necessarily in cash. The husband, though, interrupted her internal debate. He was saying something about bringing more monies in tomorrow to place in trust with her to fund in advance his wife's anticipated property settlement. *See there, drug money!* her mind shouted to her again, this time adding, *money laundering! Better research it!*

36

She silenced the thoughts once again until she had seen her new client out. After dealing for the rest of the afternoon with a few small matters, she returned to mulling her unusual new client's matter once again. *Alright,* she thought, *maybe he is a drug dealer. Even so, he may have lawful objectives that she could help him achieve.* Well, that was a start. He had, after all, only asked her to help provide for his about-to-be-ex wife, which depending on the source of his largesse could not only be a lawful but also an unusually moral objective. She didn't have to *like* him to represent him as a client, if she respected and approved of what she was about to help him do, and if she did it lawfully. She decided to do the money-laundering research.

The divorce complaint, hand delivered to her by her fisticuffs nemesis, was in her hands midday the next day. He had brought it over to her office personally just to gloat that he was going to *bring her playboy client down,* as he put it to her in her office waiting area, when handing her the tidily printed and impressively stamped summons on top of the complaint. She smiled back at him confidently, ignoring the challenge and instead asking him cordially how he was feeling lately. *Remember,* she reminded him when he looked back at her blankly, *you were sick for that hearing a couple of months ago.*

Hah, he replied, he hadn't been *sick* but instead out on the lake with a buddy of his. *Don't you ever get tired of this crap?* he asked her, in explanation of his duplicitous absence from the hearing at which his law partner had, properly, resolved the mess that he had made of the case. Although irritated that he had misrepresented to her and, through his law partner, to the court the reason for his absence, she just smiled back even more broadly, while saying, *well then, I hope you stay well.* Heap coals of kindness on his head, she thought to herself.

The moment that he left, she returned to her office, picked up the telephone, and called his law partner, asking if they could meet *right away. You mean tomorrow?* the law partner replied. *No, right now, today,* she answered. And in minutes, she was on her way to the busy coffee shop down the street from the courthouse, where the two of them spent an hour discussing their new clients' unusual matter. *Gosh, I like him*, she thought, when they were done. She headed straight back to the office to get to work on the matter.

One month passed, and then a second month, as she worked furiously on the matter. During that time, she received from her combative opposing counsel the usual barrage of outrageous settlement demands, burdensome discovery requests, and harassing motions. While she would usually have cautiously and firmly countered every such tactic, in this instance, she ignored them all, even managing to adjourn and delay the requisite court hearings. She had more-important work to do on the case, and her work didn't involve stalling.

She met periodically with her handsome, composed, and always-in-control client during this time. Each time, she gave him a full report of her dealings with an alphabet-soup of federal and state agencies, updates that she took pains to detail in writing for him—and for her, just in case. At no time did he acknowledge in the least that he was involved in anything other than fruit trading and distribution. Yet he also took in perfect stride each of her disclosures of the several serious matters on which she was working for him, in pursuit of his sole objective of providing for his beloved about-to-be-ex wife.

Their professional relationship at first seemed to her unusual, even bizarre, as if they were somehow navigating completely different universes. And indeed, they were, as she increasingly came to discover. At the same time, she came to appreciate that they needed and respected one another. She needed clients to serve on significant matters. He needed a sensible, smart, creative, and thoroughly practical lawyer, of which the community had several. But he also needed a lawyer of deep wisdom and surpassing composure. She didn't yet count herself as the latter, but she also felt that in this case she might somehow prove herself qualified beyond her modest ambitions. Time, though, would tell.

Each time that she and her client met, he brought more bundles of cash to fund the property settlement that he desired to provide for his wife. He would stack the bundles on her desk and slide them over to her. She would dutifully count and record the amounts, hand him a receipt for the total, and then after seeing him out, carry the money as casually as she could manage in her paisley shoulder bag down to the local bank for deposit in her trust account. By the time the sixty-day waiting period to take a divorce judgment had passed, the deposits had funded an amount that would easily secure, for a very long time, most beautiful young women whose husbands were sadly divorcing them.

Shortly after the sixty days had elapsed, she stopped stonewalling her combative counsel on his several pending motions. They would now appear together in court for the first time in the case, clients in tow, to address his furious aspersions over her abject failure to respond to discovery, secure assets, and comply with the court's scheduling order. They would engage in the first of what would likely be many battles until one of them, doubtless *her* rather than him, given her complete failure in tactical maneuvers to this point, had succumbed entirely. She dressed early that morning in her best court outfit.

She and her client sat at counsel table in the empty courtroom, waiting for opposing counsel to appear so that they could let the judge know that they were ready for the grand skirmish, for which they had agreed to secure a special hearing time outside of the usual cattle-call docket of motions. Her client's wife sat alone at the other counsel table, waiting sadly for her fisticuffs lawyer, who finally showed up, red-faced, suit coat unbuttoned, and shirt-tail untucked as usual. *Get him in here*, he muttered to her without looking at her. She rose curtly, made her way to the chambers door, opened it, and nodded to the judge's secretary inside.

At the same moment as the judge took the bench, the door at the back of the courtroom opened. In walked a small parade of serious-looking officials, at the end of which was opposing counsel's law partner. The officials, all in black suits, white shirts, and dark ties, except for a marshal in federal uniform, stood in the front-row gallery benches, waiting for the judge's signal. The law partner swung the rail gate open to stand a seat next to his startled partner at counsel table with their petite client. *You may be seated*, the judge said, and then turning to her, added respectfully, *Counsel?*

Opposing counsel rose quickly to object, blurting out, *Your Honor, these are my motions*, but the judge was already raising his hand to silence opposing counsel, who would ordinarily have continued with his bluster but for the unusual company that had inexplicably joined the hearing. For the next half an hour, she methodically outlined one agreement after another into which the parties and various state and federal agencies had entered, establishing the terms of an exceedingly difficult resolution.

After each recitation, the law partner would rise to present to the judge the executed agreement, for the judge to acknowledge or sign. Periodically, the judge would ask for oral confirmation of the executed agreements from one or another of the officials in the back of the courtroom. Each in turn would place their appearance on the record to acknowledge the negotiation and approval of each agreement.

The combative lawyer sat agog throughout the proceeding. She and the law partner had worked out everything, not just the usual divorce terms but also the parties' many state and federal obligations. She and the law partner had even confirmed with those agencies their right to retain reasonable fees out of the excessive retainers that the husband had insisted on paying on his own behalf and for his wife. The wife would receive only a fraction of the sums that the husband had her deposit in her trust account, but that fraction was still significantly more than most wives of her age and station would have, whether divorced or not.

All that was left when she had concluded her recitations was for the judge to take the requisite testimony supporting the divorce. Husband took the witness stand, raising his right hand to affirm to tell the truth. *Yes*, the marriage had broken down such that they could not achieve the objects of matrimony, he answered her question dejectedly. *No*, they could not preserve the marriage. *Yes*, he and she had signed and approved the judgment of divorce.

Finding the husband's testimony sufficient to satisfy the statute, the judge declared the parties divorced. With the husband still sitting silently on the witness stand, the judge granted the wife's unusual request for a change of both her first and last name. The judge then ordered the record sealed, another unusual order in ordinary divorce cases, except that this case had been no ordinary case. The judge turned to thank and excuse the husband, who still sat silently on the witness stand.

Looking down and over at his beautiful but now-tearful wife seated at counsel table, the husband, though, had something more to say. The judge paused, looking to the husband's lawyer, who silently nodded her assent. Taking his cue from the silent exchange, the husband continued. The marriage did not break for lack of love and devotion, he explained, looking once again at his wife. No, his ... and here he paused before choosing the word ... *employment* had interfered and was now to take him away indefinitely. He loved her fiercely, he said, and remained wholly devoted to her but could not for now fulfill the objects of their matrimony. He dropped his head as she sobbed silently at counsel table.

You may step down, the judge said firmly now to the husband. As the husband rose from the witness stand, the marshal in the gallery also rose, making his way through the rail's gate to meet the husband at counsel table. Handcuffs in place, the marshal led the husband away through the courtroom's side door leading out to the secure hallway. *Court in recess*, the judge said formally, followed by a rap of the gavel. The wife then rose, her formerly fisticuffs but now contrite counsel rising solicitously with her to escort her from the courtroom.

She met the law partner behind the podium, thanking him for his cooperation. As the two of them walked out of the courtroom together, he invited her up the stairway to the roof. Once there, he pulled a cigarette from somewhere inside his suit coat, lit it, and leaned on the railing to look out across the town's quaint skyline. *How will your partner be?* she asked him kindly, adding that he'd probably throw fits over having been duped and left out by his own law partner.

Him? the law partner replied. *Oh, he'll be alright. He's not such a bad guy*, the law partner added. A pause ensued, as if the law partner was thinking about his law partner, or perhaps thinking about her, with fresh insight. *You know*, the law partner finally resumed, *we each have our own role, and sometimes the roles work well together.* The law partner paused again, as if wondering whether to say more. Finally, he added, *he sure made the right call in this case ... when he told the husband to go hire you.*

Us

Lizz Robinson

Here, a law student tells an intergalactic tale of a reporter charged with vague crimes for telling the truth, writing an account for his long-awaited defense lawyer.

December 15, 2559

Well, here I am. It's been a long couple of years, but things are finally starting to look up for us. I spoke with an attorney on the phone who was willing to help. After all these months, I can still hardly wrap my head around the fact that someone is actually willing to help. He told me that he'd be here as soon as he could but wasn't sure how long it would take to get through. In the meantime, I'm supposed to write down my story. I guess that's what this is— well, it's more like *our* story.

Even though it's fairly common knowledge these days, I'll start with how they got here. I think that will help me keep my head clear and keep the facts in line.

I don't remember the month anymore, but about fifteen years ago, they made contact. They came from space, a place which we thought we had all figured out. We had satellites and space stations, and thought we were alone. It's sort of crazy now to think that we were once that arrogant. Or maybe we still are?

They sent us some warnings, manipulating our machines to let us know that we weren't alone. That we were going to have guests real soon.

It took some getting used to at first, but get used to it we did—at least, those of us who knew. We tried to meet them on the edge of our arm of the Milky Way, but they didn't want that. They wanted to get to Earth as fast as possible. They were dying, and we had something they needed—we just didn't know it.

So anyway, we spent some time stalling them, trying to figure out what they were and how they found us. Although, thinking back, it was more like we were trying to figure out how they hid from us for so long. Like I said, we thought we knew it all. After all, we'd done so much, and figured out so much—how could we not know about them?

Okay, maybe I should back track for a minute. I'm getting ahead of myself, and the attorney said to write it all down, sparing no detail. We thought we knew a lot, because we did know a lot. We humans had figured out how to save our planet. Previous generations had almost destroyed it and the creatures that lived on it. We had a great big war, you see, over things as stupid as who owned what land and things less stupid like human rights. It ended with us nearly killing ourselves off—so we had to change. That's something humans have always been good at—adapting.

We banded together first to learn how to feed ourselves without creating byproducts that poisoned our atmosphere. Then we figured out how to clean our oceans and reuse what we'd pulled out. I won't bore you with the details, as anyone can pull up a hub and figure those things out—but they're worth mentioning as background information.

Anyway, it took a couple hundred years, but we got the ocean temperatures to stabilize again. We began to see sea ice start to grow, and the things that needed the ice began to thrive again. Unfortunately, we couldn't save all species, but we do have the ability to clone them—if we could only get our ethics committees to sign off. We've been waiting for over forty years now for them to decide, but again, that's a different story. This is just the background.

So, after we'd picked ourselves up and dusted ourselves off, that's when we first heard from them. They had been watching us and finally liked what they saw. They wanted to meet us, and they wanted it to be on Earth. That's why we sprinted to the edge of the Milky Way—they were already on their way.

What we found waiting for us at the edge was unlike anything we ever expected. The ships were nothing like ours, made from materials for which we didn't even have names. Who would have thought, after all that time, that we'd discover our periodic table was mostly unique to the Milky Way. Sure, we recognized a couple elements, basic building blocks of life. The rest, though—it was startling to say the least.

They had been studying us long enough to have picked up some of our programming languages. They sent code to us, with greetings and basic informa—

December 19, 2559

with basic information. It took some time, but we finally let them in. We had all sorts wanting to screen them, from scientists to the new wave of politicians. We had to make sure it was safe to let them get close to Earth, after all.

This is where I come in. I'm a civilian reporter, and I work for one of the few non-government agencies left after the war. I generally write about global happenings, letting people know what's going on in the other Hemispheres. I was a part of a team invited to meet the new arrivals.

The meeting wasn't nearly as easy as it sounds. The anatomy of our two ships were so different, that we had to figure out how to get from one to the other. We didn't have ships that could stand the pressure on their loading bays, and we didn't have loading bays that could open enough to let in their transport vessels.

It took a couple of years, but our scientists came up with a mechanism to attach the two ships. Our technology was different, but with the help of the hub, our two species could work together to come up with a solution. They didn't have a quick way to get resources, but we did. So, we shipped in some engineers and supplies, and got to work. It was pretty boring at first, but then Big Brother decided to let us reporters communicate with the team from the other ship, via a hub port.

Once we plugged in, our languages were translated by the hub port itself, so that we wouldn't have a language barrier. The arrangement allowed us to be candid, asking whatever questions we wanted. That's how I met her.

I was put in contact with one whom I can only describe as their head of PR. It seems so long ago now, I can't believe I ever thought of her as only *the PR person*—but I did.

She said that she didn't have a name that could translate, so I should just call her Sandra. It was just as good as any other name to me at the time, so I didn't question anything. I didn't know at the time that she had been catching radio waves of our movies, her favorite of which was *Grease*. I would never know how much her name would mean to me, or how she only chose it after I'd told her my name was Danny.

We started with sharing basic information, asking where was their home. We had a permitted list of questions, but we exhausted those rather quickly. Sandra impressed me, the way that she really knew how to have a conversation. For a being about whom I knew nothing—not even the way she looked—it was uncanny to find wit, intelligence, and a sense of humor. I knew I liked her right away, even though we were just communicating via hub port.

They called themselves the Dao, saying that they were the first of a wave of ships looking for a new place to live. They were refugees, in a way, but I wouldn't relate that to my team. Their planet was dying, and they couldn't figure out how to reverse the process like we had. They figured that if they could look at Earth to figure out what we'd done, then they could use that technology for their own world. I thought this was a great idea and told Sandra so. After all, humans had changed. We worked together, and we cared about other living things. Surely, we would be happy to share what we had with other sentient beings.

It's funny, I look back and feel bad for myself. I had no idea just how naïve I was.

I spent almost every evening having private conversations with Sandra. We talked about everything, from grass on Earth to the sky from her planet. She was scared that we were taking so long, because she knew that her planet was dying. The Dao needed us, she told me, and they would do pretty much anything to secure our help.

Once the engineers had the door figured out, we invited the Dao to come aboard. They graciously accepted our offer, but Sandra warned me that they would have to wear special suits. Their bodies weren't attuned to our atmospheric pressure or temp-

December 26, 2559

Had to stop again. The people here aren't really on board with what I'm doing, writing down my story. Luckily, my attorney got me some special privileges, so I'm able to keep writing. I must do it in the common area though—not allowed to have writing implements in our cells. Plus, it's so cold in there, I don't know if I'd be able to take off my gloves long enough to write very much.

You see, once I met Sandra in person, everything changed. At first, she was simply this creature in what can only be described as a *pod.* They came out of their ship like that, to protect themselves. They stayed with us for a while, but I still had to use a hub port to communicate with her. At that point, we had been talking for close to three years. I had written some articles and sent them home. Apparently, the people of Earth ate it up. The other reporters wrote some too, but the government would only release so much of what we wrote.

That first night, her tone changed. She said that she hadn't expected me to look so Dao. That I had been not much more than a console to her for a long time but that seeing my face changed things. We spent the whole first day just talking on our hub ports as I led her and her team around the ship. They had a load of questions, and I did my best to answer as many as I could. Engineers with us answered a lot of the more technical stuff.

At the end of our tour, she thanked me for helping her around the ship and giving her a tour. Then she told me she thought I was handsome in a soft and hairy sort of way. Frankly, I was dumbstruck. Luckily, she sent it over a private communication, so no one else heard what she said. Or how I responded.

The private communication sort of reminded me of stories from pre-hub civilizations that would use this thing called the *internet* (sort of like an early hub) to communicate. They couldn't plug into it and share emotions like we can, but they could exchange words.

People used to date and meet up that way. Sandra's words to me that night—they were what I would imagine people used to feel after getting to know someone online.

After Sandra and her team had been with us for a couple of weeks, they invited us back to their ship. We had shared some rudimentary technology with them, so they thought it would be polite to return the favor. Three of my team got to go, and Sandra pulled some strings to make sure I'd be one of them. For the first time, I would get to see what she looked like.

I was pretty nervous as I strapped into my suit. Apparently, the atmosphere on the Dao ship was a lot like the bottom of our ocean, as far as pressure and temperature went. I had shaved that morning, so my prior six-inch beard was no longer protecting my face from space atmosphere. I remember worrying that Sandra wouldn't recognize me—until I realized that she wouldn't be able to see through the reflective helmet of my space suit.

It took about two hours for our suits to adjust to the pressure in the doorway. That's one of the reasons it had taken the engineers so long. The difference in pressure was extreme. Our engineers had designed our equipment pressure for the vacuum of space, not for the compression of the deep ocean.

When we could finally walk into their ship, I don't think any of us really knew how to react. First, we saw no color. The Dao are all color blind but see more than us with a mixture of echolocation and 3D vision from three eyes.

Although I was pretty shocked at my first look at an alien, I remember trying hard to determine which one was Sandra. To my eyes, the Dao all initially looked the same: four flexible legs, human-like torsos, and two arms. Longish necks, and uncannily human faces—plus the third eye on the forehead. They wore uniform clothes, which I suppose made sense on a ship. Their skin was all different shades, which was probably the most human part of them. One of them stood off to the side, holding her hands together in front of her in the most human gesture I'd seen since entering the ship. It was Sandra, and I could tell she was nervous for me to see her.

I sent a message to her from my hub port. I'm a bit ashamed to say it wasn't my most eloquent moment. What I said was, "Hey."

What else could I say? The moment I saw her-

January 5, 2560

I don't know what the point of this is. My attorney still hasn't been able to meet with me. There's some issue with immigration or something, I don't know. My days are blurring together, and every day, I start to think it might be my last. I might just talk to someone and tell them whatever they want to hear. I can feel myself getting to the point where I would say anything, if it meant I could see Sandra again. If it meant I didn't have to be cold anymore.

I've been in prison for so long, I almost don't know how long. If not for this journal, I don't think I'd even bother to count the days. I am still waiting for my trial, to hear my formal charges. They don't know what else to do with me, so they stuck me in this prison in the Northern Territories of the United Western Hemisphere. I guess they figure that there will be fewer Dao sympathizers here and that maybe I'll tell them something they want to know. At least, that's what Sandra thinks.

I've lost count of how long it's been since I've seen Sandra. She's the one who found the attorney for me and coordinated to get him here. If he ever shows up.

January 15, 2560

I've got to keep writing. I got a hub chat from Sandra last night, and she felt so—hopeful. She said the attorney was on the way but that he been stopped in immigration. Apparently, a bunch of government red tape, or something. I guess I'm not surprised. She also said that he was coming with a team because apparently Big Brother is preparing to hold a whole bunch of charges against me. She said they range from slander, to kidnapping a foreign diplomat, to harboring an illegal immigrant. Creative, right?

I used to think that with the unification of humanity the government and people would have open communication—that things like slander, libel, and defamation would be issues of the past. After all, hadn't we learned to stop keeping secrets from each other? Apparently not.

See, on our journey back to Earth with the Dao, I had written an article. In it, I had criticized a government-sanctioned news broadcast, which was supposed to prepare the people of Earth for the arrival of the Dao. I said some things that came from a deeply emotional place, but you know what? Everything I wrote was true.

Apparently, the agency decided that what I had written was not only false but that it cast them in a pretty bad light. They lost a lot of subscribers, and humans began to do this thing called *thinking for themselves*. Questions were being asked, and information was being doubted. Unfortunately, some of what I had written, the government of the United Western Hemisphere had been trying to keep secret— or at least that's what they told me when they arrested me.

I suppose it didn't help that as soon as I could, I took Sandra to experience a human sunset, to meet my mom, and to enjoy a human cup of coffee from Starbucks. She had developed a taste for it on our ship, and I wanted her to have a real caramel macchiato.

So here I am, rotting in a frozen prison.

I would, for a moment, like to examine the bright side. The Dao scientist team is developing a new, more-mobile suit for them to wear while outside of their pressurized compound farther south of my northern hellhole. They are saying that within two years they should be able to make it as thin as a membrane. It seems that some of the elements on our periodic table are pretty exciting to them, and they think they'll be able to use them for this new bit of technology. I also got an image on the hub of Sandra meeting a dog for the first time. It was pretty cute, especially since until that point I was the furriest thing she'd ever seen.

Okay, those two things were my silver lining. You have to find hope where you can, especially when your attorney advises you to keep your mouth shut until he arrives. Messiah, miranda, and self-incrimination are things to take seriously, according to him.

The Dao aren't being allowed out of their compound for much, but they do get a lot of visitors. At least, this is according to Sandra. A whole bunch of people don't want them here—and a whole bunch of people do. She told me that an attorney came to speak with them about immigration, which is a word she didn't know before that day. They have been assigned refugee status, since their world isn't really habitable anymore. A lot of people are nervous that more ships are coming—another bit of information I wasn't supposed to share.

I've been worried about her, but she said that being able to talk with me once a month on the hub keeps her feeling sane. I told her I feel the same way.

January 20, 2560

I know that I probably did some things I shouldn't have done. I said some things that I may or may not have agreed not to say. But those things I needed to say. I don't understand why we haven't learned from our past. Keeping secrets and releasing inflammatory information has never served humans in the past. As a journalist, it was my duty to tell the people the truth. I felt that I owed it to them.

All I ever thought I wanted was to write a big story. I wanted people to know my name, to know who I was. I thought that I could be the biggest name in news since the last war. I never anticipated finding Sandra and, with her, finding a cause for which I felt so strongly. It was always more like a game to me, like something to conquer. Now I know the truth of having a cause about which to be passionate.

The Dao have nowhere else to go. Their planet is dying, and unless they figure out how we saved ours, they won't be able to save theirs. I have been doing a lot of research during my free time, and it seems that some humans want to send them to another planet. Someplace like Jupiter or Venus, where the pressure would be more suited to their anatomy. Some people want to examine them, comparing them to fish that live in the deep parts of the ocean.

I can't help but think about how this line of thought is dangerous, especially as a student of history. It took us five-hundred years to figure out how to get to the edge of our arm of the galaxy in five years. After reaching that point, it took ten years of being with Sandra to get back. In that time, I learned—

The attorneys are here.

Trust

Sam Preston

Here, a lawyer spins a harrowing tale of murders, an effort at vigilante justice, and further demise.

Lansing. Michigan's capital city: beer-soaked and deep-fried. A blue-collar town, mostly underemployed and angry about it. I almost didn't go. A storm loomed on the horizon—I could smell it. Lightening fits started at dinner and went on for hours.

I didn't mind storms. My girl—Lucy Burger—hated them.

Sleek, black, and sassy—with a heart of gold. My Lucy Burger: half-Labrador, half-Pit. Big brown eyes, muscled legs. Her tail smacked walls like a whip. Classy dame, that Burger—even if she drank out of a bowl. My Lucy Burger: half-Labrador, half-Pit. Big brown eyes, muscled legs.

She was the kind of gal you didn't let down.

And nothing let Lucy down like leaving her alone. Especially during a thunderstorm.

The actual storm arrived later that night. After it was over, Grand Rapids folk said it was the worst in thirty years. That's probably a lie. I'm forty-eight, and I don't remember any '81 storm. A fella remembers a storm like that.

This one, I won't forget.

It started like this:

Peter Francis dialed me up from the Ingham County can. Note: he was not in police custody. The cops were just asking him questions. I advised him not to talk, but he said that the facts "were as they were" and there wasn't much he could do about it.

Peter Francis. Republican state senator. Closet Case. Hypocrite. Peter Francis hurt people, broke things, and didn't care. He was a fat man in a big rig, making too wide a turn.

Peter Francis was bad company, but I owed him a favor.

So, I made that drive to Lansing; let my girl down.

Darnell Simms was working homicide. Good Ole' Darnell. "*Ebony Scrooge.*" He looked great for an old buzzard.

"You still got that pizzazz," I told him.

He cracked a smile, scratched his grizzled beard, and showed me to the interrogation room.

"I should have gone to law school," he said. "By the way, your guy here? A real doozy."

"Not my guy, Darnell," I responded. "Not by a long shot."

"Well, the suite's yours until I need it."

I thanked him, shut the door behind me.

It was a nine-by-seven room with a table and two chairs thrown in for thrills. Smelled like sweat. Peter Francis sat in the corner like he owned it. His feet were laced in loud high-tops. They rested atop the table.

"Howdy, pal," he said, bright and cheery as an Amway salesman. His outfit was too much: apricot jeans, light denim shirt, beige shearing jacket on top.

"Why are you dressed like a clown?" I deadpanned.

Peter snickered. "Oh, come on, man," he said. "Nothing wrong with dressing young. You should try it. It feels good to be hip, man."

I looked him over. "That's hip?" I asked. "I'm not so sure."

"Oh, it's hip, Posner. Trust me, it's hip. Capitol folks think I'm twenty-something."

That was preposterous. Peter wasn't any picture of youth. His face was fat, full of gin blossoms. His body was soft and doughy, as if he'd been sitting in a recliner his entire life.

"Anyway," he said. "It sure beats the lawyer costume! Nice paisley tie there, buddy."

I feigned a chuckle. "I enjoy dressing like an adult," I said.

Peter and I met in *Torts I.*

Law school, for me, was a five-year trip to the dentist. Financially, academically ... one sorry root canal after another. I worked two jobs to pay tuition, and one more for meals. Classes were three-hours a pop, foreign, with no subtitles. They'd sweat you, put your head in a vice. I could barely stand it. I graduated with mediocre grades and a whole lot of scorn.

But you know what? It was worth it. I passed the bar exam and reentered the world with a brand-new set of teeth. I could chew and taste a wide new palate of life's flavors ... none of it digestible without the law.

Peter's law school experience was different. More akin to a spa. He breezed through the program in two quick years while his old man paid for tuition, a condominium, and Peter's sleek foreign coupe.

Big Daddy Francis was a real peach. A defense contractor with physical shortcomings, he overcompensated with huge artillery. Made a fortune off Vietnam; strenuously supported every military conflict since. Viewed his family's spoils as a celebration of liberty; his son's educational pursuits were no exception. Party faithful called him "*The General*," even though the General never served.

Peter cleared his throat. His demeanor grew serious. "Thanks for coming," he said.

"It's fine. But I'm not sure I'm the guy."

"You drove all the way from Grand Rapids. You might as well hear me out." He lit a cigarette, waived his hand dismissively. "I'll make it worth your time, Posner," he said. "Trust me."

Trust me?

Trust was the dead-end road I swerved to avoid. Trust someone? Mother summed it up best: "*Don't trust anyone*," she said.

Then again, you can't always trust your mother.

"I'm listening."

Peter played the old dramatic. "The game's over for me," he said, painting the air with smoke. His saccharine expression was saturated with self-pity. "Seriously. This time it's *game over.*"

I liked Peter's sports analogy. "Have the General buy-off the umpires," I said, gamely perpetuating the theme.

"*The General?*" Peter's voice piped like a whistle. "He can't help me. He's mad as a hatter, crapping himself in a rest home. He wouldn't anyway. *The General* figured things out, back when he was lucid. Promptly wrote me out of the will. Now it all goes into a trust for my half-sister and her punk kids."

"Sister?"

"*Half*-sister. A bastard. Turns out the General knocked up a 1980 convention delegate."

"*General Family Values?* His pals down at the country club must be humiliated."

Peter paused, taking a deep drag. "Ah, who cares? I've got bigger fish to fry."

"Okay, so never mind the General. Why am I here?"

He looked up at the ceiling. "My intern is missing."

"Your intern?"

"Well, yeah." His voice cracked. "But Jerry isn't just any intern. He's—"

54

I knew where he was going and cut him off. "Are you a suspect?"

"No. Well, maybe ... I don't know." He sighed. "It's not like last time, I swear. I'm the one who reported him missing."

He went on sputtering for about five minutes, spitting out disconnected pieces of information until I finally lost my patience. I slapped him across the face, hard enough to make it sting. "Get a grip on it," I said, snubbing out his fallen cigarette with my shoe. "Nothing you've told me makes any sense. What are you hiding?"

He stood up, beckoned me to the table.

I met him halfway, which meant one step forward. "What is it?" I asked. "Spit it out already."

"You remember those kids?" he asked in a whisper. His voice was raspy, pained. "Missing kids? Back in '98?"

I really didn't. "What are you talking about?"

"Murdered young men. Disappeared from the bars. Don't you remember the old joke, the one about *Looking for Mr. Gay Bar?*"

Looking for Mr. Gay Bar.

I knew the lingua franca. Knew it well. I touched the scar on my face, running my finger across the smooth, raised flesh that trailed from nostril to earlobe.

1998. Anti-gay sentiment in Michigan was sky-high and politically fashionable. Gay marriage: banned. Health benefits: stripped. Young men, ages 18-22, were turning up dead, their ragged bodies littering the streets. Rumors circulated. Victims—all of them—were last seen at the Lansing gay bars. Disinterested cops did little to investigate. The press, owned by a conservative conglomerate, refused to cover it.

I decided to take matters into my own hands.

A mechanism in Michigan law qualifies Juris Doctors to register as private dicks. I obtained my license, hit the bars, and started asking questions. All signs pointed to one generic suspect: a clean-cut guy with sharp, eerie eyes. "Michigan Blue."

It took me a week to find him. Really, he found me. I was walking out of the bar, sober—around the corner and down the street to my car. A heavy blow caught me behind the ear, knocking me to the ground, dazed and flailing. The assailant crouched over me, drooling. He pounded my head and chest with large fists. I raised my arms, tried to shield myself. He pulled out a blade, slashed my face from nose to ear. I remembered the hunting knife, sheathed in my boot. Blood coated my face. Dripped into my mouth. Tasted sweet and hot and like iron. The knife was out of my boot and in my hand. I gripped it tight. Thrusted. The first wound was superficial, across the attacker's collarbone. Took him by surprise. Stunned, he paused for a moment, long enough for me to stab the blade deep into his throat. He rose, stumbling forward as the life spiraled out of him. Dark, gushing ribbons of blood sprayed into the street.

That was the last time I went into the night without my .38.

Peter had my attention. "The Mr. Gay Bar Murders," I said. "What about them?"

"You thought it was over," he said, pointing at me. "But it's not."

"What are you talking about?"

"The killing never stopped—and now it's come home."

"What?"

"Check the papers. They cover it now. More bodies. One in the Red Cedar, another on the MSU flood plains. A third in Old Town, discarded in the middle of Turner Street. The killer is bolder, more sophisticated now. He's dumping bodies in the open, taunting the Lansing and East Lansing cops."

I pictured the ribbons of blood, the killer staggering to his feet, then crumpling to the ground, lifeless. "The killer's dead, Peter. Believe me, I know."

"No. You killed a patsy, a *currier*. He was sent to pick you up. You were supposed to be delivered in a van, right out of Silence of the Lambs."

I shook my head. "Come on, Peter. This is pretty high drama, even for you."

"Read the papers." He spat onto the floor. "Same M.O. Same *exact M.O.*"

My face burned like it did when I gave a damn. "It can't be the same killer, Peter." In my heart of hearts, I knew that the original killer was dead.

"It's no copycat, Jay. I know."

"How do you know?"

"How? I saw the look in his eyes—eerie, crazed. *Michigan Blue*. Saw it myself, with my own two eyeballs."

"What?"

"I saw him. Two nights ago. At my fundraiser. I saw the way he looked at Jerry, my intern. Then he—Jerry—disappeared. That's when I put it all together."

"Who, Peter? Who are you talking about?"

"Chip Richmond."

If I had a lozenge, I would have choked on it. I nearly choked anyway.

"What?" I asked. "The Attorney General?"

"That's him, Jay. He's out there, killing people. And it was him in '98. He was in the Michigan Legislature back then. State senator by day, killer by night. Then you killed his delivery man. He laid low. Term limits hit. He ran for Congress, won. Moved to Washington. Raped and killed there for years, until they eliminated his seat after the Census. So ... he came back to Michigan, ran for Attorney General, won. Now he's back in Lansing. *Mr. Gaybar* is alive and well in 2011, Posner. Right here in Michigan."

I didn't know what to say.

"It's him, Jay, and I'm telling you: he has ears and eyes all over Ingham County. He could be listening right now, for all I know."

Three quick knocks rattled the room. Darnell entered. "My apologies," he said. "We need the space, Jay. Can you wrap it up?"

"Yeah, five minutes." The door closed and I turned to Peter. "What do you want me to do?"

"Be my attorney. Represent me."

"I'm not a defense lawyer, Peter."

"I don't care. I want your representation. And I want you to investigate the A.G."

I looked at my watch. "I'm not committing to anything, Peter." I needed to get home, tend to the dog. Poor Lucy Burger.

Peter seemed to expect my reluctance. "That's fine," he said. "They haven't charged me with anything."

"Let me digest this, Peter."

"Okay. You'll see, Jay. Trust me. You'll see. Talk to you tomorrow, then?"

I rubbed my chin. "I have a Rule 341 meeting in the morning. Call me after lunch."

"Connect the dots," Peter said as I made my way out. He drew two fingers across his Adam's apple, making a cutthroat gesture. "The guy you killed was a patsy."

I tried to piece it together during the drive home. I telephoned Fritz, my hot-shot paralegal. He was relaxing in his Eastown apartment, watching the game. I apologized for ruining his night and asked him to run a couple searches for me.

"No problem," he said. "I'm at my computer now. Westlaw?"

"No Westlaw. Just Google. I'm looking for news. Let me know when you're ready."

"I'm ready. Go ahead."

I rattled off the modus operandi of the *Mr. Gaybar* killer, which Fritz matched to several unsolved Washington cases between the years of 2002 and 2010.

"What about Lansing and East Lansing? Run the M.O. for this year."

He pulled three more, all from 2011.

"They're identical," Fritz said. "Males, age 18-22, white, short and thin. Raped, strangled, slashed across the face. Ligature marks on neck, cigarette burns on back. Rapist wore a condom."

"Unbelievable," I said, groaning. "Thanks, Fritz. See you tomorrow."

I hung up, knowing I'd been played by Peter Francis.

Whether I decided to represent him or not, our conversation was confidential. I couldn't disclose one word of it without his informed consent. And what was there to disclose? He hadn't admitted to anything. He'd pinned it all on Michigan's forgettable Attorney General—a hapless placeholder if there ever was one.

And the intern—this Jerry What's-his-face? Probably 18-22, white, short and thin. Was he still alive?

Chances were slim.

I sighed, resolved to another sleepless night. At least I had Ms. Lucy Burger to keep me company while I stared into the dark.

Thirty miles out of Lansing, the sky finally broke. Sheets of rain smacked my windshield. I slowed down to 20 mph just to stay on the road. Wind was rocking my car side-to-side.

So much for making good time.

Poor Lucy Burger.

I was doing 35, blowing all over the highway. Visibility was nothing. If my concentration hadn't been sapped, I might have noticed the Cadillac, but at that point, I had no clue.

Then I caught a glimpse of the pedestrian. How? I don't know. He was out in the middle of nowhere, wafting around like a scarecrow, trudging through the grass just off the highway.

I pumped the breaks, pulled to the shoulder, and waited for him to catch-up.

He ducked into my car, dripping wet. White fella, my age. Blondish-grey hair, parted on the left. Air Force flight jacket, authentic. His skin had a friendly glow to it. Must have been the interior lights.

"Thank you so much for stopping," he said. "I was out walking, got caught up in the storm."

"What a night for a walk!" I said.

He smiled, offered a shrug. "Not too great for a drive either."

"Yeah, tell me about it. I was out on business, up in Lansing."

We made small talk. He wasn't going far. Only about five miles or so. Nice guy. He knew I was an attorney and a dog person. Funny, since I don't remember mentioning either. His name was Jim Dressel. Air Force pilot, Vietnam. Said he worked at the Capitol years back. Stopped working up there a good twenty-five years ago. Now he had a part-time job doing something else.

His exit came up fast. I pulled over. His tone grew serious.

"Listen," he said. "There's a car following you. Cadillac, government plates. Nearly stopped when you did, then waited up the road."

I strained my eyes. "Is it still there? I can't see more than twenty feet ahead."

"No. He didn't wait this time. Went down *M-6*. You headed to Grand Rapids?"

"Yeah."

"Be careful, he might circle around. *M-6* to *131* to *196* ... it's a back-door route."

"Yeah, I know that drag."

"He might know where you live. Guys like that ... well, you shouldn't underestimate them."

He stepped out into the rainy night. I thanked him for the tip. He smiled, closed the door, and slipped back into the storm.

I was still driving slow; about 35 minutes from home when my phone rang.

"Jay Posner," I said.

"Yeah, Jay, it's Darnell."

"Darnell? What happened?"

"It's your friend, the senator."

"Did you arrest him?"

"No ... he's dead."

"What?"

"Senator Peter Francis. He went home and was murdered. Didn't even make it inside. Brains all over the sidewalk."

I should have trusted Peter Francis. What were the odds?

I called Fritz. "Can you get to my house in five minutes?" I asked.

"Yeah."

"Got the key?"

"Yeah."

"Okay, good. Go over there. Get Lucy Burger."

"You want me to take her out?"

"Yes, take her out of my house—to yours."

"Take her to my house?"

"Yes, take her to your house. For the night. And do it fast. Got it?"

"Yeah. Pick up the Burger, bring to my house, for the night. Do it fast."

"That's right. Five minutes. Can you get there in five minutes?"

"Yes. Keys in hand, heading out now. What's going on?"

"An unexpected meeting with the Attorney General. Long overdue."

"Okay. Ms. Burger and I will see you in the morning."

"Good, Fritz. Thank you."

The rain let up, but lightning continued to crackle across the midnight sky.

61

I pulled my .38 out from the seat console and picked up the pace.

Law and Allure

Mo Fawaz

Here, a lawyer practicing disability and discrimination law for government and nonprofit agencies writes of the ups, downs, and ups again of family-law practice.

"You know that obtaining sole legal and sole physical custody of your child is going to be an uphill battle, right? The law favors joint custody unless the other parent is practically not fit to be a parent. You have to understand that, in custody battles, the court looks for the best interest of the child."

"Hey," the woman screamed. "My ex is definitely not fit to be a father! I mean, he failed to make dinner when it was his turn to do so twice within one week – what a good father and role model would he be for my little Sam? He would starve him to death! So, ya see, it is Sam's best interest to be with me!"

"Right," Mark said, trying to tactfully explain. "Listen, Ms. Ah ... Smith. The court uses the best-interest factors to determine the best interest of the child. These factors consider many things, such as stability, mental and physical health, permanence, the child's preference, morals, any criminal record – domestic abuse, for example, whether witnessed by the child or against him." He stressed this last one a little, knowing that the father had a record of domestic violence some four or so years ago. He handed her a sheet with all the factors and another sheet with a bunch of questions.

"I will give you a few minutes to answer these questions while I run to the back to do something really quick, okay?"

63

Mark did not wait for an answer. The woman should have completed the questionnaire before meeting with him, but his assistant forgot to email the form to her — the assistant's third such mistake within two weeks. He and his assistant must have a talk, he thought, although recollecting that his assistant probably worked twice as hard as he did and that she, on multiple occasions, brought his attention to mistakes that he would have otherwise made if it were not for her knowledge and experience. He was lucky to have her, he thought, but why so many mistakes lately? He should have a talk with her to check on her well-being at least. If he could ever find time to talk, that is.

Finishing his email, he rejoined the client, smiling to disarm any objection at his absence, while remarking, "You have seven children, correct?"

"Sure do!" The woman proudly smiled. "It shows that I'm such an experienced mother and it is best for the child to be with me and his siblings! They all love each other, though they seem to fight with one another all the time."

"Seven children from six different fathers, correct?" he rejoined. Mark was trying to show the mother the weakness of her case. What will the judge think of a woman who has seven children from six different fathers? The woman was but 31, for God's sake! What does that say about her sense of responsibility and moral background?

"That's correct." The woman played with her fingers. They were small, pointed fingers, and her hands were so soft – Mark wondered whether this woman had ever washed dishes in her life. She continued, "Looks like all men out there are scumbags – don't you think? None of them know how to properly treat a woman."

Mark nodded. Last he checked, he was a man. He must be a scumbag for taking such a case, he thought. But everybody deserved representation. And the father was not a good father, either. But he at least had no other children. No matter, Mark thought, he was going to do his best, and, moreover, he had a good shot because the man was an idiot and had a record of domestic violence.

Mark's gaze shifted back to his client in front of him. She wore her long red hair loose – he wondered how long it took her to straighten it in such a manner. This woman had seven kids and yet had time to take good care of her physical appearance. She was wearing a tank top that showed significant skin and tight shorts that appeared to be made of the same fabric as Mark's boxers. The shorts did not appear to be any longer than his boxers, either, he thought, wondering whether this woman thought herself at a night club rather than a law office.

"Make sure you dress conservatively tomorrow," Mark ordered. He tried to sound firm. "Judges are somewhat old school and they do not appreciate it when they see women dressed in revealing clothing at the courtroom."

Mark then remembered that the word conservative is not quite clear enough. "This means a dress or skirt that goes below the knee at the shortest. Ideally, wear a suit." He stood up to imply the end of their meeting.

"By the way," he said, and then paused. "I don't think I asked how you heard about us? Who referred you to me?"

Lacey Smith smiled. Her smile was different. It seemed like she was trying to say something but did not have the guts to say it.

No matter, he thought, sometimes, if something is too embarrassing to say, he may not want to know what it is anyway, recollecting how one of his clients, Dalia – now what was her last name? He could not remember. He remembered how Dalia looked like she wanted to say something. Mark thought there is something important that he needs to know for the case at hand, so he insisted that Dalia tells him what was going on. He assured her that he will not be offended. It turned out Dalia wanted to ask him out on a date. He almost had a heart attack. His hand mechanically went to his chest as if he was recollecting the sense of shock.

Just then, Lacey perked up. "Ah – Dalia Emery. She is my neighbor, you know. She told me you were so good. Is it true that you helped her get custody of her daughter in a very contested case with her millionaire former boyfriend? That dude was so powerful, ya know. How did you pull that off? Did you bribe the judge or something?"

Lacey giggled. Her cheeks were turning a little red, too. Mark wondered what the woman was thinking.

Mark again placed his hand on his chest. What was wrong with these people? As a matter of fact, what was wrong with him? Why was he attracting such weird clients? Dalia asked him out on a date; Cima Crooks surprised him with a kiss on the lips; Tiffany Green exposed herself in front of him; John Jones spit in his face; and now this woman, Lacey Smith, thinks he bribed the judge. Gosh, he hoped she was not passing around such a rumor. That is so against the Model Rules of Professional Conduct!

"I most certainly did not bribe the judge. I would never as much as think of it – like – ever!" He emphasized his statement multiple times. There was no way he would let such a statement pass without making sure this woman understands that he has no power over any judge whatsoever. Just to be sure that she understood, he ended with, "I haven't any influence over judges, Ms. Smith."

Mark knew that he was speaking in such a cold tone of voice that could be perceived as rude and condescending. He hated to be so mean, but, as it turns out, this manner of speaking is often perceived as confident and powerful. People like to feel that their attorney is powerful and confident. When the attorney appears confident, his or her confidence seems to translate into a sense of peace with the clients. They feel like they have somebody who is powerful looking after their interests.

"I know the law – yes," Mark affirmed. "I know the judges and understand their language. I know where to stop and what points to emphasize, yes. But that's the extent of it." He wanted to say something more – anything to distract his thoughts. He hated to tell people when their cases were weak, or not so strong, but he had a duty to do it. He must be honest to the utmost extent possible.

"I must emphasize to you, Ma'am, that our case may not be the strongest – not for sole legal and physical custody, at least. I told you this will be an uphill battle, you know. But I'll do my best. That's all I can promise."

Mark extended his hand to Lacey, implying that he had to leave the room.

"I have a meeting in – like – five minutes," he said. "I will see you tomorrow at 8:30 in the morning. And again, remember, wear a suit – a conservative suit. The hearing starts at 8:30, so please be there at least 15 minutes before. Being on time shows the judge that you respect your appointments."

He wanted to say that being timely reflects a sense of responsibility, but responsibility and Lacey Smith were quite the enemies. After all, what responsible person gets seven kids from six different fathers by age 31?!

It was Mark's first hearing for sole custody since he passed his Bar Exam. He had practiced family law as a junior associate in his law school's clinic, and he even had many cases since getting his license to practice law. However, Lacey's was his first case for sole legal and physical custody since graduating his junior-associate position in the clinic nearly two years before.

His last case for sole custody, back at the clinic, was quite a success. The father, however, had made his job much easier because the father had been abusive to the kids. The mother, at the time, was not a good mother, either, but she was the lesser of the two evils.

In this case, Mark thought, Lacey Smith may not be the best mother. But was the father any better with his record of domestic violence nearly four years ago? Probably not, he thought, but it was likely not enough to award Lacey Smith sole legal and physical custody, either. Worse, Mark thought, opposing counsel was Bradley Brunner. Mark had never faced off with Brunner, but Brunner's license number showed that he had been a lawyer for the last 35 years. He probably knew more about the ins and outs of the field than Mark did.

Mark reached to the back of his head and tried to massage the tension. This was going to be a tough case, and he will probably have to write it off as one of the losses in his record. Sadly, it seemed like his losses often taught him the most. He always wondered what he could have done differently to get a different result. Unfortunately, in the hypothetical world, it is all about guessing. After every loss, he sat at his desk and reviewed the entire case. He always kept notes on whether he should have emphasized any point more than he did or whether he should have called an expert witness.

The courtroom was practically empty. Excepting the parties involved, nobody was in the room. Outside, it had been so cold that he wondered whether he should have been in his bed, drinking coffee and reading the paper. Fortunately, he only had such temptations when he had difficult cases or clients. The cold weather certainly did not help.

Entering the courtroom, Mark looked at his client and almost groaned. Lacey dressed conservatively all right. She was wearing black tights and a mini skirt. She wore a tank top that, true, appeared dressy but still showed way too much skin. She wore her red hair loose, like she had at their last meeting, and she wore stiletto heels.

Mark could only pray to God that the judge did not kick out Lacey for contempt of court. She plainly intended to seduce someone, from the look of her auburn-red hair on her shoulders, he thought. Was the woman trying to use her beauty to gain the judge's sympathy? If her goal was to do so, then it would definitely fail. Judge Creek was not that type of person.

The hearing began with his direct examination of Lacey.

"Ms. Smith," Mark asked, "Can you please tell me the age of your youngest child?"

"He's two, but he's so sharp. You would think him five or six. Wanna see a pic of him? He's in my phone. Just look here – look – ain't he so adorable?" She leaned forward toward Mark, holding the smartphone toward him. Although at the podium some distance away, Mark instinctively stepped back, bumping into counsel table.

Gathering himself, Mark sighed. He was used to clients like Lacey Smith, but, no matter, he wanted to be done to go home and sip some warm coffee. Another hour of this torture and he would need to sip rum instead. Not that he ever drank alcohol. That is probably why many attorneys seem to abuse alcohol, he thought, touching his head. He opened his water bottle and took a generous gulp.

The time allowed him to recompose himself before the next question. It only took him a few seconds to drink the water, but he wondered whether this short time felt like eternity to the judge and Lacey. His gaze accidentally shifted to Lacey's legs. He could see her purple underwear from beneath her mini-skirt. He blushed and quickly looked the other direction.

"Ms. Smith. Can you please tell me who attends to the needs of your child?" He looked at the notebook in his hands. He was not looking for anything in particular – just wanted to hide his face behind something – anything.

"What an offensive question!!!!" she shouted. "Of course, I do! You think this scumbag ever cares?"

Lacey pointed her finger at the father in a threatening manner before continuing. "Naughty naughty! He even drank my child's milk once. Can you believe it? It was breast milk that I had saved for my little baby!" Her look changed to a smirk. Mark wondered whether her outburst was heading. Maybe this dispute had more to it than his client had told him. Every matter has more to it, he had already learned.

"Who feeds the child every day?" Mark continued.

"You think my baby ever eats if I wasn't there? This jerk would feed him sometimes, but I would be telling him a story to make him stay!"

Lacey shook her head. The look on her face was changing to anger. He could not quite comprehend this woman or what was going on. Mark wondered whether it was a good idea to have the couple in the same room. He crossed his fingers, hoping neither party would start a fist fight. He had seen a lot, but a fight in the courtroom would be something he had never seen before. Another twenty or so questions and he would be done with this woman, but then she would have to be cross-examined. God help him then.

Mark completed the direct examination without further outburst. Cross-examination began.

"Ms. Smith, it's true that you have seven children, correct?"

"That's correct, sir. It shows that I'm such an experienced mother. My baby Sam must be with his siblings."

Lacey looked at opposing counsel with half-closed eyes. Her eye lashes appeared so long. Her hand then moved to straighten her hair. Opposing counsel suddenly seemed attracted to her. His tongue licked his lower lip unconsciously, while his eyes focused on the woman's legs. Or maybe they were focused on her purple underwear.

69

Mark wondered whether the judge had seen Lacey's underwear or not. Postponing the hearing is never taken lightly, so maybe the judge decided to act as if he did not notice. Mark looked at the seething father and unconsciously shifted his seat further away.

"These seven children come from six different fathers, Adam Grigg, Alex Brown, Fred Tanner, Tom Howe, Bobby Price, and Jeff Lambert, correct?" opposing counsel continued.

Ms. Smith was shaking her right leg in a dancing-like manner now, clearly trying to seduce opposing counsel. Mark wondered how opposing counsel could sound so sharp when his eyes were on the woman's legs as if she were on the dessert menu. No matter, Mark appreciated the attorney's strategy of naming every father. He clearly intended to emphasize this point for the judge. He thought it was a good strategy and decided to adopt it in future cases.

Lacey simply nodded, adding suggestively, "I don't know. Men are so attracted to me. I just don't know how to push them away sometimes." She shrugged, exposing more cleavage.

It was all like a dream, no, a nightmare, Mark thought.

Suddenly, the father stood up at counsel table, saying to his own counsel, "Look here! You're flirting with my girl! I saw you licking your lips. You must be the man with whom she cheated on me!"

The father grabbed opposing counsel by his tie. Fortunately for counsel, it was a clip-on tie that promptly gave way into the father's hand. Counsel darted in the direction of the courtroom door without saying a word. Counsel was moving well for a sixtyish man, Mark thought. He wanted to step over to help him, but opposing counsel had already reached the exit and left the courtroom. The bailiff must have been in shock, too. By the time he reached the father, opposing counsel was already gone.

The judge, elected just six months earlier and still new to the bench, looked perplexed.

"Don't be jealous, Baby," Lacey Smith said, getting up from the witness stand to run to and hold the father in a tight embrace. "I was just trying to make you see what you're missing. I wanted you to feel jealous – that's all."

Lacey giggled as she and the father of her youngest child fell into a tighter embrace. Her lips locked with the father's lips as if they were on their honeymoon. The judge coughed uncomfortably.

"Forgive me, Your Honor," Lacey Smith finally said in her most seductive voice, as she and the father released their tight embrace. She lifted her hands up in surrender. "No need to determine custody any more. We're back together – forever. Right, sweetheart?"

Deciding to Sue

Graham Ward

Here, a lawyer with decades of litigation experience, mostly but not exclusively paid by insurers to defend tort lawsuits, explores the biases and intricacies of lawyer and client decision-making, through an archetypal first consult with a new personal-injury client.

"I just want you to know I'm not one of those greedy people who sue all the time."

I hid a painful laugh at the client's comment, made barely a moment after the client had first perched on the chair across from my desk, as if ready to take flight at the first peek of the devil's horns that I was presumably hiding in my graying-at-the-edges hair. She was plainly making every effort to show her reluctance at even visiting my office.

I smiled warmly back at the client, hiding no horns but only my disappointment at the client's presumption. I knew that the client meant no offense to me—didn't mean to cast *ambulance-chaser!* aspersions at my peculiar niche within a broad profession. She was upset, confused, and fearful, like nearly all my clients at their first meeting, what we lawyers call the *intake*. Well, see there—maybe we *are* a little carnivorous in my niche, I thought, this time with a little better-spirited silent laugh.

Having recovered my self-deprecating humility, I began with her my long-practiced intake art. While I was interviewing this pert but deeply troubled client, I realized more clearly than before that she was also interviewing me. My question, as always, was whether I would *take her case*, as we lawyers think of the intake exercise. *Taking her case* meant asking her to sign a contingency-fee agreement, which meant that I would work for free unless I garnered her a recovery, in which case I would take a third of that recovery. Of course, if she had been considering offering me an hourly retainer, then my objective would have been quite different: to gain her trust and confidence. After all, if I faced no financial risk in serving her, and instead she was offering to *pay* me, upfront no less, then I had no decision to make, only the payment to secure. I winced. *See there*, I thought again, *you are greedy, you devil, you!*

I silently shook off the thought, more eager now to gather the many pieces of information that I would need to decide whether to engage in a more complete investigation or to decline the matter. As I did so, though, I was more conscious than usual that the client had her own decision to make, which was whether to retain me. What was *she* thinking? They hadn't taught me that in law school, that law practice often involves what marketers call a *beauty pageant* or *dog-and-pony show*.

Doubtless, the client across my desk was looking still for my hidden horns. But probably, she was also wondering whether she could trust my skills and judgment, whether she could get along with and respect me, and whether I shared her own commitments, which plainly involved a substantial degree of integrity and consideration for others. She was also trying to understand the justice system, not just how it operated but more so what commitments it represented. Of course, she, too, may have been hiding horns, that is, using feigned rather than genuine reluctance at pursuing a claim to hide her own greed.

In any case, as we spoke, I mixed subtly in with my questions brief explanations of the justice system's goals, the role that liability insurance plays, and the effect of her *not* pursuing a claim—that the insurers (those greedy insurers!) would make a little larger profit for having kept *her* compensation. Even as I explained so, I thought again, *see there, you devil, you! Manipulating her for a fee, you are!* But I knew, too, that the client on the other side of my desk, now somewhat relaxing, would benefit from my little bit of education, which after all was true even if offered not just for her but also for my own purpose.

73

As our mutual inquiry continued, I thought about why clients, even badly injured clients who know that the law offers them compensation, feel the need to excuse in advance their pursuit of that remedy. They plainly perceive some degree of socially unacceptable behavior, from the fact of their presence in my office. They may even feel that because another has injured them, they are somehow *different* than others, maybe even *less valuable* than others, a sort of victim mentality like the Stockholm syndrome in which they come to trust their victimizers more than those who would relieve them of their victim status.

As the client told me her story, answered my questions, and listened to my not-always-subtle bits of wisdom on the justice system, I realized that she was like most of my other personal-injury clients in another way, beyond her reticence to avail herself of my services. She worked for a living. She didn't live in the so-called *finest* of communities with the so-called *best* of people. She was instead a member of the nation's backbone, yes, those on whose backs the rest of us enjoy the so-sought-after best and finest. Bad things, unfortunate injuries, workplace accidents, and their untoward results, happen to those who work for a living, not those who acquire, amass, and control the capital that fuels the work.

For the first time, then, I realized that her reluctance at seeking redress may have been in part due to her *guilt* at not already being a member of the elite on whom she would depend, and on whose laws she would depend, for relief. She, too, had driven past the same billboards as everyone else, displaying the tort claimant in handcuffs and an orange prison suit, with the insurance lobby's caption "defrauders go to jail" beneath it. Corporate campaigns against litigiousness and frivolous lawsuits, promoting tort "reform," had not only molded the courts and legislatures, and public opinion, but had even permeated the self-concept of the injured.

Or if not guilt, then maybe she harbored resentment at resorting to elite favor to ensure her basic provision. She perceived that the law was not hers or was no longer hers but instead the captive of others who had more education, wealth, and influence in the boardrooms, academies, courts, and legislatures.

And so, with this client, as with clients who followed her, I began to explain that every case, in the grand tradition of the common law, is unique, rising and falling on its own merits within long-established rules and principles, pursued in an unbiased judicial process. The injured client on the other side of my desk was not wrong or bad in seeking redress of grievances within a civil-justice system but was instead pursuing ancient remedies and enforcing ancient rights that had ordered every civil society.

At this point, the client naturally brought up the McDonald's hot-coffee case, or I should say the corporate campaign that followed it because the case itself was something quite different than publicly portrayed. Yes, I acknowledged to the client, a badly burned customer, one with horrible third-degree burns across her lap, had won an overly large verdict against the company, although one that the trial judge promptly and properly reduced. But no, I further explained, the woman hadn't stupidly spilled ordinary coffee on herself, as the corporate campaign implied and the public assumed. The coffee, far hotter than industry standards, had spilled from a loose lid as the worker had carelessly handed it to her, just as the corporate defendant had faced similar claims from many other badly injured customers.

The corporate campaign had deployed behavioral psychology in such an effective way that the documentary *Hot Coffee* intended to correct its misimpressions made barely a splash. We should not be surprised, though, I told the client, because after all, Madison Avenue marketing campaigns employing similar strategy have successfully created perceived needs for whole categories of non-essential new products.

The client then told me briefly about an experience that she had with another lawyer whom she had consulted before seeing me. She had telephoned the lawyer, who had promptly assured her with great confidence that she had a *great* claim, even though the lawyer knew little to nothing about what had happened. The lawyer insisted that she make an appointment to see the lawyer right away.

"What happened?" I asked.

"I made the appointment just to get the lawyer off the telephone but then never kept the appointment. I wasn't going to see a lawyer that I couldn't trust, who obviously just wanted to get me in the door."

"And so, you came to see me?" I asked again, although with a little too much pride.

"No, I did nothing," she answered. "I didn't want to deal with *any* lawyers after that introduction."

I decided to explain to her that the lawyer had indeed done both her and himself a disfavor. He might have created a wrong impression in her mind that she had a good claim when she didn't, wasting substantial amounts of her time and trouble. He was also making trouble for himself if he had to break the bad news that her claim was not what he had initially represented. She might then file a grievance against him or even sue for malpractice, while complaining to friends in ways that would ruin his reputation.

The client did sign my contingency-fee agreement. I did not promise her anything. I even resisted estimating the value of her claim, knowing that my estimate might well be high and that it would inappropriately mold her perception about her case, in what behavioral psychologists call *anchoring*.

We met again two weeks later after the client had gathered some information about which I had asked, and after I had gathered other information with her authorization and done some needed research.

At this second meeting, I felt that I had a good handle on the case *as she perceived it*. After all, where you stand determines what you see. Yet, again I resisted the strong temptation to tell her the probable value of her case. We agreed that we were nearly ready to contact the wrongdoer's insurance claim representative, whom my investigation had identified. I would not, though, do what many lawyers would do, which would be to demand disclosure of the policy limits and, perhaps, make a policy-limits demand. While those tactics are common, and one does in high-value claims typically need to know the available insurance, I didn't want to anchor the client's perception at an inappropriately high level, sacrificing my integrity and client relationship in the process.

Moreover, I knew how the claim representative would respond to my request to disclose and pay the policy limits. The claim representative would likely have other information that I did not yet know, contradicting certain aspects of the client's presumed claim. The claim representative could justly have countered with a refusal to disclose the limits because they were not relevant, and counter with a nuisance offer. I would then have caused the claim representative to anchor the insurer's perspective at nuisance value.

So, I explained to the client the problem of one-sided information and the anchoring effect. The client understood that we were better instead to develop both sides' information before locking the opposing sides into place around their initial evaluation. One finds much easier getting the right figure in place initially than changing an initial figure, even when new information warrants the change. From a behavioral-psychology perspective, we routinely hold too long and too fast to initial positions.

I also explained to the client that exaggerated demands and low-balled offers encourage the claimant and insurer to see one another not only as adversaries but as manipulative adversaries, even lying adversaries. In fact, neither side may have lied about known facts or concealed and manipulated information. They may have made reasonable evaluations, but if they hadn't first shared information, they would have been making one-sided evaluations. We didn't need the insurer to identify either of us as the greedy, money-grubbing, scheming claimants that corporate campaigns portray. So, together we decided to first make a full exchange of information before making a demand or asking for an offer, or even asking for a disclosure of the often-important policy limits.

We also considered involving early an independent professional skilled in dispute resolution. To get the proper outcome, one based on rights and rationality rather than manipulation and misinformation, we would want someone who understood these perspectives, biases, and decision-making principles. We would want someone who understood the unintended consequences of ineffective, ill-timed, and poorly conceived strategy, tactics, and communication.

The client initially resisted, saying, "I thought that's what you guys, the lawyers, do."

I agreed that some lawyers are indeed skilled in just that way and, not just skilled, but also able to employ that skill even while representing and advocating for a party. Yet I also pointed out to the client that some systems, like worker's compensation and medical-malpractice claims under tort reform, provide for similar pre-suit exchanges of information and communications to facilitate early resolution.

In using these approaches with my clients, I encountered some resistance from my law partners, who still thought about dispute resolution primarily in political, adversarial, and economic terms, without knowledge of cognitive biases and behavioral psychology. A justice system need not operate in that manner, I would explain to my law partners. We don't have to be so individualistic, even egotistic. We don't always need to produce winners and losers. Material ends, more and more money, do not always produce what our clients truly seek, which often has instead to do with addressing the loss of unique and precious abilities, and the concomitant loss of unique and precious love, society, and companionship.

Indeed, I would point out to my law partners that we served clients, or could serve clients, whose cultures and commitments were not so materialistic and individualistic. We could serve clients in ways that decreased adversarial relationships and increased harmony.

Some of my law partners agreed that when we meet with new clients, we should take care to recognize opportunities to act as learned professionals and to serve as ministers of justice. They admitted room for educating clients not only about the specifics of their case but also about the assumptions and biases that permeate and in some instance poison and mislead our decision-making.

We agreed that such sensitive service is not always easy. Some of my law partners saw their current practices as sound and any reform as foolish. Yet most of my law partners agreed that pursuing and defending cases in an adversarial manner, up to and through trial, also created substantial risk for misunderstanding and wrong outcomes. If we are not careful, then we can let the present system not only unnecessarily create winners and losers, but we can also turn losers into winners and winners into losers.

Nearly all my law partners agreed that we could do better at using the best voice to create understanding, foster respect, and pursue restorative principles that more closely resemble truth and justice. Earlier acquisition and sharing of information was one key. We need to stop expending most of the resources at the last minute before trial, when parties are entrenched in win-at-all-costs mode.

We need to exchange more information in non-adversarial manner, even before claimants file suit, with the goal finding restorative opportunities that meet both short-term and long-term needs.

This one reluctant client helped me see that the law alone does not provide a sufficient answer. She taught me that I needed to reach more deeply into other disciplines to improve communication, discernment, strategy, approaches, and outcomes. She helped me see that healthy, creative, well-studied reform may determine whether our society continues to look to the civil-justice system as its bedrock institution for adjusting, preserving, and promoting private rights. We may need fewer winners and losers, and better justice.

Next

David Tarrien

Here, a law professor and dean, writing instructor, and former practitioner in education and disability law uses an abbreviated prose form approaching poetry, to explore a new lawyer's concern in facing the bar exam.

He turned away from the open door.

What will I do now?

Did I do anything?

What the hell –

Is it –

God.

Up and out ...

How on earth did I –

Okay, settle down –

Can't be as bad as all that – can it?

There will be questions – what do I say? Blank. There were 24 – no ... 25 ... Christ. Trespass? Battery? Murder? I don't know; shit – what am I going to tell her? What am I going to tell him? Can't do it again – no way. Won't ... do I have a choice? I have no choice ...

I ate a hamburger. What the fuck? I'm a vegetarian. Needed it – out of my element; extreme stress. Willful. Premeditated. Knock it off; no excuse, no duress, no way, know how. I can be an accountant --- no, I can't.

I need a drink – a bar! The bar. Passing by the bar. Pass the bar. Fuck.

The end of the world? End of a chapter? End to end? This is crazy.

Go home. Avoid questions. Answer all questions. What are your issues? What is the call? Why so many? Stop.

Enough. Too much? 42? Stop.

Three months? Jesus that's a long time; what if ...

what if I don't ... don't panic.

You will.

But what if I don't?

You will. But if not ... What. Next.

The Lawyer as Client

Sarah Rae Miller

Here, a lawyer known at her firm as the technician, who also teaches out of love for children and volunteers out of compassion for others, writes of how becoming a client could encourage a lawyer to learn to show clients compassion.

As she sat down at her desk that morning, she noticed the two chairs designated for clients that sat on the opposite side of her desk. They were hand-me-downs from her Grandpa John. *I should really replace those*, she thought to herself, *with something a little more comfortable.*

Another day at the firm posed the usual tasks, except today was a little different. The night before she had stayed up late to pray about her marriage. Her husband, who was also an attorney, had flown to Texas for a deposition over a month ago and hadn't returned. He worked as in-house counsel for a major hospital and was gone frequently but never for this length of time. Her mind started to race as she opened her email. Maybe God will change his heart, she thought as she read an email from her boss sent at midnight the night before.

She couldn't let her mind go there—not now, and she had settled her circumstances with God the night before. Tom, her husband, would most likely leave her for Heather, but until then, she was committed to him and their covenant.

"Good morning!" Lacey chimed. Lacey was Jaime's friendly, hard-working assistant. Sometimes Jaime believed that Lacey worked harder than the attorneys.

"Good morning, Lacey. How was your evening with AJ?"

"It was great. We went to Bob Evans and had the loaded potato skins--AJ's favorite!" she replied as she rubbed her stomach.

"And how are you feeling this morning?" Jaime teased.

"Oh. I had to take a few Zantac, but it was worth it as usual."

Lacey also struggled in her marriage, but Jaime didn't feel comfortable asking Lacey for advice. What kind of advice was Jaime even looking for? She was the advisor. Jaime quickly changed the subject after glancing at her schedule.

"Lacey, this morning I meet a new client. From what her ex-boyfriend told me, she has a few questions about filing for divorce."

Lacey didn't even flinch at the ex-boyfriend part of Jaime's description. "Yup. I have the papers ready if she's interested. And I think we can waive a couple of the fees. It should be pretty routine."

The night before, Jaime's neighbor had called and said his ex-girlfriend wanted to divorce her husband. Jaime told her neighbor to have his ex-girlfriend come into the office first thing, and she could answer a few questions to ease her nerves. Jaime sent a quick text message to Lacey when she hung up with her neighbor and asked her to have the divorce papers ready, and, as usual, she did.

"Thanks, Lacey. Her name is Kate. Send her in when she gets here."

From the sounds of it, Kate was a submissive wife. Her husband kicked her out of the house—and Kate willingly left. Why didn't Kate try to stay in the house? Jaime was often questioning her client's motives, logic, and reasoning—not in a judgmental way but more out of curiosity, as in, *if I were in her circumstances, I would have called the police and stayed in the home*. Whenever her thoughts turned judgmental, she quickly repented and moved on.

Jaime had some experience in family law, especially divorce proceedings. In law school, she volunteered at a family law clinic for a year. The work was fascinating. Well, the clinic patrons were fascinating, while the work was routine. Divorces were easy. It was the people who were complicated.

Jaime had one patron who thought she had been divorced for nine years, and when she went to remarry, she found out that she was still married. *I still don't know why she didn't ask the court about her final judgment of divorce,* Jaime mused. *If she didn't receive the papers, wouldn't she call?* Jaime's curiosity got the better of her again.

The law firm at which Jaime practiced had a family law attorney, but Jaime's work was primarily municipal. The County of Macomb had long retained the firm as corporate counsel. Jaime spent her days advising on property disputes, contract negotiations, and ordinances. But, when friends and family asked for legal advice, even outside of municipal law, she did her best to help.

Jaime heard Lacey greet Kate in the lobby. Of course, Lacey's greeting was a warm one. Better to receive a greeting from Lacey than from Jaime. Jaime was almost too calm and cool for people. She knew it made them uneasy, but she didn't change her ways because she was comfortable, and it was how she best did her job. At least, that's what she thought.

Kate walked into her office. She wore a t-shirt with cutoff jean shorts and flip flops. Her cigarettes poked out of her purse and her blonde bangs hung just above her eyelashes.

"Kate, nice to see you. Come in." Jaime stood, but didn't leave the spot behind her desk.

"W-where should I sit?"

There were only the two hand-me-down chairs in the office, in addition to the chair in which Jaime sat. *Should I make a joke to help her relax?* Jaime thought.

"You can sit on my desk if you'd like," Jaime said with a smile.

"I-I'll just sit here." The chair creaked loudly as Kate sat in the hand-me-down chair.

Ugh, Jaime thought, *I totally need to replace those chairs.*

Kate looked around the twelve-foot by twelve-foot office. Jaime followed her eyes for a moment, then asked, "Did you find the place alright?"

In law school, Jaime learned to say that to a prospective client. Apparently, it made them comfortable.

"Yeah. I used to live around here, so I knew where you was talking about."

"Great." Jaime replied softly, then paused briefly to let Kate continue to look around the office. Kate had probably never been in an attorney's office, or maybe she had, but it wasn't Jaime's place to pry. But then again, part of Jaime's job was to pry. So, she cut right to the point. "Hey, it sounds like you want to file for divorce. Tell me about the circumstances regarding your husband."

Kate looked uncomfortable, so Jaime stayed quiet, letting Kate gather her thoughts.

"Well, my husband kicked me out last night—"

"Of whose home?" Jaime cut in.

"Um, my Ma and Pa's."

"So, your mom and dad own the home in which you and your husband reside?"

Kate simply nodded her head.

"Are your mom and dad still living?" Jaime used to flinch when she asked this question, but not anymore. After drafting so many wills, preparing questions for trials, and reading transcripts, not much made Jaime flinch.

"Yeah," replied Kate.

"I'm glad to hear that," Jaime said in effort to sound thoughtful.

"Did your husband threaten you physically?"

"No, he just said, 'I'm kicking you out. Leave.' So, I left."

You left because he told you to leave? Jaime thought but said instead, "Did you want to stay?"

"Well, yeah. Can I? I mean, that's my main concern right now. I don't have anywhere to stay and just want to be in our home. Not necessarily with him, but just in a place I know."

"Kate, it's your parents' home. You're allowed to be there."

"Really? I mean, I just didn't know my rights and all. So, I just left 'cause I didn't know."

Jaime was perplexed, but didn't let on so. "Yes, you may be there, but if he becomes violent or verbally abusive, you need to call the police."

Kate nodded. As usual, Jaime let the silence linger. As she did, she noticed Kate clutching her pack of cigarettes. She's nervous, Jaime noted.

After a few more questions and responses, Jaime walked Kate to her office door. Kate held the necessary divorce papers in her hand. "Please don't hesitate to contact me." Jaime sounded like one of the memoranda that she wrote to the County Administration.

Lacey quickly stepped in and picked up the conversation from there. "You okay, Hun? What're you doing the rest of the day? Did you see the new Farmer's Market down the street? Stop by for the maple-glazed donuts. They are the best!" Lacey always knew how to make people feel like they were long time friends.

Jaime stepped back inside her office and checked her personal email. She found only a message from Tom—her husband—with the subject line reading only *Papers*.

Dear Jaime,

I am sorry for our circumstances, but I have decided to file for divorce. You will receive the divorce papers from my counsel Edwin P. VanHalen. Please contact Mr. VanHalen with any questions or concerns. Again, I apologize.

Tom

Jaime's eyes filled with tears as she looked away from her computer and out her office window. She saw her boss pull up in his black Mercedes. She knew he'd stop in her office, so she fought back the tears. God had prepared her for this email the night before when she spoke with Him. *I will praise you through this storm*, Jaime thought just as her boss glided into her office.

Her boss, Greg Williams, was also quiet and calm but in a much less intense way than Jaime. Greg sauntered into the office with a quiet, "Hey." He walked right behind Jaime's desk and leaned into the window. "I got some new wheels this morning," he said looking out the window.

"Yeah? Your car looks the same."

"Bike wheels," Greg replied as he pretended to grab two handle bars.

"Ah. Makes sense. You going for a ride then today?"

"Nah. I have the soup kitchen this afternoon. Homeless people need their dinner." Greg sauntered back out of the office. Jaime heard him say the same quiet, "Hey" to Lacey as he passed her desk.

Jaime thought of Greg's email he had sent at midnight and jumped up to follow him. As she caught up to him in the long hallway, he said to her, "Hey. Stop in my office when you get the chance. I want to talk to you about that email."

"Is now cool?" Jaime sounded so informal with her boss that it took her by surprise.

"Come on in," he said as they approached his office.

Jaime had a love-hate relationship with Greg's office. She loved the dim lighting, mood music that always played, silly family pictures, and chairs in which you could fall asleep. Jaime imagined that a therapist's office felt very similar. On the other hand, she was not a fan of how much work she gained every time she entered the office.

"Have you heard of Sheryl Crow?" Greg inquired as he dropped a file stack on his desk.

"Yeah, but it's been awhile since I listened to her." Again, her informality startled Jaime.

"You gotta hear her new song," Greg said as he adjusted the volume to the large speakers. Sheryl's melodious voice filled the room as Greg spun around in his chair.

"So, what's going on?" Greg asked. Jaime never knew how to respond to this question from Greg. He always asked it like a concerned father would after hearing his daughter's heart had been broken. Does he mean with Tom and I? Jaime avoided the subject and stuck to work.

"Well, I saw your email about Rick and the Board of—"

"Hang on a second." Greg turned his phone on speaker and dialed a number. "Bonnie, hi, it's Greg. Do you still need help at the soup kitchen today?"

Bonnie replied, "Greg! Hi, yes! We are looking forward to seeing you!"

"Great. Be there at one."

As Greg hung up, he looked at Jaime apologetically. "Sorry," he said.

"No worries." Jaime was a little too comfortable in the chair and tried to sit up straighter. She grabbed one of Greg's candies and popped it in her mouth. What was wrong with her? Greg returned to his concerned-father mode and said, "You know we would do anything for you." The tears filled Jaime's eyes again because she knew that Greg was watching out for her and more importantly praying for her and Tom.

As she drove home that evening, Jaime thought about the email from Tom. She was too tired to cry anymore, but tears seemed to naturally stream down her face as she thought about calling the attorney, Mr. VanHalen, and not her own husband. What would she say? Should she, an attorney, get an attorney?

Jaime thought about her latest trip to her doctor's office. She had teased her doctor about who his primary care physician was. Her doctor had laughed at the question but responded nonchalantly, "I have my own primary care. A surgeon can't operate on himself, so he'd have to have a surgeon. It's the same kind of thing, you know?"

Jaime thought it a valid point. But what about an attorney? Do I hire someone to tell me what I already know? She felt her face scrunch up as she thought over her dilemma.

When she unlocked the door at home, Mandy, their border collie, jumped to greet her. "You're almost as friendly as Lacey!" Jaime said in a baby voice, knowing that Lacey would not appreciate that comment.

Yet as she stepped into her house, it all felt different. She slumped to the floor and let Mandy lick her and step on her work suit. Now that divorce was an actuality, what would she and Tom do with Mandy? Mandy was her baby; she and Tom had no kids. They got Mandy on a trip to Indiana for Tom's college alumni party.

"So technically you are marital property," Jaime said to Mandy who cocked her head at Jaime's words. *Wait!* Jaime thought indignantly, *my dog isn't marital property!* Although she knew that the law considered Mandy so, Jaime couldn't label her beloved dog as marital property. She stayed on the floor for the next hour with Mandy and let the tears flow.

The next morning Jaime had a free hour and decided to stop by a friend of her dad's law office. He was older, wiser, and specialized in family law. Jaime figured she could ask him a few questions, although she didn't really know what to ask because she had all the answers.

What am I doing here? Jaime thought as she sat in the shiny, modern lobby. A slender woman in a red suit and extremely high heals approached her. *Is she an attorney?* Jaime questioned.

"Mr. Matthews will see you now."

Jaime stood and followed the woman, thinking, *Well, obviously not.* This firm was much bigger than her firm. The hallway was humming with attorneys, assistants, and corporate-client representatives, and probably expert witnesses, too. Jaime hoped she wouldn't see anyone she knew. What if they asked her why she was there? Again, the question of whether an attorney gets an attorney to handle legal matters entered her mind.

The overly high-healed, slender woman stopped at the door to Mr. Matthews' office and simply extended her arm. Jaime followed it like she would a traffic signal and kept going. The office was large with two desks and a credenza. The two desks were both suited for an attorney. There were chairs—*five, six, seven*, Jaime counted. After all the courtrooms, conference rooms, and even judge's chambers she'd been in, this office was the most overwhelming.

Mr. Matthews hung up the phone as she stood in the middle of his office.

"Jaime." He stood from his desk. "Janice!" he yelled for the red-suited woman who had just dropped Jaime off. In the doorway, he muttered a few words to the woman. It made Jaime uncomfortable. Were they talking about her? She tried to ignore it while she continued to stand in the middle of the office.

Mr. Matthews glanced at Jaime. "Have a seat. I'll be right there."

Jaime didn't know where to sit, so she slowly walked toward one of the two desks, irritated now that Mr. Matthews had left with the overly high-healed, slender woman Janice.

"Yeah. Right there is fine," Mr. Matthews said when he returned after a few moments and Jaime was just taking a seat. "So, you haven't been here in awhile—or maybe ever? Did you find the place okay? Parking can be a pain." Jaime didn't know whether to laugh or cry that his inquiries were the same as those that she had asked Kate the day before and every other new client. While she had thought the questions helpful, she suddenly realized that they were not.

"Yes. Just fine."

Mr. Matthews looked at his computer and clicked a few things. Jaime didn't know what to do while he fiddled distractedly and, she thought, somewhat rudely. So, she looked around the office. Although Jaime usually preferred silence, here, it lingered a little too long. *What is he doing? Why isn't he talking?* Jaime thought.

He interrupted her thoughts, "I'm sorry to hear about you and Tom. Devastating. Did you get the papers?"

"Uh, no, I—"

"Well, had you considered filing?"

"He filed."

"Oh, but you haven't gotten the papers?"

"No, I just—"

"Okay, you'll need to let me know when you do. We want to get every dime that we can from him. It's really a shame."

We do? Jaime thought. It had been less than twenty-four hours since she received the news from Tom, and even though she was hurt, she wasn't planning to ruin Tom's life in this divorce.

"So, how's your dad?" Mr. Matthews asked.

"He's doing well. He's on the building committee for our church, and it's a large capital—"

"Hang on. I need to answer this. Sorry."

The phone had rung only once before Mr. Matthews had answered it. Jaime grew even more uncomfortable. Even though the office was cool, she felt sweat forming on her neck. She needed to leave. She wasn't prepared to hire an attorney who treated her divorce from Tom like a dog fight. Thinking of her dog Mandy, she abruptly stood, saying over the telephone call, "Mr. Matthews. I apologize."

He put his hand over the mouthpiece of his phone as she spoke.

"I need to leave," she added, and before he could say anything, Jaime turned and walked out of his office. She heard him resume his conversation on the phone just as she reached his office door.

The hallway was a relief—until she saw Ryan, a law school friend, in fact probably her closest law school friend. They had lost touch over the years, but she thought of him often.

"Jaime!" he hollered down the hall and waved. She instinctively walked toward him.

"Hi, Ryan."

"What're you doing here?"

Did he have to ask that question? Jaime first thought but then promptly decided to tell him the truth in an edited version. "I was seeing Mr. Matthews."

"Are you two friends?" Ryan was intuitive and knew there was more going on. He wouldn't pry out of vain curiosity but he would out of genuine concern and a desire to help if he could.

"Sort of. Our families are friends."

"Oh," Ryan said with a frown. "Well, come into my office and tell me what you've been up to." She had the time, and Ryan was always easy with whom to talk, so she followed him.

Ryan's office was much smaller than Mr. Matthews' office. He had shelves of books, which he undoubtedly referenced every day. There was a candle burning in the corner that smelled like toasted marshmallows. *Fire-code issue*, Jaime thought.

"Have a seat." He gestured toward a single chair covered with a plaid blanket. "Mind if I stand? My back's been bothering me."

"Not at all."

Ryan grabbed a magazine from a stack of papers on his desk and handed it to Jaime. "Here. I've been saving this just in case I ran into you." Ryan would have saved this magazine for a decade or more. He was too thoughtful to be an attorney. "I know you get stuck with a lot of marijuana work, so I thought I'd pass it along."

The article was about how to start a marijuana business and keep it going, despite municipal pushback of the kind that municipalities routinely retained Jaime's firm to give. Jaime looked up at Ryan who was grinning.

"Ha. Very funny," Jaime said as she tossed the magazine back onto Ryan's desk.

"So, tell me. Really. What're you seeing old Matthews for?"

Jaime had no choice but to be honest, and she was okay with telling Ryan. He always had her best interest in mind and kept her confidences. "About Tom and me. We've grown apart, and last night, he emailed me that he had formally filed for divorce."

Ryan pushed himself off the wall he was leaning against, walked over to Jaime, and put his hand on her shoulder.

"I am so sorry, JR." He hadn't called her JR since law school. It stood for Jaime Rae. "What does Matthews have to say about it?"

"That he can help me take it all from Tom. But that's not what I want to do in this—I don't want to hurt Tom. Matthews just didn't listen, so if he talks ignore his banter."

"Matthews has done this so much that he doesn't think he needs to listen. He's on autopilot."

"I didn't even know if I should get an attorney," Jaime said, hoping Ryan would give his input.

"Of course you should!" Ryan was not one to withhold his opinion, so Jaime didn't know why she even needed to hope. "Don't you think a second opinion would be beneficial? I mean, you're not a family law attorney, so why would you even think about representing yourself. I mean, if a dermatologist has vision problems, don't you think he'd see an ophthalmologist? Yeah, he's a doctor, but he can't diagnose a vision problem—he's a skin specialist!"

Ryan probably went with the dermatology analogy because he had skin issues and spent a lot of time at the dermatologist's office, Jaime thought briefly before replying, "Yeah, I know—"

"And even if you were a family law practitioner, don't you think it's a good idea to get a second opinion? Your emotions are too invested because it's your own marriage. You might miss something. You need someone there to watch out for you. You know? And make sure you're okay and getting what's coming at you from the legal perspective."

Those words rang in Jaime's ears as she left Ryan's office. *You need someone there to watch out for you.* Jaime thought of Kate.

After she left Ryan's office, she stopped by the resale store. Jaime wasn't frugal, but she appreciated a bargain. The store smelled familiar, and the cashier looked at her like an alien.

"Are you lost?" the attendant asked innocently.

Jaime laughed. "No, I am on my way to work, but really need two new chairs for my office."

"You're not going to find anything new here," the attendant responded. "But just yesterday a lawyer who's retiring dropped them two off. They're pretty nice." The attendant pointed behind

93

Jaime as she spoke. Jaime turned around and saw two gray suede chairs with rounded backs and silver feet.

"Hmm. Those look comfortable." Jaime held back her excitement. They looked too good to be true. She sat in them. Her feet still touched the floor while she leaned back.

"I'll take them," she said without looking at the price. *Thank you, Jesus*, she said under her breath as she stood and faced the chairs before fishing out her wallet from her purse. Her mind wandered to Kate again, and Jaime wondered how she was doing.

That evening Jaime received a text from Ryan. It read, "Great to catch up today. Sorry about you and Tom. If I can help in any way, please know I'm here for you." Ryan started to sound like Greg.

Jaime opened her Bible to Exodus 14:14: "Be still, and know that I will fight for you."

Well, that makes at least three, Jaime thought.

Yet who was watching out for Kate? Did she know the Lord? Jaime pulled her phone from her purse to see if she had saved Kate's number from her neighbor. She had, and so before she could change her mind, Jaime sent Kate a text. Jaime would never have done that with a client, but Kate wasn't exactly a client.

"How's your heart?" Jaime texted. That was what Jaime asked her friends, and they always knew what she meant, but Kate might not.

"My heart is fine. Why?" Kate texted back. Clearly, Kate didn't get it.

"How are you doing?" Jaime tried again.

"Okay. It's hard."

As Jaime sat on her back porch, she caught a glimpse of a girl with blonde hair at her neighbor's house. Is that Kate? Jaime peered around the trees. It was Kate. Jaime's instinct was to hide, but she had a new perspective, and so instead she said a quick prayer, *Lord, forgive my disregard of Kate, her circumstances, and feelings*. Thinking of Mr. Matthews, Jaime resumed her prayer, *Let me be a light to her in this time of darkness*. Then thinking of Ryan, she resumed again, *Let your truth and your word guide her, comfort her, and give her peace in this storm*. Finally, thinking of her Savior—the all-knowing, all-wise, all-loving Counselor who simultaneously held all authority—she concluded, *Fight for her, Lord, as you fight for each of your children. Amen.*

Jaime ran outside toward Kate. As she strode toward Kate with an inviting smile, she felt something bulky in her pant leg. Kate waved at Jaime in surprise. As they hugged briefly on the neighbor's patio, a pair of Jaime's underwear fell out of her pant leg onto the patio right in front of Kate. Kate looked down at the underwear and then up at Jaime, and they both burst into laughter. *How's that for an ice breaker?* Jaime thought, laughing even harder.

At that moment, Jaime concluded that while it's tough to be an attorney, it's even harder to be a client, meaning that to be both an attorney and client at the same time is impossible. Jaime decided to retain counsel for her divorce. She knew Tom would have to account for his conduct before God someday, so Jaime did not plan on making the divorce difficult as a form of revenge.

Her experience as a lawyer-client made Jaime empathize more with her clients, not inhibiting her lawyer skills but making her more Christ-like—and Greg-like and Ryan-like. She started by inviting Kate to try out her new office chairs on Kate's next visit to her office.

"I absolutely love this song," Kate beamed as she grabbed a piece of candy from the bowl on Jaime's desk. Jaime leaned back in her chair and turned up Sheryl Crow a little louder.

An Expert's Cross-Examination

Tipler McGee

[Here, a longtime insurance defense counsel uses the form of an expert witness's cross-examination at trial to explore how lawyers give account through the mouths of adverse witnesses.]

THE COURT: Cross-examination, counsel?

MR. HAMMOND: Thank you, Your Honor.

Mr. Garner, turning your attention first to your qualifications to opine that my client's press was defective and unreasonably dangerous, you do hold an engineering degree, is that correct?

MR. GARNER: Yes.

COUNSEL: But that degree is an undergraduate or bachelor's degree, correct?

WITNESS: Yes. I earned it from –

COUNSEL: Hold on, Mr. Garner, we'll get there. You don't hold a doctorate, do you?

WITNESS: No, but I was going to say –

96

1 COUNSEL: That's alright, Mr. Garner, you've answered my
2 question.

3 MS. LUCTOR: Your Honor, if the witness has a clarification –

4 THE COURT: I think he's answered, Ms. Luctor. Uh, do you have a
5 clarification?

6 WITNESS: I was just going to say that my degree is from a college
7 accredited by the Northwest Association of Schools and –

8 THE COURT: That's fine, Mr. Garner. Let's just answer the
9 questions for now.

10 MR. HAMMOND: So, you don't hold a doctorate?

11 WITNESS: No.

12 COUNSEL: And you don't hold a master's degree in engineering,
13 either, do you?

14 WITNESS: No.

15 COUNSEL: And yet several of your engineering-department
16 colleagues at Manion do hold graduate engineering degrees, don't
17 they?

18 WITNESS: Yes, but –

19 COUNSEL: That's alright, Mr. Garner, we've got it.

20 MS. LUCTOR: I think that was going to be a clarification, Your
21 Honor.

22 THE COURT: Well, Ms. Luctor, we tried that a moment ago, and it
23 didn't work so well. Let's just leave it for your redirect, shall we?

MS. LUCTOR: [Shrugs.]

MR. HAMMOND: How long have you worked for Manion, Mr. Garner?

MR. GARNER: Nearly fifty years. I retire later this summer.

COUNSEL: Well congratulations, Mr. Garner. Well earned, I'm sure. Are you going to be the only one of the five Manion engineers who will testify in Manion's defense in this case?

MS. LUCTOR: Objection, Your Honor. Argumentative.

THE COURT: Well, we are having a hard time getting started, ladies and gentlemen of the jury, aren't we? [Jurors laugh.] Objection sustained, though. Mr. Hammond, could we move along a little with the next question?

MR. HAMMOND: Yes, Your Honor. Mr. Garner, you didn't design the press that injured my client, did you?

MR. GARNER: No, but – Well, I guess I'll just wait on that.

COUNSEL: And you haven't designed any other press, have you?

WITNESS: Well, that one I've got to explain. I mean, I've designed parts of presses. It's not like we sit down and suddenly sketch out a whole press, you know.

COUNSEL: Exactly, Mr. Garner. And as to those parts of presses that you have designed, you've not designed the part that malfunctioned in this case, either, have you?

WITNESS: No, I haven't, not exactly.

1 COUNSEL: Yes, Mr. Garner, in fairness to you, you have designed
2 press components that work with the part that failed in this incident,
3 is that correct?

4 WITNESS: Yes, Mr. Hammond, but what do you mean by failed? I
5 mean, the controls actually worked, you know, they just didn't –

6 COUNSEL: Yes, Mr. Garner? They just didn't what, Mr. Garner?

7 WITNESS: Your client's fingers still got cut off.

8 COUNSEL: I'm sorry, Mr. Garner, but I didn't quite hear you.

9 WITNESS: I said your client's fingers still got cut off. I don't mean
10 all of her fingers, but, well, you know what I mean.

11 COUNSEL: You mean that your employer's press cut off three of
12 my client's fingers?

13 WITNESS: I – I –

14 MS. LUCTOR: This is argument, Your Honor, not a question.

15 THE COURT: I think we get your point, Mr. Hammond. I mean,
16 we know it was three fingers. Could you move along again? You
17 were making good progress there for a minute.

18 MR. HAMMOND: Sure, Your Honor. Mr. Garner, you have
19 testified before in these types of cases, haven't you?

20 MR. GARNER: I have.

21 COUNSEL: Yet although you've testified several times before,
22 you've never testified for an injured person, have you?

23 WITNESS: No, but –

1   COUNSEL: Hold on. Your testimony has always been for the

2 defense, hasn't it?

3   WITNESS: No, that's not exactly true. I've –

4   COUNSEL: Hold on, Mr. Garner. When I took your deposition in

5 this case, didn't you tell us – and you were under oath – that your

6 testimony had always been for the defense?

7   WITNESS: I did, but I should have said that – well, I mean that I

8 meant to say – sometimes my testimony helped the other side. I'm

9 not all one-sided or something, you know.

0   COUNSEL: I think we know what you mean, Mr. Garner. You're

1 just going to tell it like it is, and whomever it helps, it helps, right?

2   WITNESS: Exactly, counsel. I just tell it like it is.

3   COUNSEL: Well, then, Mr. Garner, could you please tell us how it

4 is that your employer's press cut off three of my client's fingers?

5   WITNESS: You want me to – I didn't mean I was going to explain

6 everything. Are you asking me to –

7   MS. LUCTOR: Your Honor, object to the form of the question as

8 calling for a narrative.

9   THE COURT: Always at the ready, huh, Ms. Luctor?

0   MS. LUCTOR: Your Honor.

1   THE COURT: Well, counsel, now, I think that Mr. Hammond asked

2 a fair question, maybe a little open ended, and maybe Mr. Hammond

3 will even regret giving your client – I mean the engineer Mr. Garner

1 such latitude to explain. But let's see what he has to say. Mr. Garner,
2 you may answer the question

3 WITNESS: I don't remember what he asked.

4 [Jurors laugh.]

5 THE COURT: Do you think that you could help us out here a little,
6 Mr. Hammond?

7 MR. HAMMOND: I can ask a narrower question, Your Honor. Mr.
8 Garner, would you please tell the jurors why the controls – I won't
9 say failed. time, so we don't get into a dispute over words, but why
10 they worked as designed but still cut my client's three fingers off?

11 WITNESS: Now, that's another matter. Your client – can I call her
12 by her name? Missy, as they call you, or you'd prefer Ms. Collins?
13 [Ms. Collins shrugs.] Well, sorry there. Um, Ms. Collins was starting
14 to – she was going to take the part out of the die, but then she
15 changed her mind, and when you start and stop, you sort of lose
16 track of where you were, sometimes, and then she – what was next?
17 She –

18 COUNSEL: Maybe I can help, Mr. Garner. I wasn't asking you
19 what my client did but what the press did.

20 WITNESS: Well, the die definitely closed.

21 COUNSEL: On Missy's fingers, right?

22 WITNESS: Yes. She should have been watching.

23 COUNSEL: Well, since you bring it up then, even though I didn't
24 exactly ask –

MS. LUCTOR: Your Honor, he did ask. Now he's badgering the witness.

THE COURT: We get it, Ms. Luctor. Go ahead, counsel, and do try not to badger. They're not very kind, those badgers. [Jurors laugh.] Unless you're in Wisconsin. Nothing against Wisconsin Badgers. [Jurors laugh.]

MR. HAMMOND: Mr. Garner, you said my client Missy should have been watching. Do you mean to say that the press controls – they were two-hand controls, weren't they?

WITNESS: Yes, two-hand controls. But that doesn't mean –

COUNSEL: Hold on, Mr. Garner, I don't want to have to badger you. [Jurors laugh.]

Would you please just tell the jurors the purpose of two-hand controls?

WITNESS: Sure. They're to keep the operator's hands out of the press when it closes. I helped invent two-hand controls.

COUNSEL: We'll get to that, Mr. Garner. Let's follow the questions. Yet if two-hand controls are to keep the operator's hands out of the press, then they didn't exactly work that way here, did they?

WITNESS: No. They worked like they were supposed to work but didn't keep her hands – her hand out.

1   COUNSEL: Now, you're going to have to explain that one to us,
2   Mr. Garner. When you helped to invent these two-hand controls –
3   and they're used all over the nation – the world, aren't they?

4   WITNESS: Oh, yes, everyone uses them, although we didn't use
5   to.

6   COUNSEL: And everyone uses them today to keep from losing
7   operator hands and fingers, isn't that so?

8   WITNESS: Sure, right, that's what they're there for.

9   COUNSEL: Well, so you said a moment ago that they worked here
10   but didn't keep Missy's hands – her hand out. Tell the jurors what
11   happened, then.

12   WITNESS: I mean, the design was good. They were supposed to
13   work that way. The control failed.

14   COUNSEL: Oh, so the design was good, but the control was bad?

15   WITNESS: Basically, yes.

16   COUNSEL: What is the control?

17   WITNESS: The part – the device – the design that makes the – the
18   circuit had an anomaly.

19   COUNSEL: Oh, so, an anomaly?

20   WITNESS: Well, not everywhere, because the thing had worked
21   fine for – well, for a long time – in a lot of presses. It was only in the
22   event of a power failure and machine reset. If the machine

1   automatically reset when the dual cams were between nine and

2   twelve – you know, this part of the dial – that the control could fail.

3   COUNSEL: Sounds like you know a little electrical engineering.

4   WITNESS: I'm not an electrical engineer. I'm a mechanical

5   engineer. But we read diagrams to make the mechanics work with

6   the electrical systems. So, I know what I'm doing – or saying. I know

7   what I'm talking about.

8   COUNSEL: Then how do you know that this press's control –

9   Manion made the control, too, didn't it? I mean not just the other

0   parts of the press?

1   WITNESS: Oh, right, we made everything. Well, not everything,

2   but yes, the control, and the cams, and the two-hand controls. No,

3   actually, some of the parts for the two-hand controls, like the plastic

4   buttons themselves, those we contracted out.

5   COUNSEL: Hold on. Let's not get too deep in the weeds. You

6   testified that Manion made the control. You mean its engineers did

7   the electrical engineering that produced the anomaly that cut off my

8   client's fingers?

9   WITNESS: I guess you could you say that.

20   COUNSEL: Well, let's not start guessing. How did you know about

21   this anomaly?

22   WITNESS: I read the electrical schematic.

23   COUNSEL: Where'd you get the schematic?

1   WITNESS: Where all the other schematics are. We store the old

2   ones rolled up in cardboard cans. The new ones are electronic, but

3   the old ones, as big as they are, are too expensive –

4   COUNSEL: That's alright, Mr. Garner. Let's stay on track. So, you

5   pulled out the schematic, read it, and saw the anomaly, so that you

6   could tell us about it here?

7   WITNESS: Not exactly that simple, but yes.

8   COUNSEL: Just telling like it is, letting it take us where it takes us,

9   right?

10   WITNESS: Yes. I mean, I didn't plan on pointing out the anomaly.

11   COUNSEL: But it was just there, and you told us the truth about

12   it?

13   WITNESS: Well, right. But an anomaly doesn't mean the press is

14   dangerous.

15   COUNSEL: Shall we address that, then? How is a press that has

16   an electrical anomaly that makes the two-hand controls fail in the

17   event of a power reset not dangerous?

18   WITNESS: Power in these plants doesn't just go off every day.

19   COUNSEL: Well, now I think you're arguing.

20   MS. LUCTOR: Objection, Your Honor. Mr. Hammond should

21   refrain from commenting on the testimony.

MR. HAMMOND: She's right, Your Honor. My apologies. Mr. Garner, though, why does Manion design a power-reset function into the press?

WITNESS: To reset the power. What do you think?

COUNSEL: Oh, I'm not here to think and give answers, Mr. Garner. I'd just like your answers. If Manion clearly foresaw power failures and the need for a reset function, then why did it design one with an anomaly that could cut an operator's hands off?

WITNESS: I don't know.

COUNSEL: Do you mean, you don't know because it doesn't make sense to do it that way, or that you just don't know?

WITNESS: I don't know. It doesn't – I don't know.

COUNSEL: Could Manion have designed the control without the anomaly?

MS. LUCTOR: Objection, Your Honor. Mr. Garner is not an electrical engineer.

MR. HAMMOND: I suppose he's not, even though he's already said a lot about electrical engineering. I'll ask it another way, Your Honor.

Mr. Garner, do you mechanically engineer other presses at Manion that don't have this electrical anomaly with which to deal?

WITNESS: Yes. This press is the only one with the anomaly.

1   COUNSEL: By the way, Mr. Manion, I want to be sure that we all
2   understand what you mean by anomaly. Do you have another word
3   for it, I mean, in case anomaly is not a word that we use every day?

4   WITNESS: What do you mean? Anomaly is anomaly.

5   COUNSEL: An engineering term?

6   WITNESS: Yeah – no, not exactly an engineering term.

7   COUNSEL: Any other way to put it? How about glitch? Is that
8   about the same thing?

9   WITNESS: I don't –

10   COUNSEL: How about irregularity?

11   WITNESS: Really, I don't know where you're going with this.

12   MS. LUCTOR: Objection, Your Honor, he's picking at things.

13   THE COURT: I don't remember that objection in law school, Ms.
14   Luctor.

15   MS. LUCTOR: He's arguing again with the witness, Your Honor.

16   THE COURT: How about if I just sustain that objection, Ms.
17   Luctor? Mr. Hammond, could you please –

18   MR. HAMMOND: Mr. Garner, you told us you're about to retire.
19   You wouldn't want to be responsible for an anomaly, a design – a
20   control anomaly, for designing a control anomaly that cut off Missy's
21   fingers, would you?

22   WITNESS: No, I wouldn't.

23   COUNSEL: So that's Manion's problem then, isn't it?

WITNESS: Well, I suppose so. It's not my design, and no, I wouldn't want it to be mine.

COUNSEL: Nothing further, Your Honor.

THE COURT: Redirect, Ms. Luctor.

MS. LUCTOR: Could we please take a break, Your Honor?

THE COURT: Middle of the afternoon, Ms. Luctor, and time's a wastin'. Do you have anything further for this witness? Seems to me that you might be about done here.

MS. LUCTOR: Nothing further, Your Honor.

THE COURT: The witness is excused, then. Have a nice retirement, Mr. Garner.

WITNESS: Thank you, Your Honor. I can go, then?

THE COURT: Wherever and whenever you please. As soon as you retire.

Call your next witness, Ms. Luctor.

* * *

Overheard: A Last Referral

Pinkston Maraud

Here, a transactional lawyer uses the imperative of looming death to discern the value of law practice, through the device of an overheard lawyer's telephone referral.

"Yeah, Larry, it's me. You must have caller ID. How you been, *buddy*?!" ...

"No kidding? I hadn't heard. Sorry to hear, man. But I know you. Strong as an ox. You'll pull through. You're not seeing Dr. Schaeffer for it, are you?!" ...

"No, I didn't think so. That one worked out alright for us—I mean for the client—didn't it, though? Geez, what a schlub. Everything else alright? How are the kids?" ...

"Chillin', man. Livin' the good life! And I meant to ask about Colleen, but these days, you never know, you know what I mean, man?! Glad to hear she's still at the AG's, but she's gotta be close to done there, isn't she?" ...

"Hey, yeah, Betty's fine, and yes, I've got something going on, but we can talk about that later. How's practice?" ...

"No, I said we can talk about that later. *Tell me how practice is going*, you stubborn mule, you!" ...

"I figured that you were still mining that gold vein. That stuff will never go away, will it?!" ...

"Oh, yeah, right, unless the supreme court takes it away like they've done with all that other stuff. A guy hardly has a chance any more. But at least no-fault is back." ...

"Yeah, thank God for that." ...

"Yeah, and you've always got that, too. It's all about the mix, isn't it, buddy? Well keep at it, *Tiger*. Man, am I glad that I don't have to face you in that stuff! You'd be good whatever you do! So, alright, let me tell you why I called. Do you have another minute?" ...

"Good, sure, let's talk. I got another case for you, and this one looks even better than the last one." ...

"No, no, not *that* last one, Ke-mo sah-bee. I know, I know, that one didn't work out so good, and I'm sorry, man. That one's on me." ...

"Right, right. And I *promised* that I'd never send you another bad case, didn't I?" ...

"And I've *kept* that promise, haven't I?" ...

"Alright, alright. You got me. That bad case *was* the last case that I sent you. But see, if I haven't sent you *any* cases since, then I haven't sent you another *bad one* since, have I?!" ...

"No, no, I know how you trial guys work! If you don't have the facts, then you argue the law. If you don't...." ...

"Wait a minute! How many cases have I sent you over the years?! You're crazy, man. You've made a *ton* of money from what I've sent you!" ...

"Just kidding! Just kidding! We're just havin' fun, man. I got you, man. But you're right, dude, a case is never as good as the day it walks in, is it?" ...

"You got *that* right! Open the file drawer and just *hear* the barking, them *dawg* cases!" ...

"No, not *your* file cabinets. You're *loaded*, man. I respect you! I *love* you, man. You're the *king*! And even after that last one, we're still kickin', ya know? We take the good with the bad, and it all evens out somehow." ...

"Exactly. The one *before* that last one was solid, man, wasn't it? You did a *great* job with that one. Remember the look on the claim rep's face when you slid the statement over to him and he read what it said?! I wish I'd have had that one on tape, man. I'd have played it a thousand times over by now, without tiring of it, like one of those—what do they call them, gips? Gifs, gifs, whatever they are!" ...

"Hey, seriously, though, I think I got a good one for you. You know that bank I've been doing collections for, all that little stuff that chases me all over creation but pays the bills?!" ...

"Yeah, that stuff's still going strong, and of course Ron's got that other stuff that he does, what is it? I mean, I've lost my mind when I can't even think...." ...

"Yeah, yeah, that's right, he's still doing that. You know, if it weren't for that and my little thing, I don't know where we'd be, with the building and all. I mean, we still got a good tenant, and the thing is supposedly worth a mountain of cash by now, for all the years we've had it. But for Ron and me, man, we seem to sink every extra dime into that thing, new roof, constant painting, and then the ridiculous taxes. But hey, listen." ...

"Right, the referral thing. I'm losing my mind. The bank director's, what do you call him?" ...

"No, not the CEO. The loan-committee chair! You know him. I've introduced you to him!" ...

"Yeah, that guy. He's decent, a real good guy, married forever, been at the bank forever. Anyway, he's got a son, well, *had* a son who died at a sports camp last week. Two-a-days, dehydration. You know, lack of medical attention. Of course, the family's destroyed over it. The dad, who I know real well, wants to meet with a lawyer about it soon, get some answers. I told him that I had just the guy, *you,* you son-of-a-gun." ...

"Thanks, Larry. I know that you mean that, and I'll tell the dad. We'll get it scheduled right away—well, as soon as he's ready, which could be as early as next week. In case he asks me, though, do you know anything about these sports cases?" ...

"Hold on a second, Larry. ... Yes, a diet Coke, please, and that's all. Thank you. ... Yes, I'm in my car! What did you think, I'd be shooting the breeze with you without getting something else done?! Geez. Do you want a hamburger?! You sure? I can make it a *quarter-pounder*! Virtual consumption, over the cell phone!" ...

"No, I don't think that we have much to do before we meet. I mean, I'll send you a couple of press reports that ran on it, but not much has been in the news. He just wasn't up to telling me any details, either. I mean, think of it, that's gotta be the worst thing in the world." ...

"No, I don't want to handle this one myself. And no co-counseling. Straight referral. Have I ever co-counseled *anything* with you? It's all yours, my friend!" ...

"You know me. I don't like the risk. Besides, I don't have the time, and I don't have the time left, either." ...

"Yes, it's as bad as you heard. I mean, I don't know what you heard, and miracles happen. I haven't given up hope. Betty and I are in this for the whole fight. But I'm not a fool. When it gets to this stage, I've got to be smart, too." ...

"A month, maybe three months." ...

"Yeah, it's crazy because I feel alright. Well, I feel like crap, but you know, not like I'm dying, although I suppose who knows what *that* feels like." ...

"She's been great. A real trooper. In fact, sometimes I sort of need to remind her, *hey, I'm dying here!*" ...

"No, I'm not worried about her. Well, wait a second. That sounds kinda bad, doesn't it?! Of course, I'm worried about her, but she'll be fine financially. And she's got the kids and grandkids. Shoot, you and Colleen know what's it like. They're probably better off without us!" ...

"No! I'm not seeing Dr. Schaeffer! That's funny. That *schlub*! He'd have killed me already!" ...

"Thanks. I know the group. They're good, although I hadn't heard what they did for Frank. That's great. I'm with Harradi and those guys over there." ...

"Yeah, I like them, but what can they really do?" ...

"Sure, they've made great advances, but we all could've died from a hangnail a long time ago. You know, that's why I don't worry about it so much. It'll take its course. I know I'm in good hands, but it doesn't have to work out that way." ...

"No, I think I'll stay busy with what I've been doing. Oh, sure, we'll take some trips, and I'm not keeping any late hours. And I need my rest. I definitely have days when I don't want to get out of bed. But this law-practice thing is alright." ...

"Wait a second, you sound like Tolstoy with his whole *Ivan Ilych* thing." ...

"Oh, go look it up. Google it, dummy! But you know that's not how it really works. Well, maybe *judges* feel that way, like they're wasting their lives on other people's crap!" ...

"Oh, yeah, that's great. I'd nearly forgotten about *him*. How could I?! Remember how red-faced he got when you told him?! I thought he was going to tear you in two! But all he did was get up and walk off the bench back into chambers. We were so surprised that we didn't even get our fannies out of the seats!" ...

"You're killin' me, Larry. Stop it! Stop it!" ...

"No, we *can't* talk about that! My sides are already splitting! I thought she was going to hold you in contempt! I really did! When you told her that she couldn't sanction you because you hadn't done anything wrong—and you were correct, you're *always* right, my man—I thought she was going to erupt! God, my sides are hurting." ...

"Right! Right! You could've knocked the bailiff over with a feather when she said that! Remember the bailiff? What was his name? Right! Right! Pothakerry, or something like that. Geez, he was a strange dude." ...

"Hey, look, I appreciate you taking the time. I mean, I really didn't call to have you make me feel good." ...

"Well, let's say I have no regrets. ... No, that's not right. I'd do a ton of things differently if I had another chance. But it doesn't work that way. You live life once, live it in the face of death, really, if you think about it. I don't want to get all philosophical on you." ...

"Thanks, guy. I'm alright with the law thing. I mean, I'd have loved to be, what, a *golf pro* or maybe a *sports announcer,* although I'd hate the travel. But what other career besides law is going to engage you in life the way this one does?" ...

"Yeah, right, like Dr. Schaeffer?!"...

"You're right. I've gotta leave him alone, poor guy. He hasn't butchered anyone lately, not that I've heard." ...

"Oh, that's right. I forgot. Well, good for us, too bad for Florida. But no, I couldn't take all the mess and all the whining. I've heard doctors quit when they discover that they're treating the same fifty patients their whole careers. But with us, everyone's got legal problems or, well, opportunities." ...

"Yeah, that's right, *you and I* deal with the problems. Ron and those transactional guys get to actually *build* stuff. If I had to do it over again, then I'd be a *bond* lawyer so I could look out at Ford Field or Arrowhead Stadium when its packed with fifty-thousand roaring people and say, *I built that!* You're playin' on *my* field, Tom Brady!" ...

"No, you're right. We do put stuff back together somehow, even this silly little collections crap that I do for the bank. These are real people, man, and sometimes I feel like I'm holding their lives in my hands. You gotta be careful with this stuff, even collections. You can't just grind people. Somehow, you gotta find a heart in it. At least, that's what I think. And you know, the bank's fine with that. They're people, too. That's why I don't have regrets. You? You do over it differently?" ...

"Hey, no, thanks for sharing that. I mean it. I'd never thought of it that way. That really helps, man. I'm gonna remember that for what, the next one-to-three months?! You tell me how that one works out because I don't think I've got the time to find out!" ...

"No, no, I'm joking, man. I love what you said. I mean it." ...

"Yeah, I agree. Sure, the profession—listen to me, I make it sound like the mafia or some racket or other, calling it the *profession.* But you know, whatever it is that we do.... Darn, look at the time. I am so sorry to hold you up this long." ...

"Yeah, I've been home for the past five minutes, sittin' in my car in the garage yacking at you! Betty's poked her head out *twice* to see what I'm doing. But she knows what's going on. She's seen me have a few of these conversations." ...

"No, really, it's the best thing I have left, talking with you, sharing time with Betty, and heck, even sharing time with the banksters and their victims whom I pursue." ...

"No, no, I'm kidding! Man, you are sensitive. Hey, but I appreciate that, too. I mean, you've been great. I've always admired you. You've always...." ...

"Larry, shut up and listen. Now don't interrupt. This may be the last time that you hear my voice, alright? Just listen!" ...

"Okay, you're right. You're gonna hear from me any day setting up the referral meeting. So you really do just care about the money, huh?!" ...

"Good. You finally know I'm kidding. You're finally learning how to take a joke. After all these years, you're learning something from me!" ...

"Wrong! That's sure not true! You are *so* funny, dude! But listen, I need to thank you again for helping me through that grievance crap. Damn, I *still* don't know where they got off chasing me like that. My whole career doing everything *by the book* and they've gotta come pickin' on me after something like *that*?! I mean, I could...." ...

"Yeah, yeah, you're right. I didn't mean to go there. Sorry about that. What I meant to say is just thanks for handling that. I knew you'd straighten them out, and you did. I've never been in a position like that. I mean, I've stood next to dozens, no *hundreds* or even *thousands* of clients with their butts in a sling, and I'd never really known what they must feel like, until that grievance thing. You really took care of that, and I could never pay you back, and I just wanted you to...." ...

"Alright, alright, yeah. But here's the other thing, a lot more important than you handling that grievance crap. You've always made it about more than just the referrals, just the transactions, just the money, which is probably why I kept feeding you the referrals, other than that you are one damn good lawyer! But you always made me feel human, feel alive, like I mattered even just a little bit, beyond whatever good that I could bring you. And...." ...

"Shh, shush! Listen to me, dammit, Larry! I'm not done yet! ... Good. Now listen. It wasn't just me and other lawyers and friends. You also made the *clients* whom I sent you feel human. You didn't just care about your family or your staff or your lawyer buddies. You cared about the damn clients, too. And I know where you get that, Larry, and I don't want you to ever give it up. Don't ever stop caring. If this profession starts to put out your light somehow, and I don't think that it will, but if it does, then walk away from it. Run!" ...

"You got it, brother. It was the same for me, as you know. This law stuff can be a calling, which is *corny*, I know. Please don't tell anyone that I said that!" ...

"No, I'm serious. Betty is going to ask some lawyer friend, probably *you*, to say something at my funeral—along with the pastor and family, you know. It's not like everyone even *knows* that I'm a lawyer. Or the bench-bar will have you write something for the website. You know, those things that they send out, where you go, gee, I didn't know he was that *old*, or, *what a way to go*. Not that anyone will read mine or care." ...

"No, listen, Larry. Don't say or write anything corny, and don't give them some sob story like the trial lawyer you are. Don't make it *your* show, or I'll come back and throttle you, you *meathead*, you! You know I'm kidding. Look, just tell 'em that I was ready to go." ...

"No, no, *not* sordid-and-sad, depressed-and-defeated ready to go. I mean happy to stay and do more work but happier to go. A lot of people have made a mess of their end, even some who did a great job with life. I'm not making a mess of my end. I know what I know. I have no fear to go. I know where I'm going, and you know, too. That's why I love you, Larry. You, too, make a good end of it, will you, buddy?" ...

"Yeah, yeah, right. We better go. Hang in there, buddy. Do a great job for my bank guy. I know you will. And watch out for Colleen if she needs any help, but she won't, nothing to worry there, friend. And Ron's all set with the practice. You know those transactional guys, crossing every *t* and dotting every *i*. He had the

116

key-man stuff in place and everything, so he'll do better without me than with me. Crazy, isn't it?" ...

"I don't know about that. But hey, you two should think about getting together after I'm gone. You'd make great law partners. But you'd hate this stupid building stuff, all your money going to the taxes. Wait, what am I talking about. Ron'll pay the building off with that key-man money he'll get when I'm gone. Damn, you're all gonna have it good without me!" ...

"Yeah, see you, Larry. Thanks, buddy. Bye, bye. Be good now. See you again someday, on the other side."

The Doctrine of Non-Interference

Matthew J. Levin

Here, a law student circumferences the passions that competition over law-school grades can at times, in places, and for certain students produce.

Seth Vallandingham descended the train platform and scurried through a slick alley that looped under the tracks for a block before dumping its travelers smack-in-the-middle of one of the city's busiest avenues. His ill-fitting wingtips, bought online at a steep discount, clicked stubbornly over wet pavement.

Rude stenches offended Seth's nostrils. An early-morning rain, inefficient in its haste, neglected to wash away the street's gelatinous film of garbage and urine. Homeless folk slumped in the shadows, their odors lingering in tandem with the scent of dumpsters soaked in the early heat of the sun. Across the street, towering above two parking garages, rose a luxury condominium inhabited by perfumed millionaires and their golden children.

Chicago was once a writer's town, then it was a fighter's town. These days, it was as faceless as any American jurisdiction, defined only by its divided struggles.

Seth's shoulders slumped under the burden of a backpack loaded with law texts. The trek from Giovani's place had been murderous, but the morning found him grateful for the hospitality. Tonight, he will sleep at *The Loading Zone* bathhouse, a stone's throw from work and school. There, he can study, rest..., even get laid if he so desires. Most importantly, $7/night was an unbeatable rate. Sure, the rooms were tiny, large enough for cot-sized bed and not much else. Yet, the setting was titillating, adventurous. Seth's usual room sat on the mouth of a maze that opened to a waterfall, sauna, and steam room, all encompassed by a stairway leading to additional exotic settings designed for heightened anonymous sex-capades.

A block away from the firm, Seth jerked to a halt and bent over to fix his socks, which were painfully bunched at the toes. A tubular worm, long, thick, and blushing, pulsated at his feet. Breaded in gravel, it writhed in agony as an army of ants feasted upon its meaty flesh. Seth, consumed with empathy, departed from his usual *Doctrine of Non-Interference* and, in an awkward pirouette, engaged the lip of his shoe in an attempt to flick the worm into the baptismal puddle of a nearby pothole.

The good-faith effort backfired.

Seth struggled to maintain his balance as the shoe—after slicing the worm in half—sailed into the puddle with a clumsy plop.

"Ah shit," Seth groaned. The worm, still at his feet, was now two divorced entities, each writhing in its own private hell.

Seth fished out his shoe and floundered across the last block in his sock.

The Law Offices of Gratz & Pryde sat in the middle of a dark mini-plaza, nestled between Euclid Realty and Glenshaw Glass. Seth entered, relocked the door, and turned on the lights. He made a pot of coffee and printed the day's schedules. In a stroke of luck, he found a pair of old, tattered loafers in his bottom desk drawer; he hung the wet wingtip over a broom handle in the storage room.

Norm's office was a cluttered mess. Notebooks and fast-food wrappers littered the floor. Desktop photos of his wife and two boys were drowned by wayward stacks of papers. Seth scraped yesterday's half-eaten sandwich off a client file and into the garbage.

Bobby's office was spotless. Proud photos glistened on spartan walls: Bobby with one-term Congressman Mike Flanagan and U.S. Senator Peter Fitzgerald, and another with Donald Trump, Antonin Scalia, and the Mandrell Sisters.

At 8:30, Seth opened the office. Before he could sit, the warning bell chimed—and a man of Seth's age and height, in torn jeans and a sweat-stained shirt, barreled through the door. Shaggy black locks bounced over wild green eyes like the curls of a crazy wig as he tossed a backpack to the floor and greeted Seth with a familiar sigh.

"Good morning, Mr. Vallandingham," said Eddie Chaplinski. His voice was typically raspy, nasal. Mumbling in low, husky tones, Fast Eddie referred to colleagues by their last names; it's how they addressed each other in class. Eddie was an ass-kisser. Easily distracted, perpetually congested, he liked to talk, mostly about himself.

"Oh, hey Eddie," Seth offered in half-sung sigh, thinking, *What is he doing here? It's 8:30 in the morning. Doesn't a guy like this sleep-in to, what, at least 10:30?*

Indeed, Eddie often complained about morning classes.

"Eddie, what's going on?" Seth asked. He hoped everything was alright. The last thing he needed was Eddie Chaplinski seeking him out as a confidant.

Chaplinski strode swiftly in Seth's direction, holding his bulbous belly like he was eight months pregnant. He leaned against Seth's desk, pretending to be relaxed. His demeanor was forced, and he had trouble concealing a fierce, almost embarrassed expression.

"Hey," he quacked. "What's your student number, Vallandingham?"

"What?" Seth asked, dumbfounded. *Why would he ask me that?*

"Your student number. What is it?"

"Why?"

Eddie forced a grin designed as reassurance. Except for a quick, veiled and questioning glance into Seth's eyes, he stared at the floor. "Don't worry," he said. "I'm not gonna share it with anyone." The corners of his mouth twitched. "You can trust me."

Seth tried not to laugh. "Trust you? For what?"

"Certificates of Merit came out last night."

"Yeah?"

"Yeah. And I lost."

"Okay ... What does that have to do with me?"

"Just tell me your student number."

"Forget it, Eddie. Are you nuts or something?"

Eddie rolled his eyes sluggishly; they unwittingly closed for a moment. "I'm not nuts, Vallandingham," he said, raising his arms to punctuate his words.

Seth gagged. "Jesus, Eddie," he groaned. "You stink."

Eddie sniffed the armpit of his shirt. "I haven't slept or showered," he said. "And I have a midterm this afternoon."

"You're gonna crash and burn, Eddie."

"No I'm not. I have pills." He shook his head like a wet dog, distracted. "Listen, I pulled a 97 in Property II and didn't get the award. If you beat me, fine. If you didn't, something's up. I also lost the award in Evidence and Secured Transactions."

"I wasn't in Evidence. Or Secured."

"Exactly. Both classes were chock full of idiots—*Shabby People.*"

"*Shabby People?*"

"Yeah. You know. The five students who don't study, come to class unprepared, dick around on their laptops during lecture, then blame everyone else for their shitty grades. My Evidence and Secured Trans were fuckin' owned by the *Shabby People.*"

"Yeah, huh?"

"Think about it, Vallandingham! Two classes: just me and the Shabby People—and I lose both awards!"

"Well—"

"Vallandingham! Listen to me. I had a 95 in Evidence. That's a tough fucking class."

"Yeah. That's what I got when I took it. Next highest grade was an 82."

Eddie slapped his knees. "See!" he said. "Same thing with Secured. I pulled a 96. Who scored higher? I guarantee none of those Shabby fuckers got more than a 75."

"You think it's rigged?"

"Do I think it's RIGGED?" he slapped his knees. "What do you think?"

"Grading is anonymous. Professors don't see our names."

"Ah, bullshit! Midterms are a total unmasking. And Professor Goebels ... did you know that he uses half-grades to demark the students he dislikes?"

"What are you talking about?"

"On the midterms. If Goebels doesn't like you, he gives you a 6.5 instead of a six or seven. A *six-point-five!* In the grading scheme, the half-point means nothing, zilch. But in the Goebels scheme, it means *everything.* When he sits down to tabulate final grades, that 6.5 serves as his personal reminder: *this is a student I dislike: liberals, gays...*, even intellectuals like me, Vallandingham! And then he grades you under a whole different standard, with no rubric and no comments."

Seth considered their Property grades. He scored a 98, one-upping Fast Eddie's 97. *Bingo!* he thought. *That award is mine. I got the highest grade!*

"You listening, Vallandingham?"

"Yeah, I'm listening. I don't know if I got the Property award."

"Property II."

"Yeah, Property II. Don't know, and I'm not concerned about it."

But Seth was concerned about it. The seed was planted and growing in his head: *the Merit Award is the perfect segue to getting back with Jay.*

"Dammit, Vallandingham!" Eddie brays. "Let me check and see! Just tell me the last three digits of your student number. Six-one-six? Are they six-one-six?"

"No."

"No, you won't tell me, or no, the last three numbers aren't six-one-six."

"No on the six-one-six."

"You wouldn't lie to me now, would you, Vallandingham?"

The bell chimed and Robert "Bobby" Gratz strode through the door, cutting to his office with such velocity that he nearly knocked Eddie to the floor. Cell phone clasped to his cheek, Bobby chirped in showy agitation, waving his hands in conversation. His crisp new suit, probably Armani, crackled under fluorescent light. As always, his grey hair was perfect. His skin? Not so. Forty-eight seasons of sun and personal abuse had taken their toll, rendering his appearance older than your average Branson, Missouri tourist.

Bobby hovered in his office doorway. "Jesus, Jesus, Jesus!" he screamed with vigor. "Do you have any idea how much time I've put into this? Yeah? Well, then you can't do that. It's that simple." He paused, cupping the phone as he nodded toward Eddie. "Who's the homeless guy?" he asked Seth.

"He's a friend."

Bobby didn't seem to hear, or care. "No charity cases," he barked. "We're not the Department of Social Services." And with that, he kicked his office door shut.

Eddie was long gone by the time Bobby freed himself. "Let's meet," he said, striding to the window. "Where's Norm? I need to be in court later."

Seth shrugged. "I don't know. He's usually here by now."

"He has a key. Lock up and we'll meet for twenty minutes, tops." Bobby always said *twenty minutes, tops*, but the meetings were usually longer. Sometimes, if expense reports were on the agenda, they could last over an hour. Bobby was the kind of guy who expensed everything. Every meal, every taxi, every indulgence. The escort "massages" were Norm's breaking point. "*Hey, a happy ending is a happy ending,*" Bobby quipped. "*Don't be bitter at me just because I'm getting laid. You wanna be bitter at someone? Be bitter at the Ice Lady.*"

Ice Lady was Bobby's sobriquet for Norm's wife Irene. It was one of many rhetorical weapons he employed against Norm and his fat blandness, his failed marriage. As Norm attempted to navigate choppy marital waters, Bobby enjoyed jerking the wheel. "*Take 'Ice' out for a nice dinner,*" was his unsolicited advice. "*Keep her wine glass full and let her talk—and talk. That's what women want, Normy. That's what they want."*

Seth never injected himself into their spats, but his respect for Norm was equal to his disdain for Bobby. Norm was bland, but he was also fair, and he was honest. This was a vast departure from Bobby, who was manipulative, incessant, loud, and preoccupied. One was continually repeating himself to Bobby because Bobby never listened the first time.

Norm, for his part, was a worrier. He fretted—and rightfully so—about Bobby's wild streak: the women, the gambling, and the Trump sign he'd occasionally hang in the office window. *"Please remove it, Bobby,"* he'd beg. *"This is Chicago, not Tazewell County. Cosmopolitan people frown on that shit."*

Bobby's response: *"They don't respect our rich white prez? Ah, fuck 'em."*

Bobby's professional privilege and Norm's resentful tolerance for it were borne of the same circumstances: Bobby's friendship with Cal O'Leary, the powerful Chicago alderman. The O'Leary connection accounted for 90 percent of Gratz & Pryde's billing. O'Leary—tall, thin, and bald as a buzzard—lurched over Chicago's real estate market like a gentrified Nosferatu.

Their scam was taut, professional, and full of conceit: when developers needed a zoning change, they came to Gratz & Pryde. At $500/hour, G&P *"petitioned"* City Hall in the form of a property list submitted to O'Leary, who would then rubber-stamp the re-classification in exchange for a 50 percent kick-back, and a guarantee that his wife, a local realtor, would be entitled to all listings sired by the re-zoned property.

Norm, shoulders shrugged in apology, once admitted that the O'Learys harvested more than $2 million/year from the scheme, half of it unreported income.

Seth and Bobby were about to sit at opposite ends of a long table when a pair of fatty hands jostled the front door.

Norm, his red cheeks bloated from struggle, tapped urgently on the glass. A raisin-faced man in overalls clawed at his suit lapel and—like a cat pulling a whale—jerked him back toward the curb.

Seth jumped to his feet and jerked the door open, startling the mousy fellow, who scampered away, shouting obscenities over his shoulder.

"Ahem," Bobby cracked. "What was that about?"

Norm brushed himself off, poured a coffee, and joined them at the table. "Guy said I cut him off."

Bobby grinned. "Did you?"

"I wasn't thinking, almost missed the alley. He was in the way."

The conversation quickly shifted. "I have the Ambler motion at eleven," said Bobby. "Should be done by noon. The rest of my week is all zoning reform."

"I have that gay marriage intake," said Norm. "Seth, what are their names?"

Bobby snickered. "Gay marriage intake?"

"*Divorce.* I meant gay *divorce.* What's their names, Seth?"

"Russell-L'Anse."

"What?" Bobby interjected, "Is that one guy, or the last name?"

Seth folded his hands, maintained a professional manner. "Joe and Kent *Russell-L'Anse,*" he stated. "Russell-*hyphen*-L'Anse is their last name."

Bobby chortled. "Well, that's gotta be a record for quickest death of a hyphen!"

Norm bit his lip. "Listen, Bobby," he said, shaking his head. "These are Seth's friends. Right here in the neighborhood. Our office here happens to be in Boystown. But hey, if you don't want the local business, we can send them downtown to the two Annes."

Bobby groaned. "Fuck the two Annes," he said. "And why call it *Boystown*? Why not *Wrigleyville*? Go Cubbies! I mean, what ever happened to the good ole' days, when 'Boystown' meant Spencer

Tracy and Mickey Rooney? You know, Father Flanagan, underprivileged kids, and all that sweet bullshit?"

Seth scratched his head. "I'm not sure what you mean. Tracy who?"

Norm clasped his fingers. "We need to welcome these clients, Bobby. Not shun them. There's a huge opportunity here. These gays, they're no dummies. They get the good degrees: doctor, lawyer, *masters of this, masters of that.* And then they leave those godforsaken places like Michigan, Iowa, Indiana ... and move here." He took a sip of his coffee. "What do you wanna do? Chase them back to the wilderness?"

Bobby waved his hand. "Okay, okay. To each his own. When it comes to divorce, one's man's *Russell-L'Anse* is another's *Rupert Murdoch.* What's the deal with you homos, anyway? You think marriage is so great? Why? You're guys, after all. Go get drunk at the gay bar and pair up at closing time. Seems a lot more sensible to me." He looked away and sighed, lost in thought for a moment. "Okay, anything else?"

This was the point in the meeting where Seth felt like a hostage negotiator. He spread a stack of invoices over the table. "Mr. Horne called yesterday," he said.

Bobby groaned. "Oh Christ."

"Yeah. He's not happy." Seth made eye contact with both partners. "From what I see, you each sent him a different March invoice."

Norm rubbed his chin. "We double-billed him?"

"Not exactly," Seth clarified. "The invoices are completely different."

Bobby snickered. "I forgot to charge him for services rendered last October," he said.

Norm turned to him, palms up. "And you're just remembering this now?"

"No, I remembered it last month. So, I adjusted his bill accordingly."

Norm jerked away from the table. "I've got work to do."

"Fine," said Bobby. "Meeting adjourned."

"Wait," Seth warned. "What do you want me to do with Mr. Horne?"

Bobby clicked his tongue. "Make something up," he said.

"Make something up?"

"Yeah ... What's that ethics test you aced?"

"The MPRE?"

"Yeah. Do they offer that in Illinois, or just states like Michigan and New Jersey?"

"Uh ... it's national ... the *Multi-state* Professional Responsibility Exam."

"Well, here's some advice, kid: forget that bullshit. This is the real world. Make something up and get our fucking money from Mr. Horne."

As the day expired, Seth's interest in the Certificate of Merit blossomed into an obsession. Even so, he did not check the school's website at work, keeping a personal oath to work separate from school.

Did I get the award? He wondered. *I must have.* A hungry curiosity lingered inside him.

Six o'clock was too early for Loading Zone check-in, so Seth wandered into *Czech Point*, a thickly carpeted, softly lit bar around the block from campus. He grabbed a booth just off the bar and ordered a ginger whiskey. Here, in *Czech's* perpetual twilight, it could have been morning, noon, or 1954. It was the perfect spot for contemplation.

Two years of law school convinced Seth to revisit his old habit of drinking. It wasn't social. Drinking—for Seth—was simply a way of coping with old demons that, while muted, still lurked in the hidden crevices of his mind.

Seth's imagination tingled with the second drink. Nostalgic images flickered, teasing his emotions: high school, baseball, the *Grand Plan.*

A natural phenom, Seth could uncork a 92 mile-per-hour fastball at age 14. Unsatisfied, he toiled endlessly on the mound, developing a complementary slider and a soft knuckle-curve. Nurturing a vendetta against Little League coaches (who benched him in favor of lesser-talented sons), Seth put thousands of hours of self-practice under his belt, destroying hundreds of baseballs, backstops, and pitch-nets in the process. A vengeful loner, he grew further incensed as teammates and coaches casually spat anti-gay epithets like the shells of infinite sunflower seeds.

By sophomore year, Seth was the unhittable ace of his high school team, representing a community that proclaimed itself the *Shining City.* Wealthy and conservative, these were Seth's people. They loved him with passion conditioned on strikeouts and wins; their American pride intolerant of any deviation from expectation.

Seth's true humanity, if known, would spur righteous hostility and outright abandonment. He numbly accepted this cold reality; it was unavoidable. To cope, he strategized, and concocted a plan.

Real impact.

Junior year, Seth carried Shining City to the state championship, where he mowed down the first nine batters. The opposition had no chance against him; they were unarmed and cornered. Under a veil of nonchalance, Seth's adrenaline pumped like a horse in the derby. The taste of victory danced on his tongue. He wanted that trophy. He wanted that prize. But most of all, he wanted that uncensored post-game moment with the press, when he'd thank his coach, teammates, and community ... and say how much it meant to him as a gay person to be such an integral part of it.

It never happened.

The fourth inning was interrupted by an ear-piercing crack—like a gunshot—then a scream. Seth crumpled to the ground, his arm snapped in half under the pressure of a 3-2 slider. Few bystanders would forget the gruesome disfigurement. Tony Palsgraf, Seth's closest teammate, walked behind second base and vomited into the shallow outfield grass.

Seth didn't remember much about the hospital, where doctors successfully removed a cancerous tumor from his humerus. Somewhere between consciousness, he lost the ability to hear. Doctors called it a psychosomatic effect of trauma.

Following discharge, Seth learned to read lips. His arm sat in a cast for 12 weeks and in a brace for 15 more. OxyContin, Percocet, and Hydrocodone soothed his pain. When he turned 18, he applied for, and received, a medical marijuana card.

The drugs carried him through high school, but his throbbing arm healed at an angle, like a half-broken branch. Even in deepest August, Seth wore long-sleeve shirts to hide the deformity.

Seth was deaf and listless in college, living at home and perpetually hung-over when he met attorney Jay Posner on a gay-dating app. Jay was moderately tall, with neatly-trimmed, honey-colored hair. Debonair, athletic, and balanced, Jay was well-versed in the arts and sports, a rare combination anywhere, at any age. His caramel complexion and chestnut eyes complemented three-piece suits as well as they did shorts and a tank-top. He was also a survivor: the half-moon scar of a hate crime ran from cheek to ear, disrupting an otherwise flawless appearance.

Age . . .

At first, Seth's parents were taken aback—Jay was their senior by a few years. Those reservations were soon blunted by Seth's new sobriety, good grades, and level demeanor.

The relationship nurtured Seth's self-confidence. He developed an identity, coming out to his friends and exploring the complexities of those relationships, as well as the conflicts and rewards they presented. He adopted the philosophy of Harvey Milk, holding himself out to friends, family, and acquaintances as a walking, breathing reason to choose humanity over hate.

That June, Jay bought prime seats for a White Sox-Cubs game. Although Chicago was only a three-hour drive, they flew into the city and hired a limousine to the game. It was Seth's first post-injury exposure to baseball; a morbid sense of foreboding quelled his initial excitement. He cringed at the first several pitches, waiting, expecting to hear that awful snap.

But that didn't happen. Instead, his ears filled with the sounds of summer: the buzzing crowd, the barking vendors, and the snapping ... of hardball against leather, building a crescendo to each sweet crack of the bat.

Something lifted, opening Seth's auricles to pulsing vibrations for the first time in years. He squeezed Jay's hand and wept openly; it was the best weekend of his life.

Three halcyon years gave way to graduation. Jay encouraged Seth's application to law school, but subsequent acceptance cast a shadow over their relationship; monogamy faded with Seth's Chicago departure. Seduced by Big City Opportunity, Seth found each day riddled with moral conflict.

Seth's dissonance subsided when he fell for "Ten-inch" Thomas, a long-legged dancer prone to Slimfast lunches, junk food dinners, and gritty, profanity-laced slang.

Under Thomas's spell, Seth ignored Jay's texts and let his calls go directly to voice mail.

His grip already tenuous, Jay interpreted Seth's behavior as a message to let go—so he did.

"*Jay's old ass don't matter,*" Thomas would say, watching himself in the mirror.

Seth didn't exactly believe that, but his best instincts were seduced away by Thomas's youthful, lazy smile ... at least until last week, when Seth found dozens of foreign condom wrappers under their bed.

So here I am.

Seth ordered another ginger whiskey as a new idea formed: *I'll give my Certificate of Merit Award to Jay.* It was the perfect opportunity to break the ice. Jay loved academic achievement more than anyone; he could barely contain his excitement when Seth made the Dean's List his first semester.

He'll flip with pride over this!

Seth would frame the award, ship it with a sticky note affixed: *I did it because of you. Forever grateful, Seth.*

Jay would call him, flattered.

It was the first step toward a long-term healing process. He'd get Jay back, earn his trust, and never let him go again.

Seth barely finished the thought before an unseemly sight startled him to attention: Professor Goebels ducked into Czech Point and shuffled nervously to the bar, where he was met by Daisy Duff-Gordon, the law school's current class president. Daisy, her big bouffant flowing outward in a zillion shades of salon-streaked blonde, sat on her stool just as she did in class: with an air of unbridled entitlement.

Seth pulled his Sox cap low and focused on the dialogue-heavy scene. His lip-reading skills, albeit a bit rusty, proved quite handy.

Professor Goebels ordered a stinger, then set an object—the size of a Swiss army knife—on the bar and slid it over to Daisy Duff-Gordon. "There you go," he said.

Daisy flipped her hair and offered a wolf's grin. "Oh, Peter!" she squealed. "The multiple-choice questions?"

The professor's face tightened. "Yes, they're all there," he said, clearing his throat. "Every single one—all departments. Quite comprehensive, actually."

"And the answers?"

"All there, of course—right on the thumb drive. If it's not on the drive, it's not on the final. I can't fix it like Property II, but this really lifts the oxcart out of the ditch."

131

Daisy clapped her tiny hands, bouncing with delight. She leaned into the professor and kissed him before crawling into his lap to play with his tie.

"You know," Goebels said authoritatively, "This place is actually owned by a German family."

"Oh, I don't care much about that," Daisy sighed.

Seth paid his tab and slid out the alleyway exit. Twenty minutes later, he was naked but for a towel around his waist, sitting on a bathhouse bed, finishing a tax law assignment. The smell of chlorine and fresh men permeated the air.

Seth's evening graduated from homework to the confines of the whirlpool spa. Sadly, the labyrinths, once bustling with eager flesh, were empty but for a few random stragglers. The availability of quick-sex through cell-phone applications diminished business considerably.

He wrapped his room key, which was affixed to an elastic chain, around his deformed arm, tossed his towel over a steel rack, and descended five marble steps into the opaque water. Held inside cavernous walls, the pool bubbled like lava, releasing steam into the mood-lit air. Seth waded his way into a private crevice, where he found a seat on a perimeter shelf. Water, warm and welcoming, rose to his shoulders. Events of the day played in his mind like the backlit images of a silent film.

Jay. The Certificate of Merit. Eddie Chaplinski. Daisy Duff-Gordon. Professor Goebels ...

Daisy cheated ... I can't let her get away with it ... That award is mine. I earned it, I deserve it ... I'll frame it and send it to Jay ... Jay will call me ... The award is mine ...

I must do something!

Seth closed his eyes, splashed water over his face, and reviewed his case against Daisy Duff-Gordon.

* * * *

There were no excuses, defenses, or mitigating circumstances: Seth fully intended to break into Daisy's apartment. She lived in a familiar, U-shaped, 18-unit three-story, directly across the courtyard from Thomas. Seth knew the place well: accessing her unit was routine.

He reached over the property's five-foot gate, released the latch, strode unnoticed across the courtyard, and ascended the deck stairway. Daisy's backdoor was locked, so Seth popped the screen and pulled himself through the kitchen window.

The apartment, decorated with large photos of Daisy in various life-poses, was a mess of dirty clothes and candy wrappers. Even so, Seth found the thumb drive immediately; it was sticking out of Daisy's laptop on the kitchen table.

He reached out to snatch it, then stopped.

What does this accomplish?

Seth leaned against the icebox. Bathed in a glow of twilight from the open window, he reconsidered his options. *Honor Codes, Rules, Responsibilities* ... there was something languid about the hum of the appliance against his shoulder.

A quick, loud crack startled him upright. Then rattling at the front door.

Shit!

Seth ducked into the main closet, heart racing as he pulled the twin doors shut.

Is it her?

Plodding footsteps echoed through the airless apartment. Floorboards moaned; a brief eclipse engulfed the closet as the intruder lumbered past. Seth held his breath.

That can't be Daisy.

After several minutes of meandered wandering, the intruder entered the bathroom and urinated into the toilet from a standing position.

Seth leaned forward slowly, took his best view through the door crack.

Eddie Chaplinski!

Chaplinski traipsed into the kitchen. A faucet whooshed, followed by the clicks and beeps of a laptop barraged by the hard taps of angry fingers.

The front door jangled, its hinges moaned. High-heeled shoes clicked on tile.

"What the hell's going on?" cried Betsy Duff-Gordon.

"You fucking cheater," growled Chaplinski. His voice cracked with agitation.

"What?"

"The thumb-drive. I knew you cheated. Now I know how."

"What?"

"Your student number's last three digits are 6-1-6. You cheated your way to the Merit Award ... and you don't know a goddamn thing about Property."

A slight pause, then: "Maybe I know more than you think."

"Okay. Contrast *joint tenancy* with *tenancy in common.*"

"Oh, please. Really?"

"Yeah, really." Chaplinski's voice rose to a startling crescendo. "And what's the difference between a *reversion* and a *remainder*? Huh? See! I knew it. You don't *know*. And you got the highest grade?"

"Sure, I know it. I'm just not, like, good with essay. I'm better at multiple-choice, way better. Did you ever think about that?" She paused, searching. "The school will clear me. Besides, you probably think a woman's place is in the home," she added, weakly.

"Not my home," snapped Chaplinski.

"Get away from my stuff! Leave! Get out!"

Chaplinski lifted her laptop like a pizza and whipped it against the wall.

"No, no, NO!"

Eddie wrestled Daisy's cell phone away and fled through the front door.

"Stop, you son-of-a-bitch!" Daisy rummaged through her purse, groping as she hustled after him.

Seth stepped out of the closet, intending to play peacemaker as the odds of violence escalated down the hallway.

Yet he halted amidst the echoes of physical confrontation. Applying the *Doctrine of Non-interference*, he turned around and departed swiftly down the fire escape, through the courtyard, and out the gate.

His cell phone collected three bars of service in the alleyway, plenty of reception to call Jay and begin his apology.

Affidavit of Counsel

Samuel J. Tosca

[Here, a personal-injury lawyer uses the formal convention of a prevailing-party fee request to tell the story of a young black man's demise in a police excessive-force case and the challenges of the complex and difficult civil-rights litigation that followed.]

State of Michigan   )
) ss.
Cass County   )

Jackson Hewlett, a competent person first being duly sworn, deposes and says as follows:

1. I am the plaintiff Estate's trial counsel in this wrongful-death, police excessive-force case pursued under 28 USC §1983.

2. I make this affidavit supporting the prevailing-party fee request, following the verdict and judgment in the Estate's favor, and will testify at any hearing on that fee request to the truth of the matters that this affidavit states.

3. The Estate has petitioned for a fee award under 28 USC §1988 showing that it prevailed on every significant claim in this case despite aggressive defense by skilled counsel representing the defendant government agency at public and insurer expense.

4. The Estate through undersigned counsel made multiple pre-suit and in-suit demands for the relief sought, including in amounts substantially less than the jury ultimately awarded, in good-faith efforts to avoid the necessity of this litigation, yet to no avail because

of the defendant government agency's decision to defend this case without offer of any relief.

5. The litigation, trial, verdict, and judgment were thus necessary to compel the relief the Estate sought and obtained in this case, without which the Estate would have obtained no relief, and the public would have gained no benefit from this case's vindication of important public and private rights.

6. The undersigned counsel is aware of no circumstances unusual or special to this case that would make the court's fee award unjust.

7. To the contrary, the trial proofs showed that the defendant government's position lacked substantial justification in law or fact.

8. Specifically, the involved officer shot the Estate's decedent at close range from behind while decedent had his hands behind his back and was stationary facing up against a wall in compliant, submissive, and defenseless posture, after having realized that an armed officer was in his pursuit and that he faced a mortal risk.

9. The single bullet from the officer's firearm pierced the decedent's lower back and traversed decedent's trunk, exiting decedent's anterior lower abdomen, severing artery and foreseeably causing decedent's painful and horrifying bleed-out death.

10. The officer's deadly act thus indisputably involved the use of more force than was reasonable under the circumstances, decedent presenting no threat of harm to anyone, equivalent to a summary street execution.

11. The officer's deadly act was further indisputably an unreasonable arrest and denial of due process leading directly to the decedent's sudden loss of liberty and life, violating to the worst possible degree, and permanently terminating, decedent's Fourth and Fourteenth Amendment rights.

12. Although unnecessary to support the verdict and judgment, trial proofs further showed that race discrimination may have motivated and animated the officer's deadly act in that decedent was a young black male while the officer was an older white female shown and known to have previously expressed racial animus, without department remonstrance or other response.

13. The rights that the Estate asserted in this case were important rights to the decedent's two infant children, decedent's girlfriend and mother of his children, decedent's mother and grandmother, and other family members surviving decedent, each of whom had reasonable expectation of decedent's future love, society, companionship, services, and support.

14. The rights that the Estate asserts in this case were further important rights to the community in which the incident took place, insofar as a history of similar incidents have divided and oppressed the community, having deleterious social and economic effects from which the community has not been able to recover.

15. The jury deliberated just two hours, reaching a unanimous verdict on the only count with which the court presented it, confirming the complete vindication of decedent's rights and full acceptance of the Estate's constitutional claims in this case.

16. The jury further awarded more in damages than the undersigned counsel requested in closing argument, reflecting counsel's compelling presentation of evidence in the most meaningful and motivating manner, without exaggerated appeal, trick, or artifice, as the court properly expects counsel to try cases.

17. Beyond representing the Estate in the preparation, pretrial, and trial of this case, the undersigned counsel has further handled the probate proceedings necessary to maintain this wrongful-death action under state law, including obtaining an order appointing the personal representative who authorized and directed this action.

18. On the defendant government's payment of the judgment in this case, or payment by the municipal-liability league insuring the defendant government, the undersigned counsel will further secure and account for the funds according to probate order that counsel will also obtain.

19. To provide the court with the information necessary for it to follow the requisite lodestar method for awarding fees, undersigned counsel represents and attests that he and his associate reasonably expended the hundreds of arduous hours of high-level law services shown in the attached itemized billings.

20. The undersigned counsel and his associate recorded the information used to compile the attached itemized billings,

contemporaneous with the services that those billings reflect and that counsel and his associate in fact performed, consistent with best practices for timekeeping and billing.

21. The services the billings reflect and that counsel and his associate in fact performed represent usual, customary, and necessary services for the specialized pursuit of civil claims of this extraordinary type involving the death of an innocent citizen at government hands.

22. The undersigned counsel further attests that the partner and associate rates shown in the attached itemized billings represent reasonable hourly rates for the specialized work that this case required, in that the rates are market rates for the relevant market for this specialized work.

23. At the hearing, the Estate will call as witnesses supporting the fee request the undersigned counsel, counsel's associate, a local practitioner as to the unavailability of local counsel, and the expert statistician who prepared the State Bar's most-recent economics-of-law-practice survey.

24. These witnesses will confirm that the attached billings reflect customary, average, and reasonable rates that lawyers practicing in this specialized field and related fields charge for equivalent services.

25. The petition requests specialized rates rather than customary and average local rates because local counsel was unavailable, unwilling, or unable to perform for the Estate.

26. While the local bar includes competent and masterful lawyers in other fields, members of the local bar lack the experience, expertise, and specialization required to handle a publicly notorious wrongful-death case involving government use of deadly force.

27. Because a competent or even masterful general practitioner could not have competently handled this case, the Estate could not obtain qualified counsel at normal local rates and thus needed to retain the undersigned counsel who possesses skills, resources, experience, and specialized expertise necessary to cases of this extraordinary type.

28. Specifically, the undersigned counsel has thirty years of experience as a civil litigator representing parties in complex personal-injury and wrongful-death cases, including these civil-rights cases against government agencies and officials.

29. Multiple substantial trial wins in state and federal courts, and substantial settlements in publicly notorious cases like this one, demonstrate undersigned counsel's special skills and expertise in the selection, investigation, pleading, discovery, pretrial, and trial of these cases.

30. While counsel's associate does not have the same experience, the undersigned counsel recruited, hired, and employed his associate to develop the experience and specialized skills and expertise, which the associate has ably demonstrated in this and other cases.

31. The Estate's retained expert statistician has adjusted the hourly rates for undersigned counsel and his associate to match lawyers having similar graduation and licensure dates, and similar experience in this specialized field.

32. This case further presented novel and difficult issues, requiring exceptional representation and creating exceptional litigation and financial risk.

33. While the claim on its face appeared simple in that the officer shot the defenseless decedent in the back from close range, the officer maintained in defense that his firearm's discharge was accidental in that decedent allegedly bumped the firearm.

34. The undersigned counsel successfully addressed this substantial and unusual fact issue by obtaining expert reconstruction, animating the event as demonstrative evidence, and presenting expert testimony confirming that the officer's story was impossible and therefore false, in that decedent's coat did not have the requisite powder burns from proximate firing and instead had powder burns consistent with a near-range firearm discharge.

35. The undersigned counsel had further to cross-examine the involved officer using specialized skills to demonstrate the factual impossibility and thus the falsity of the officer's trial testimony, and its inconsistency with deposition testimony that undersigned counsel skillfully obtained and internal investigation reports that undersigned counsel successfully argued were subject to discovery.

36. Moreover, the Estate's decedent was an unemployed and twice-convicted individual having already at young age had two children out of wedlock and who may have been unlawfully possessing or delivering controlled substances just before or at the time of the incident, thus creating substantial risk of undue prejudice.

37. The undersigned counsel successfully addressed these substantial and unusual fact issues by obtaining the court's order in limine as to decedent's unemployment and convictions, and limiting instructions as to the possession and delivery evidence, and by making opening statement and closing argument, and skillfully conducting jury voir dire witness examinations, to give appropriate context to such evidence.

38. Further, the undersigned counsel successfully obtained an order of recusal as to the prior judge assigned to this case, after that judge made comments publicly about this case, creating a serious risk that the judge had an actual bias that could affect rulings, prejudice rights, and create an appearance of impropriety and miscarriage of justice.

39. The undersigned counsel operates his small law firm independent of any public, charitable, or other government or philanthropic funding, and instead as a for-profit professional corporation.

40. Because counsel's law firm specializes in injury and death cases representing individual and estate claimants, the firm must fund the important law services that it offers to the public through recoveries that the firm's clients make, under contingency-fee agreements.

41. These clients would not have access to law services and to the justice of the courts without the exceptional risk that firms like counsel's firm accept, when representing clients on contingency-fee bases.

42. A fee recovery in this case and other like cases is essential to the undersigned counsel maintaining his law practice, employing his associate, and ensuring access to justice consistent with the lawyer's oath administered in this state.

43. To the extent if any that reputation of counsel remains a fee factor and question of interest to the court, the undersigned counsel has received awards or recognition from local and state bars, and public-interest and advocacy organizations, for offering law services like those in this case.

44. The undersigned counsel further offers substantial public education for no charge, at conferences, workshops, and continuing-legal-education seminars, and through the print, television, radio, and social media.

45. To the extent that the nature and quality of the lawyer-client relationship bears on the value of representation, as case law supports, the undersigned counsel duly gained the trust and confidence of decedent's mother, who is the Estate's personal representative.

46. Decedent's mother, the personal representative, does not hold a high school diploma and, while fully competent to manage the Estate's affairs with the help of skilled professionals, requires an additional level of education, advice, and support in that management.

47. The undersigned counsel and, in particular, his associate have provided the personal representative with that additional level of expert education, advice, and support, and have thus maintained her trust and confidence throughout these highly charged, emotional, complex, and difficult proceedings.

48. In providing these valuable professional services to the Estate, the undersigned counsel and his associate were necessarily forgoing other valuable professional employment and representation, turning down or not pursuing representation in other matters of substantial potential economic and social value.

49. If as case law supports the court awards fees commensurate with the request, then the undersigned counsel and his law firm will exercise an election in the contingency-fee agreement with the Estate not to recover any portion of the damages awarded in the judgment but instead to receive the awarded fees alone.

50. That election, while reducing the total fees that counsel and his firm would receive if they elected their alternative option of receiving one third of the total recovery including both damages and

fees, would enable the Estate and its creditors and beneficiaries to recover one-hundred percent of the damages that the jury awarded.

51. The Estate's creditors, who by law would recover only from the portion of damages awarded for decedent's conscious pain and suffering, include only local emergency medical-care providers and retailers with whom decedent maintained credit.

52. Thus, the substantial portion of the total damages awarded would go to the adult beneficiaries or into trust for the benefit of decedent's two minor children, as the probate court hears and approves of the beneficiary distribution.

53. The undersigned counsel understands and in good faith believes that the adult beneficiaries have agreed, and that the probate court is likely to approve, that the substantial portion of the total damages be held in trust for the benefit of decedent's two minor children, with the expectation that the children will receive education including college education that would not otherwise be available to them.

54. The undersigned counsel further understands and in good faith believes that the adult beneficiaries have agreed that if awarded the distribution that they expect from the probate court, that they intend with a portion of those funds to establish a community fund to train and educate law-enforcement officers and the public in these most-important civil rights.

55. If the adult beneficiaries do so establish a community fund to train and educate law-enforcement officers and the public in these most-important civil rights, and counsel receives the requested fees, then the undersigned counsel intends to contribute a portion of those fees to the community fund for the same public benefit.

56. The undersigned counsel and his law firm have advanced substantial sums in the investigation, discovery, trial, and other pursuit of this case, as the attached itemized statement of account indicates.

57. Those sums comprise expert witness fees, deposition and transcript costs and court-reporter fees, fees for the preparation of animations and illustrations, fees for records and copying, court filing fees and jury fees, travel costs, and other costs, all of which are

either taxable as court costs as indicated or are recoverable expenses under counsel's contingency-fee agreement with the Estate.

58. The sums that the undersigned counsel and his firm expended in this case represent an additional risk that counsel and his firm incurred in that they would have lost those sums out of pocket if the Estate had not prevailed in this case, beyond the substantial lost value of their time incurred in this case.

59. While the undersigned counsel has the skills, expertise, standing, and reputation to which this affidavit attests, counsel and his firm do not win all cases and instead occasionally fail to recover, such that counsel and his firm must finance those losses out of fees earned in cases in which the firm's clients prevail, like this case.

60. The court's judgment in this case specifically reserved the fee issue that the Estate's petition presents, such that the court now has the authority, procedural opportunity, and evidentiary basis for granting the fee request.

Further affiant says not.

_____
Jackson Hewlett

Subscribed and sworn to before
me this 26th day of July, 2017:

_____
Mary A. Schrodinger, Notary Public
Wayne County, MI
My commission expires: 07/10/18

Broken Promises

Bart Demeter

Here, a lawyer with substantial real-estate experience and who also teaches college writing courses tells a poignant story of a new lawyer coming of age when facing up to his law partner's misconduct.

December's clouds move over Michigan like a cold steel tarp. The sun, the blue sky, the grass, all evidence of life before winter won't be seen again until cruel April. Pulling into his spot, Thomas parks and then stares at the reflection of gray clouds in the charcoal-black hood of his Lincoln. The smell of his coffee competes with the hint of new leather reminding him that he has sixty-nine more payments.

The car's quiet purr is only slightly louder than the sound of his breathing. In front of him, the little brick building's shingle, Parker and Darmstadt, Attorneys at Law. Not ready to face the harshness, Thomas sits a while longer. He punches up the climate control on the Lincoln's fancy computer screen and sets it to a reasonable seventy-two degrees. He feels around in his blazer's breast pocket for his smart phone; two more texts, David, and one from AT&T reminding him he owes $278 before the 6th.

Rather than read David's, he looks at the 6 AM text again. "36574 : Account balance below $200.00. Account 57.34 current balance." Thomas hopes that when he reads it this time it won't be real. His mind races over the day's schedule. "Three closings scheduled... that account had nearly two million wired into it last night." He thinks about the possibilities; bank errors, Trans Union's wiring goofs,

145

reporting delays..., David. He hopes it isn't David. "God, it better not be David." The thought reminds him he still had not read his text.

"Don't worry about the account, I got it: 6:15 AM."

"What does that mean? I got it."

David, all at once, best friend, law partner, confidant, and now—embezzler?

"I got it?" Thomas mutters in a mocking caricature of David's confident voice.

The possibilities all at once narrow. Thumping his head on the steering wheel, Thomas runs a dozen worst-case scenarios through his mind. Then a mantra recalled from law school, "When in doubt, rat your buddy out." The ethics professor insisted they repeat it over and over. "When in doubt, rat your buddy out."

"As if it was so effing simple," his voice sounds cracked and dry.

Even though the professional ethics class was four years ago, he recalls the rule as if reading it from the book: Model ABA Rules of Professional Conduct, Rule 1.15, Subsection A:

> A lawyer shall hold property of clients or third persons that is in a lawyer's possession in connection with a representation separate from the lawyer's own property. Funds shall be kept in a separate account maintained in the state where the lawyer's office is situated, or elsewhere with the consent of the client or third person. Other property shall be identified as such and appropriately safeguarded.

Some of the ethics rules were complicated. §1.15—Pretty simple, don't take stuff that isn't yours.

"I'm overreacting."

Thomas thinks about simplicity and then of his life at law school. Coffee and study in the morning, quick lunch, go to class, study until bed. Tomorrow, do it all over again. In fifteen weeks, a three-hour test. There were no complications outside of sheer exhaustion and mental breakdown. Read the case, learn the rule, perform when the Professor calls you out. At the time it seemed impossibly hard, but in truth it was the easiest thing Thomas faced since. Law school was routine; all he needed was the force of will to keep jamming the

146

information and processes in his head. There was a right answer at the end of all the cases, most of the time.

Thomas liked simple. That is why he wanted to practice real estate law. By and large, he lorded over a title agent, made sure no one screwed up the county record search, and wrote checks. It wasn't glamorous—it was steady, safe, and had a routine that Thomas preferred. His partner, on the other hand, focused on the big stuff, personal-injury litigation. David always fancied himself some sort of Wild West gun-for-hire. He embodies the clichéd square-jawed lawyer on television, "I'll fight for you in court." A kind of over-the-top-confidence that Thomas admires, but doesn't really want. For all the bluster, a fair amount of the time David is a gunslinger for nothing. Mostly he maintains the image of success and talking to people who want revenge more than recovery.

Thomas stares at phone again, trying hard to quell the burning in his stomach.

"Too much coffee?"

As he scrolls through the bank transactions on his phone he sees withdrawals he never made and deposits he didn't expect. The burning in his stomach intensifies, creating a strange taste in his mouth, the same kind of nervous bile he had on the day he was sworn in. He tracks that thought back into the Courthouse where five other newly minted lawyers in fresh suits and crisp white Oxfords prepare to pledge their life's efforts to the law. Relatives and invested onlookers fill the court's pews. Five right hands raised.

"I do solemnly swear that I will support the Constitution of the State of Michigan...."

He felt his parents' eyes on him. So proud. The first college graduate and the first professional in the family. His mother had a few college classes, but she never finished, life had gotten in the way. His father worked hard injecting plastics since graduating high school. Now both of them witnessed his ascension into life that they had only seen in television dramas.

"I will maintain the respect due to the courts of justice and judicial officers...."

Their pride was to be expected. College, for him, was their dream, one that Thomas unenthusiastically pursued. It wasn't until he imagined a future with a girl he met in college that he began to take life seriously. When Thomas announced he wanted to go to law school, they were as unprepared as they were thrilled. His four-figure student loan payment testified to that.

The sharp crunch of tires pressing in the newly fallen snow jars Thomas away from his musing as David pulls in the spot marked David E. Parker, Esquire. Thomas looks over to see David's grinning face through the window of his Audi.

"What are you sitting here for?" he mouths. Tapping his showy watch, "Time's a wastin'."

Thomas grabs his coffee. As the car door opens, Thomas struggles with hating the slap of cold but loving the sound of the wind in the trees.

David holds the door for his partner and smiles. A blast of wind flips over his tie, revealing the Salvatore Ferragamo label.

"Okay, sorry for the morning's drama, but it's solved. The money will be back in the bank by 10:00 am. There was a little hiccup, but no worries."

"No worries?! As if that just explains it? There was two million dollars in that account. What the hell happened to it?"

"Nothing happened to it." The look of relief on Thomas's face makes David laugh a little. "It was just making us some money overnight," he says with the laughing smile still on his face.

"What? You can't be that stupid. You know what happens to people who embezzle." David's face no longer looks relieved.

"It's only embezzlement if you get caught." David looks at Thomas seriously. "You're the one always bitching about money. Take a hard look around." His voice toughens as he speaks. "You and I don't generate enough to pay for all this shit."

"So what did you do?" Thomas asks.

"I made us money. Us." He points to himself and then Thomas.

"How?" Thomas's tone drums with profound disapproval.

148

"Nothing illegal. Geeze."

"You raided an escrow account, clients' funds, it's illegal."

"It sounds terrible when you say it like that. What I did was trade foreign currency markets while resources sat dormant." David pauses. "It's not like I have a wife to go home to like you, so I started dabbling. The money is back in our account before business. You've never complained before today."

"I never noticed before 6:00 this morning. How long?"

"Just after the Turner case."

"Jesus. I need a minute to think."

"What's there to think about Tom? I made us nearly 100k. That's what's been paying for lights, the rent, and all the other crap that makes this place run, not to mention your student loans. Try and remember that."

Thomas stares at David for a moment, but looks away without comment. David never flinched.

Thomas retreats to his office, sits, and thinks back to the pathetic little office they first had. It is a good thing that most of his real estate clients operate by phone. Amy at Chicago Title, the elderly gentleman at Stewart, Bette at First American, all good clients whom he'd never actually met. Had they seen the used file cabinets supporting an honest repurposed door that held his law school laptop, they would have thought twice. It was David's first litigation win that emboldened the two to lease their first real furniture, a phone system, and new computers. In theory, Thomas's work kept the lights on, while David provided image and hope for a plentiful future.

David insisted on the upgraded office machines, fancy office furniture, and pricey coffee service. His argument was simple. "If we don't show that we are successful, clients won't ever give us the chance to be successful. You gotta fake it till you make it, man." And he would flash his winning smile to close the argument. In truth, Thomas was never sure they needed all this extra stuff, but he certainly enjoyed having it.

149

What an odd pair we are, he thinks. His mind races back to the day the two met in undergrad.

"Hey! Hey you." A voice calls from atop a ladder.

Thomas looks up to see a silhouette of a young man standing on a tall ladder, the light through the window blinding him to any details. He looks like he wants to hang a giant black and white Kappa Alpha Phi banner across the student union's pillared walkway. What is unclear is how he planned to do it.

"Little help… please and thank you." The young man's smile and tone is infectious.

"Uh yea, sure thing."

The two struggle with the banner, eventually managing to secure it across the columns.

"What is Kappa Alpha Phi?"

"Seriously? What's your major?"

"I haven't decided yet."

"Ahh, one of those. Still haven't figured out why you came to college? It's a pre-law fraternity, but it's co-ed. All us up-and-coming lawyers belong. Helps with LSAT, and we do community stuff."

"You already know what you want to do after college. I'm not even sure what I'm doing now."

"Of course, man, you gotta have a plan. And the plan is retire by thirty-five. What's your name?"

"Thomas. You didn't strike me as a plan kinda guy, I mean with the sign and all. How did you plan to do that by yourself?"

"Good one. I'm David. I'm a big-picture guy. I'll hire out people to handle the details. Hey, why don't you come to our party tonight?"

"Ahh, I'm not really into the party scene."

"Tell you what, I'll introduce you to some pre-law girls—super-hot; smart, funny, and gorgeous is a hell of a combo. Did I mention super-hot? C'mon, you know you want to." He flashed an infectious smile.

"Okay, I guess, but I'm not signing up for some creepy wanna-be-lawyer cult."

"Excellent, it starts at 9:00. I'll see you there." David handed Thomas a brightly colored flyer with a map to the party's location.

Even to this day, Thomas hates going to parties. There was always some initial excitement, but as the hour approached, he reminded himself how much he didn't like being in crowds, how much he really didn't like loud conversations, and how he hated the stench of cigarettes and beer breath. Over the next couple hours, Thomas thought up every conceivable reason not to go. In the end, the thought of meeting some hot female up-and-coming lawyer won out.

Thomas arrived at the party exactly at 9:00, with his exit excuse already well-rehearsed. The house looked like any other off Grand River Ave. except for the large Greek letters above. David greeted Thomas at the door.

"Ha, I didn't think you'd come," flashing his trademark smile.

"I figured you might need help with hanging decorations."

"Oh, you have jokes now. Did you spend all evening thinking that up?" he said laughing. "Let me introduce you to a few people."

David led him into a noisy room of loud music and even louder conversations. The evening, for Thomas, was a blur of people whose names he wouldn't remember, stories of places he would forget, and red cups brimmed with cheap beer. With Thomas trailing behind, David floated from one group to another, introducing, socializing, and networking. Even with several beers in him, Thomas never felt that kind of ease, and rarely said anything other than "Hello" and "What's up" with a nod. Mostly he listened.

As the room quieted and the music dimmed, Thomas found himself on an over-used couch talking to a small group of intense people. Beer-fueled debates of politics, philosophy, and unstable ideologies continued until late into the morning. When the conversation stalled, David reenergized it by championing a point no one had thought of. Thomas, with the aid of a girl with intensely blue eyes, ganged up on David's positions. Of course, as soon as he was pinned down, he would add yet another complicating element.

"Intellectual intercourse," he called it. For Thomas, it was his first real college discussion experience, allowing him to try out the ideas he only encountered in class. It woke an intellectual hunger in him and cemented their friendship—eventually leading Thomas into law school.

A conflicted flash of admiration and anger crossed Thomas's mind, jarring him out of his nostalgia.

"Retired by thirty-five," he mutters.

Thomas looks out of his office window—gray sky.

The speaker on his phone alerts, "Tom, can you come to my office, I want to show you something."

Thomas knows he's in for a sales job. David only calls him Tom when he is trying to convince him.

"I'll be there in a few, I'm working on the noon closing." He purposely keeps his tone even so David doesn't worry.

A moment later David knocks.

"Tom, what tortured logic is your brain attempting?"

"For the love of God," a phrase he uses only for his most irritated moments. "David, I need a few minutes to think. I don't work like you. I need time."

"Fine. We'll talk after lunch. I have Thai coming in for lunch."

"I have a closing at noon, 1:30 and 3:00. I won't have time until at least 4:00, if not later."

"You want me to do one?" he replies.

"No, I've got it." Thomas says, trying to mirror the tone he imagined from the 6:15 text. Crap, he is really heaping it up, Thomas thinks.

Sitting down, he prepares to seriously consider the situation, going so far as grabbing a pen and pad to sketch out pros and cons. On one side, do nothing; on the other, report his friend and partner to the Bar. Not since asking his then-girlfriend to marry him had he pulled up paper and pad to sketch out a problem. Even then, his marriage list never made it to the con side because, wisely, David had come by and knocked it off the common-room table.

"What are you doing?"

"I'm considering marrying Heather," Tom said.

David looked at him as if he was observing a struggling infant.

"You are the dumbest smart guy I have ever met."

"What? Why?"

"First, you think something like love can be written down and quantified like a problem to be solved. And two, you would write down the cons. You really are a moron." He launched into one of his bumper-sticker philosophies. "Don't write anything down you wouldn't want to see in the paper tomorrow. Plausible deniability, man, what would happen if she found your list?"

"Thanks," Thomas said, realizing he hadn't considered the unintentional hurt his list could cause.

"Anyways, what is there to think about? You two have been married since I hooked you up back in undergrad."

"You never hooked us up."

"Didn't I?" David ended the conversation with a tight grin.

As Thomas thinks back, David had been the influence that had brought about many of the best things in his life. Until they had met, Thomas had no idea what he wanted to do, no real motivation, and certainly no plan. Now he had a wife and a career, a real purpose in life. If any one person had earned his unwavering loyalty, it was David.

Thomas's frustration boils over and his keyboard takes the brunt; a few ungentle keyboard strokes pull up his HUD-1 program. Trying hard to concentrate, he reviews his upcoming closing appointments. Releases, mortgage, deed, easement, truth-in-lending form, abstract report, marketability letter, policy, and many required acknowledgements, all affixed with various yellow and pink tabs, indicating where seller and buyers sign. As he moves papers from one stack to another, he comes to a stack of checks written to the many interested parties. His mind snaps back to his partner's misuse of funds.

The rest of the day is a blur. Thomas attempts to concentrate, but his mind returns to the awful realization that at some point, he is expected to betray his friend and report his actions to the Bar. David Parker, Esquire, will lose his license to practice law, and Thomas will be a world-class traitor.

Thomas's phone's speaker blurts a metallic, "Meet me in the closing room."

Thomas forces himself from his desk to join his partner. The men sit awkwardly across the dark, polished table, Thomas's leg bouncing irritably.

"Listen, the way I see it, Tom, you have two choices. You're an ungrateful son-of-bitch without a vestige of loyalty, or you forget about it, and we make a success of this firm."

"Yeah, but you forgot disbarred and put in jail."

"You're such a drama queen. Do you really think those giants in their high-rise buildings didn't fudge things a time or two on their way up?" David says, pointing in the general direction of downtown. "It's not like I'm ripping anybody off. Just the opposite. The money I've made will keep us in business."

"We were in business just fine until you had to have all this," Thomas gestures widely.

David looks at Tom intently.

"You mean when we used doors for desks?" David's look was one of disgust. "What do you want me to do?"

"I'm not sure, David. I'm not sure."

"You know, it's funny. We've never argued, you always backed my play."

"You're right, I trusted you."

"Then trust me now."

Thomas walks out of the room wordlessly, taking notice of the leather waiting-room furniture as he passes. Outside winter presses on unabated, unending steel-gray skies. Inside the car, Thomas fumbles in his breast pocket for his cell phone and wonders how much worse this winter will get.

Opening Doors

Tonya Krause-Phelan

Here, a law professor and dean with substantial experience defending individuals charged with serious crimes illustrates how appearances may not be what they seem, warranting a presumption of innocence.

1

Loud, pulsating music wafted out into the crisp night air as the graffiti-marred steel door swung open. Tipsy from drinking several pints of beer, and dizzy at the prospect of connecting with some beautiful women, two young men stumbled out of the door and into the alley behind O'Connor's Pub. The two men, Drew and Ty, headed toward Michigan Avenue to hail a cab, exchanging friendly banter as they walked. Both college seniors, Drew and Ty had known each other since their freshman year when they met at orientation and became roommates. They had been inseparable since then.

Ty, a tall skinny redhead with curly hair and freckles, was intelligent, kind, and very serious. He attended college on a full academic scholarship, which was a good thing given that his parents were poor. Ty dual-majored in philosophy and art history, was on the debate team, and volunteered for Habitat for Humanity. He was also very shy and didn't date much.

In contrast, Drew was tall, with dark hair and brown eyes. He was a good looking young man in a rugged way. He had a disarming smile and a sarcastic sense of humor. The only son of a single mom,

Drew was admittedly spoiled and self-absorbed. Even so, he never wanted for dates. Most women found Drew charming and friendly.

Drew's dad walked out when Drew was six, and his mom had been trying to make up for it ever since. Growing up without a dad, Drew had developed a strong sense of right and wrong. To that end, he was a criminal justice major and was toying with the idea of becoming a cop. Although law enforcement called to him because of his profound sense of justice, he was insightful enough to know that his chosen major frustrated his mom, a criminal defense lawyer.

As they approached Michigan Avenue, Drew stopped, unsteady on his feet, saying, "Dude, hold up a second. I need to take a leak."

Drew knew he'd drunk too much, but drinking had been the evening's entire point. Drew and Ty had gone to O'Connor's Pub specifically to drink as much alcohol as possible, trying to keep up with the amount of alcohol they thought their friends were drinking down south on spring break.

Speaking of spring break, Drew was still angry with his mom for not giving him the money to take his spring break trip, especially considering he was in his senior year. But what angered Drew most was the tongue lashing his mom had given him. Drew recounted the lecture as he put his cell phone in his back pocket, unzipped his jeans, and began to relieve himself. Drew had called his mom at her office. Big mistake. She was in the middle of a meeting when he called; she hated to be interrupted at work.

"Gray, Ryan, and Prendergrast. May I help you?" the receptionist asked.

"Hi Stacey, this is Drew. Is my mom available?"

"She's in a client meeting. But let me see if she can step out for a minute."

Drew started to tell the receptionist not to interrupt his mom's meeting, but she placed Drew on hold before he could get the words out.

"Drew," his mother asked coolly.

"Hey Mom. Sorry to call you at work," Drew apologized.

"This better be important."

Drew closed his eyes, took a deep breath, and exhaled before he spoke. "Well, it's not important in the solving-world-hunger kind of way. But, it's important to me. This is my senior year, and it's my last chance to go on a spring break with my friends. I was wondering if you'd send extra money with my check this month so Ty and I can go to the Bahamas."

Annoyed at the interruption, Drew's mom measured her words. "I'm not paying for a trip to the Bahamas where you'll spend a week in a drunken stupor trying to hook up with every cutie you see. You've avoided being an adult long enough. I want you to spend spring break finishing your resume and applying for jobs. You graduate in two months! You need to have a job by then."

"You could have just said no," Drew said mockingly.

"I mean it Drew. I'm using tough love. It's time to grow up. Now I need to get back to my meeting."

Drew had never understood how his mom could represent guilty people. "Yeah, I know. You've got to get back to helping your guilty, scumbag clients. They've always been more important to you than I am."

"Drew, spare me the drama. I'll talk with you later." With that, the phone went dead.

Drew was still so angry about the conversation that as he relived it, he repeated the words out loud, in a sing-song snippy voice, "I mean it Drew. I'm using tough love." He finished peeing, zipped his pants, and pulled his cellphone out of his back pocket. He held the phone up in front of his face, changed the direction of the camera lens, and took a selfie. He then texted the photo to his mom with the caption, "Spring Break Memories. Having a great time! Wish you were here."

Ty, who'd gone ahead to the street, yelled, "Come on man, I have a cab for us.

Drew yelled back, "Alright, already. I'm coming."

With exasperation, Ty hollered, "Drew! Now! The meter is running."

Before he started walking toward the cab, Drew tapped on the response his mom sent. Her message said, "Very funny. Did you get a lot of work done on your resume while you were at the bar? At this rate, that's where you're going to be working when you graduate."

Drew paused for a few seconds to think of a pithy reply. He decided to record a message instead. Drew smiled as he hit the video camera's record button. "Hey, mom. Here's lookin' at you! Hope you're having a good time representing those scumbags!"

2

Officers Cameron Brody and Jalon Jones were on routine patrol. They had been partners for five years and had a comfortable relationship. Over the years they had worked every shift and every section of the city. But this night, neither of them were happy about their shift. After all, they worked in a college town, and Saturday nights were known on the force as the "Beer Brigade." Although Saturday-night shifts usually involved nothing more dangerous than some intoxicated co-eds yelling at each other or trying to cop a feel on their date, the Saturday night shifts almost always ended up with someone puking in their back seat or, worse, on them.

Officer Brody feared that this night would be worse than normal because the local university was on spring break. As he drove, Brody told his partner Jones, "A lot of the college kids will have already left for a spring break. But I think the students who are still in town will be determined to spend a week in a drunken stupor. They won't want to feel like they're missing out on the spring-break experience."

Officer Jones nodded his head in agreement. "Yeah, we'll probably be throwing a lot of people in the drunk tank."

Yet drunk coeds weren't the most important thing on Officer Jones's mind. Earlier in the day, the shift sergeant had confronted him about Officer Brody. Apparently, the sergeant had found some discrepancies between Brody's and Jones's reports regarding some recent cases. Because all the cases involved drugs, and because Brody had been acting erratically lately, the sergeant asked internal affairs to investigate Brody. The sergeant told Officer Jones not to say anything to Brody, but Jones was loyal to his partner and wanted to give him a heads-up.

Officer Jones turned his head and took a long look at his partner while he continued to complain about the college kids and spring break. Jones reached up to make sure his bodycam was off, then turned the dash-cam off, too. Jones motioned for Brody to turn his bodycam off. Jones knew he would have to explain to the sergeant why all the cameras were off, but he'd cross that bridge when he came to it. Once Brody's bodycam was off, Jones took a deep breath.

"Hey Cam, we need to talk. Internal affairs is investigating you."

Alarmed, Brody asked, "What are you talking about? For what?"

"What do you think? You've been acting weird lately. And apparently our reports for some drugs cases don't match. I think the sergeant thinks you have a drug problem."

Brody's brows furrowed and he bit his lip.

"Shit," thought Jones. Whenever Brody lied, he bit his lip. Jones's heart sank. He hadn't wanted to believe that his partner was in trouble or that he'd broken the law, but there it was. Jones decided to approach the issue head on.

"Brody, tell me what's going on. I'm your partner, and I'll have your back. But I can't help you if I don't know what's going on. Plus, I need to protect myself. I've got a wife and kids to support."

For what seemed like a long time, Brody didn't respond. When he did speak, his voice was low and measured. Through gritted teeth, he said, "You're my partner, man. But you need to mind your own business."

Just then, Brody and Jones turned on to Michigan Avenue, the town's main strip. As they did, dispatch notified them that a fight had broken out in the alley behind one of the bars. The dispatcher told them that they were the closest patrol unit to the location.

"Shit," Officer Brody said, "And so the fun begins."

"Hey, we're not done talking about this," Jones replied. He had decided to give Brody more information about the investigation so that Brody knew how serious the situation was. "The DEA and internal affairs are doing an audit of the evidence room. They've already asked why our reports differ in that big coke bust we did two months ago. They know some cocaine is missing from the evidence locker."

Without saying a word or looking at his partner, Officer Brody switched on the overhead lights and drove about halfway down the alley. Still not looking at Jones, Brody said, "Are you accusing me of stealing or lying?"

In a quiet voice, Jones said, "Look, I just need to know what's going on? I'll have your back, but I need to know."

Brody looked at Jones suspiciously. "Why? Are you working for internal affairs?"

Incredulous, Jones said, "Why would I violate departmental policy and turn all the cameras off if I was working for internal affairs? I'm trying to help you."

As Brody parked the car in the alley between O'Conner's Pub and The Alibi, the two bars most frequented by college students, Brody looked at Jones and said, "Just drop it." As they got out of their patrol car and started to walk down the ally, Brody suddenly said, "Hold up, man."

Standing just a few feet in front of the patrol car, directly in front of the headlights, Jones said, "What's up?

"Wait, I'm just grabbing my flashlight," Brody lied. Deciding that his partner was going to die in the alley, he reached into the patrol car, bending at his waist. Making sure Jones couldn't see what he was doing, Brody put a backup pistol in his front-pocket holster. He stood up and said, "Okay, now I'm ready."

The partners walked about twenty feet down the alley. Right between O'Connor's Pub and The Alibi, they noticed a young man standing in the alley. Not only did the officers not see a fight, the young man was standing in the alley by himself. Officer Brody, in an agitated voice, said, "I think he's got something in his hands."

Squinting down the alley, Jones cautioned Brody, "Hold up. I think it's just a cell phone.

Brody ignored Jones and yelled, "Drop it! Drop it!"

Drew, startled, looked up and said, "It's just my cellphone, man. Chill." Drew, not recognizing the severity of the situation, chuckled. "I'm making a message for my mom."

Officer Brody yelled, "Drop it and put your hands up! Now!"

Now scared, the young man replied, "Man, don't shoot. It's not a gun; it's a phone."

Jones, worried that his partner was misreading the situation, tried to calm the situation down. "Brody, it's not a gun, it's a phone. It's a phone."

By then, Brody had solidified his plan. He was convinced Jones was a snitch for internal affairs. He was damned if he was going to let his partner rat him out. It was probably a matter of time before internal affairs figured out how he was stealing cocaine from the evidence room, doctoring police reports to cover his tracks, and selling the drugs. But they'd have to figure it out without his partner's help. A pretty decent aim, Brody needed to hit two targets with 100 percent accuracy tonight.

Brody's attention snapped back to the situation at hand. Jones was yelling, "Brody did you hear me? The guy's just holding a cell phone."

Ignoring, Jones, Brody screamed, "Drop it!" one more time before he fired the gun he had been pointing at Drew. As the bullet struck Drew, his body spun from the force of the bullet. As Drew fell to the ground, Brody saw Drew's cellphone fly out of his hand and land underneath one of the dumpsters in the alley.

Jones turned to Brody and screamed, "What the fuck are you doing, man? He didn't have a gun. He was holding a cell phone." Jones then realized, too late, that Brody was reaching into his pocket. "Brody, don't! Please."

In one swift and fluid movement, Brody reached into his pocket, pulled out his backup pistol, and shot Jones in the head, killing him. Brody knew he only had a few seconds before he had to call dispatch. He wiped off his backup pistol, an unmarked, untraceable pistol he'd stolen from the evidence room a few days ago. Brody went over to Drew's motionless body, picked up his hand, and wrapped Drew's fingers around the pistol. He went to the dumpster to retrieve

Drew's cell phone, but he couldn't find it. Brody didn't have time to look for the phone. He had more immediate details to which to attend.

Brody stood up and walked back toward the patrol car. Even though Brody decided to protect himself by killing Jones, he still couldn't bring himself to look at his partner. Turning his back on Jones's lifeless body, Brody clicked on his shoulder radio and screamed, "Shots fired. Officer down! Hurry, hurry!"

3

Trying to calm the cabbie's growing impatience, Ty said, "My friend had to take a leak. He'll be here in a second."

Rolling his eyes, the cabbie said, "Fine. I'll hold the cab as long as we run your credit card first."

Ty handed the cabbie his credit card, saying, "I'll go get him. I'll be right back," and jogged off toward the alley.

As Ty turned into the alley, the flashing police lights stopped him dead in his tracks. He saw Drew with both hands in the hair, his left hand holding his phone. Ty could hear a cop yelling, "Drop it!" and Drew frantically trying to explain that he was holding a phone, not a gun.

Realizing the bad situation, Ty leaned up against the bar wall trying to stay out of sight. He pulled his cell phone from his pocket to call 9-1-1 but, in a split-second decision, instead pulled up the video app and recorded the next several horrific minutes.

Ty watched in helpless horror as one of the police officers shot Drew, shot the other police officer, and then planted a gun on Drew. Ty also saw that when Drew's body hit the ground, his phone flew out of his hand and slid under the garbage dumpster. Ty closed the video app, put the phone in his pants pocket, and tried to decide what to do next.

When the officer who shot Drew walked back to the patrol car, Ty saw an opportunity. He darted toward the dumpster and grabbed Drew's phone. He allowed himself one quick glance over his shoulder. Ty saw Drew's motionless body on the ground. The copy who had shot Drew was not looking his way. Good. He kept running out of the alley and back toward Michigan Avenue.

The cab Ty paid for was gone. So were all the other cabs. They must have fled when they heard the gunshots. Ty could hear the sirens approaching, but he had no intention of sticking around to answer questions. Ty didn't want that cop to know he had seen what happened. He turned and sprinted toward his apartment. The only person with whom he intended to talk was Drew's mom.

4

Within a few minutes of Officer Brody's call, paramedics, backup officers, and homicide detectives arrived on the scene. Brody quickly and efficiently told detectives his fabricated version of events, which included blaming Drew for Officer Jones's death.

After they were done asking him questions, Brody walked over to where the paramedics were caring for Drew. Brody asked them if they had collected all Drew's personal belongings. One of the paramedics snapped, "That's not our primary concern, sir. We're trying to save his life."

"Damn," Brody thought to himself. He couldn't search for the phone right now without looking suspicious, but he couldn't take the chance that anyone would see the images on Drew's phone if he had recorded anything. Brody decide he'd come back when everyone was cleared out of the scene to look for Drew's cell phone.

Several hours later, after answering the detectives' questions, offering condolences to Jones's widow, and preparing his incident report, Brody returned to the alley. He looked under the dumpster and every piece of litter lying in the alley, but the phone was gone.

Tamping down panic, Brody returned to the police station and went to the evidence room. He asked the officer on duty to let him look at the evidence the crime-scene technicians recovered in the alley. Brody's face fell as he looked through the evidence box. The phone wasn't there, either.

Brody had to get his hands on that cell phone! After several minutes, he came up with the only other place the phone could be: at the hospital. The paramedics must have scooped it up when they took Drew from the alley to the hospital. Brody left the police station and raced to the hospital.

5

Drew awoke in the hospital. He didn't know where he was at first, but he did know he was in overwhelming pain. Drew tried to focus, but the last thing he remembered was taking a leak in the alley outside O'Conner's Pub and texting his mom. But everything else was fuzzy. Confused, Drew tried to sit up. When he did, and realized he was handcuffed to the bed, he blurted out, "What the hell?"

The nurse came in, saying, "Look who's awake. How are you feeling?"

Drew moaned, "Like I was hit by a truck." The nurse replied coolly, without looking, "You weren't hit by a truck. You were hit a bullet. It went clean through your neck and just missed your carotid artery."

A vague memory tickled at the back of his brain. Then Drew remembered a police officer telling him to put up his hands. He turned to the nurse with a look of surprise and horror and said, "Oh, my God. The police shot me!"

The nurse said, "Yes, they did. But only after you killed a cop."

"What?" Drew couldn't believe what he just heard. "I didn't shoot anyone. I don't even own a gun! This is crazy!" Drew looked on his bed stand and didn't see what he was looking for. Drew frantically was trying to twist and turn as he looked for something, but the handcuffs impeded his movement.

Irritated, the nurse asked, "What are you looking for?" It was bad enough that she had to care for this cop killer, but it was even worse that she had to put up with him claiming he was innocent.

Drew responded, "My phone. I need to call my mom." The nurse handed the young man a large plastic bag that had his belongings in it. He desperately looked through the bag, but it held no phone. He asked the nurse, "Where's my phone?"

"How would I know?" the nurse snapped. "Maybe the cops kept it as evidence."

Drew felt a glimmer of hope. "Good. I think I was recording a message to my mom when the cops came into the alley. That could prove I didn't do anything wrong!"

Just as the nurse was finishing inputting notations about Drew's vitals and conditions into the hospital database, Officer Brody walked in. "How's the patient?"

The nurse said, "He'll live. And just so you know, he says he's innocent."

Officer Brody smirked, "Yeah, that's what they all say."

When the nurse left the room, Officer Brody sneered at Drew. Keeping up his ruse, Brody said, "You killed my partner, you scumbag."

"Officer, there's gotta be some misunderstanding. I don't have a gun. I've never had a gun. I was texting my mom when you guys came into the alley."

Brody spat, "Save it, asshole. Don't say another word. I don't want to hear another word come out of your mouth. Now where's your phone?"

"It's gone. The nurse tried to help me find it in my property bag. It's not there."

Brody grabbed Drew's property bag and pawed through it. "Shit." Brody threw the bag on Drew's bed, turned, and sped out of the room without saying another word.

Drew pushed the nurse's button. He needed to call his mom.

6

In most situations, Tara Gray was an imposing figure. Today was no exception. In her early fifties, she looked at least ten years younger than her age. She was dressed in a smart navy suit and high designer heels. In all aspects, she was a force to be reckoned with. As she rushed down the hospital corridor, her heels tapped authoritatively, as if to say, "Get out of my way. Don't mess with me."

As Tara walked down the corridor, she noticed two uniformed officers outside Drew's door. She also saw Brody leaving Drew's room; he looked agitated and in a hurry. Tara rushed into Drew's room, brushing by the two uniformed officers. As she entered the room, she went to the side of the bed, leaned down and gave her son a kiss, at first saying only, "Thank God, you're alive."

She looked at her son in silence as he groggily tried to focus on her and what she was saying. When she was sure he was awake, Tara demanded, "Well? What happened? I want all the details!"

"Hey, Mom, I love you, too," Drew snarked. Yet as much as he desired their usual back and forth, rather than affectionate conversation, Drew didn't have the strength. He was also too frightened to be witty and so, dropping all pretense, pled, "Mom, they're saying I shot a cop!"

"Tell me what happened. What do you remember?"

Drew recounted what he remembered. When he reached the part about his missing phone, his mother said, "That's it. I'm getting to the bottom of this. Those cops are not getting away with this."

The young man laid his head back on the pillow. Normally, he disapproved of what his mom did for a living. After all, she represented guilty scumbags. But today Drew was relieved to know that his mom was handling this situation. She did battle every day in courtrooms across the state. Surely, his mom could get to the bottom of this mess. Drew knew he was in very capable hands.

"By the way," Tara asked, "what was that police officer doing in your room?"

Drew said, "He was looking for my phone. He also said his partner was the one who was killed."

"Did you say anything to him?" Tara demanded.

"I started to, but he said he didn't want to hear anything I had to say."

"Well that's a first, a police officer stopping a suspect from talking." Tara said. "I wonder why." Tara stepped into the hallway, angrily punching numbers on her cell phone.

166

"Chief Daly, this is Tara Gray. Is there any particular reason you didn't bother to call me to tell me one of your men shot my son?"

On the other end of the phone, Chief Brendan Daly sighed heavily. "Ms. Gray, I was just about to call you. But, I've been a little busy here. I've got a dead cop, reporters crawling up my ass, and internal affairs investigating one of my cops. Not to mention, I've been getting updates on your son's condition. I was waiting to call you until I had complete information to give you."

"I'm not buying it, Brendan." Tara was becoming increasingly irritated. "You all were trying to get your stories straight before you talked to me. I'm bringing over an emergency discovery order so all the evidence is preserved. I want to look at the footage from the officers' body cameras and I want the dash-cam video, too."

Chief Daly sighed heavily again. "About that; you're not going to like this. There is no footage to show you. None of the cams were on. No bodycams. No dash-cam."

"What!" Tara cried. "You've got to be kidding me! Why not?"

"I don't know yet why Brody and Jones weren't wearing the bodycams. Their patrol car's dash-cam malfunctioned."

Tara didn't respond for several seconds. When she did speak, ice dripped from her words. "Listen to me, Chief. I will be in your office in fifteen minutes with a court order commanding you to preserve the evidence and to put it into the custody of an independent police department. I will also have an order authorizing another department be assigned to investigate this case. There's already evidence missing and you're telling me none of the department-sanctioned cameras were on. Something doesn't smell right."

Chief Daly sighed once again. "Tara, we all want to know what happened in that alley."

7

Ty rode the elevator up to the fourth floor of Mercy hospital. He kept his head down in case there were security cameras in the elevator. When he stepped off the elevator, he noticed two uniformed police officers standing outside Drew's room. Ty saw

Drew's mom talking to a doctor on the other side of the hallway. Ty walked up to Tara and, making sure to keep his back to the officers, quietly greeted her. When Tara recognized Ty, she started to say something, but Ty held his finger up to his lips to shush her. Ty walked to the stairwell and Tara followed.

In the stairwell, Ty said, "Drew did not kill that police officer. I can prove it."

Tara searched Ty's eyes and asked "How?"

Ty recounted the events of the previous evening. "I had my phone with me when I went back in the alley to see what was taking Drew so long. As I came into the alley, I saw the police lights flashing so I decided to turn the video on. I recorded what happened. I think you should look at this."

Ty hit the play button. Tara watched in horror as Officer Brody shot her son, pulled another gun out of his pocket, and shot his partner. The video showed Brody placing the gun in Drew's hands.

When she was done watching the video, she told Ty, "I'm going to need to keep your cell phone."

Ty expected so, and immediately agreed. He looked at Tara and said, "That's not all. I have Drew's phone. I don't know his password so I can't open it up. But there might be something on it. Drew had his phone out when this happened. He dropped it when he was shot. I got it without that cop seeing me. But, I know that cop Brody is trying to find it. I went back to the alley this morning and saw him looking around."

Tara looked at Ty and said, "I'm going to need Drew's phone, too."

8

Tara had been on several cases against Wade Franklin, the prosecutor who had filed murder charges against Drew. She considered him to be a smart, fair, and ethical lawyer. And she most definitely considered him to be a worthy opponent. But today she was not talking to Wade as an adversary. After Ty had given her his cell phone, along with Drew's phone, she scheduled an appointment with Wade. Her plan was to play the footage from each phone. She was confident that once Wade saw what really happened, he'd dismiss the case against Drew.

They both sat in Wade's office in silence as Tara played the video footage. First from Drew's phone and then from Ty's phone. They continued to sit in silence for several minutes. After what seemed like an eternity, Wade picked up the phone and called Chief Daly. Wade explained what he had just watched. He also informed the chief that he had authorized a warrant for Officer Brody's arrest on charges of murder and attempted murder.

After Wade hung up the phone, he turned to Tara and said, "Of course that means I'm dropping the murder charge against Drew, but he's going to have to fall on the urinating-in-public charge." Wade's smile let Tara know he was joking. Tara, normally stoic in professional settings, cried with relief and joy.

In the meantime, Officer Brody had heard rumors that Tara had evidence that would exonerate Drew and that she was meeting with the prosecutor that morning. Brody went to the prosecutor's office and waited in the lobby. After what seemed like an eternity, Wade and Tara walked out of Wade's office.

They were both surprised to see Brody standing there. Brody searched their faces for a clue as to what happened during their meeting. But it was the evidence bag in Wade's hand that gave it away. There, in the bag, were two cell phones.

Without saying a word, Brody turned and walked out of the prosecutor's office. He could hear Wade saying that he had a warrant for his arrest. Wade told Brody to stop, but he kept walking. When he reached the stairway, Brody pushed the gray steel door open, climbed the stairs, and walked out onto the rooftop. Brody could hear a commotion behind him and people running up the stairs. Brody cleared the sounds from his mind and thought about what he had to do.

Just as the rooftop door opened behind him, Brody pulled out his service revolver, the one he had used to shoot Drew. He raised the revolver to his temple and pulled the trigger. As Brody's body slumped to the ground, the security guard opened the door and yelled, "Shots fired. Officer down."

9

Drew was awake before his alarm rang. It had been six months since that fateful night in the alley. His injuries had healed, and he was finally starting to feel like himself. His energy level had returned, which was good because he was going to need all the energy and strength he could muster for his new adventure. He jumped into the shower, dressed, and snarfed down some toast and coffee.

As he put the books in his backpack, Drew heard his mother honking from the parking lot. Drew closed his apartment door behind him and slid into Tara's car.

As Tara began to drive, she asked "Are you sure this is what you want to do?

"Yes. But I have a question for you before we go."

"What is it?" his mom asked.

"I've been wondering why you didn't have another lawyer meet with Wade. I thought lawyers weren't supposed to represent family, that it was a conflict of interest."

Tara considered this for a moment. "I see you've been doing some legal research already. Well, you're partially right. I couldn't have represented you if the case had gone to trial. But all I did was turn critical evidence over to the prosecutor, which I had an ethical obligation to do. Wade decided what to do from there."

Drew said, "Well, I'm not complaining with the results. I just thought maybe you were turning over a new leaf and only representing innocent clients for a change."

Tara chuckled, saying only, "Very funny."

When they arrived at their destination, Tara pulled over and parked the car. "Hey, before you go in, open this. It's a little something I picked out for you."

Drew pulled a metal plaque out of the gift bag. It read: Gray and Gray, Attorneys at Law. Drew smiled. "I love it. But I have to graduate from law school and pass the bar exam first, Mom."

"You will."

Drew got out of the car. He walked up the steps and pushed open the law school's door.

Psalms 22 and 23

Nelson P. Miller

Here, a law dean projects the challenges and rewards of teaching and administration, through an allegory of faith, in overlapping dream sequences.

22

What will another day bring? the dean thought briefly as he resumed his seat behind the desk in the faculty suite's corner office for another intense two-hour burst of virtual work with its many usual and unusual interruptions.

From thirty years of law school and law practice, the dean knew that human endeavors involve the most bizarre mix of characters and motives. The dean's former law practice had lifted decorum's curtain, revealing to him a much-too-clear picture of humankind's ancient and very deep fall. The dean had naively assumed that law school would bring less of the shocking, freakish, and weird than the client matters of his former law practice had involved, and more of the routine. Law school, after all, involved only education and not all of the other trials and travails of life with which lawyers help clients each day.

And indeed, law school did initially bring less of the bizarre and outlandish but only until the dean's role that he assumed after his predecessor's untimely demise once again lifted decorum's curtain. As a law professor, he had consistently seen the best of students, faculty, staff, and administrators. As a dean, he helped members of the law school community deal not just with the best but also with the worst that life brought. Those challenges included not only debilitating disease and mortifying death but also the humbling and even daunting consequences of various perversions and predilections that one might have assumed aspiring professionals and their instructors and administrators would have avoided. Knowing human nature as anyone naturally does, though, he should have known better.

Things had been challenging the last few years at the law school. A painful recession had driven national enrollment declines that led, at the dean's law school and many other law schools, to agonizing faculty and staff layoffs. Surviving faculty and staff members were doing much more than they had but under pay freezes and benefits reductions. The feds were dumping burdensome new regulations onto already-harried administrators while scaring accreditors into promulgating and enforcing onerous new law school standards. And national media and scam blogs continued to harass law school deans with distorted stories, as if law schools were training blackjack dealers rather than pillars of social order.

Things, though, had been particularly unusual on campus lately. One day after another had brought the most absurd of events. Previously sound-thinking and responsible-acting students, faculty, and staff just seemed to have somehow gone off the deep end, one after another. Some of the events were serious, some just bizarre, but all of them completely out of character not only for professionals generally but for the individuals themselves. Yes, he knew, the world has a lot of crazies, plenty of the mentally disturbed, but the strange things with which the dean had recently been dealing involved previously very stable people.

So the dean sighed heavily as he entered his computer's password for the umpteenth time that day. He'd been sighing a lot lately. He had also noticed other quietly disturbing new mannerisms, tics really. He now frequently blinked, rubbed his fingertips in his palms, and hunched his shoulders up and down. He made a brief commitment to get ahold of himself—get a grip, put a lid on it—as the computer's security screen cleared, allowing him back into the email stream that had eddied and accumulated in his brief absence.

173

Email momentarily cleared, he got started again on his report to the president about the latest strange turn of events on campus. He resumed wearily trying to summarize for the president the tangled mess that the events had created, while trying to discern and propose concise recommendations. But he quickly realized that he wasn't yet up to the draining task. Having already tried his habitual walk around the block, he turned instead to consume the donut that administrative assistant Carla had delivered unbidden earlier that morning on her ceremonial work arrival.

Maybe his drowsiness was the donut's sugar. Just as likely, it was his recent nighttime sleeplessness and the work's growing nonstop stress. In any case, he finally put his head down in weariness on the desk. He could only remember having done so once before in his career, way back in law practice. Usually, he would have just gutted it out, pushed through with the work, and made the best of it. But instead, nearly the moment that the dean laid his head on the desk, he was already dozing and dreaming.

23

His dream was of a great green field, a pasture from the cropped looks of it, although a vast and gorgeous one without any fence, surrounded by spectacular mountains. *Sound of Music*, he thought in dreamy amusement, until the white-robed shepherd in the scene caught his attention. The shepherd held a crooked staff in one hand and a short stick or rod of some sort in the other. Odd, he thought, where was Julie Andrews? He smiled at his own humor until something about the shepherd's appearance, or perhaps the shepherd's unusual direct effect on his senses, caught his attention.

The dean first noticed that the great shepherd's appearance had promptly dissolved the last bit of anxiety that the dean's weariness had carried into the dream. Indeed, before noticing the shepherd, the dean had briefly luxuriated in the lush grass, just long enough to feel rested in a way that he had not felt in a very long time, maybe ever. As he watched the shepherd approach at a distance, he resolved to return to this pasture, to mark and recall it if ever he could, for its utter refreshment. Odd, though, he thought, how could a dream be so refreshing? He *was* dreaming, after all, wasn't he?

The shepherd, though, had not simply reinforced the pasture's ameliorating effect. The shepherd seemed to have a certain command about him, as if he were not merely a shepherd but also a warrior or king. In the dean's unusually real and volitional dream, the dean thus stood sharply up, brushing the lush grass off his suit, when he saw the shepherd beckon him toward a pristine lake where the pasture met the mountain foothills. The dean picked up his black leather folder at his feet, with his free hand tapped his suit-coat pocket to be sure that he had his cellphone with him, and followed in the direction that the shepherd had already turned. Probably a meeting that he was missing, he thought, to which the shepherd was leading him. After all, he *loved* meetings, the dean thought in wry amusement but then quickly dismissed the sarcasm as inappropriate in the shepherd's presence.

As the shepherd reached the glassy lake, he turned back toward the dean, who had followed several respectful steps behind. Although the dean hesitated even to look upon the obviously regal shepherd, when he did steal a guarded glance, the shepherd's visage appeared as perfectly serene as the mirrored lake. Much like the rejuvenation that he had drawn from laying in the pasture's grass, that one glance accomplished something extraordinary within the dean, as if the shepherd had shared with him the shepherd's own fathomless serenity. The shepherd turned away again just as the dean felt as if he could hold no more of whatever deep healing his glance at the shepherd had drawn.

The shepherd led the dean on a path around the lake into the foothills. Just as the path turned into the foothills away from the lake, the dean got a brief vision of the shepherd's distant palace high in the mountains. Again odd, he thought, that a shepherd would have a palace, although at the same time he found himself analyzing how he had inferred that the palace was the shepherd's. Might make a good essay fact pattern, he mused. The irreverent thought of work stirred him awake from his brief but incredibly refreshing reverie.

22

The dean awoke, though in embarrassment, having drooled on his desk. Good thing no one had poked their head in, he thought, as the pleasant dream faded from memory. He scrubbed ineffectively at the tiny pool on his desk where his head had lain, first with a tissue and then a disinfecting wipe. To his alarm, his efforts only made the pool appear larger. His growing embarrassment reminded him of the mortifying events at an administrative meeting that morning.

He had walked into the room just after the meeting started. Settling in his usual spot, he looked around the room, trying to no avail to greet the others with a smile. Everyone seemed preoccupied with something especially serious. Oh well, he thought, administrative matters had been especially serious lately, more so than usual as the school adapted to local effects of national enrollment declines and the new heavy pressure of federal regulators. Indeed, they'd been dealing not only with the usual law school concerns of student retention, performance, and placement, and then the employee layoffs and budget challenges from enrollment declines, certainly serious stuff, but also the increasingly absurd regulator demands, things like collecting crime information at conference sites and documenting student complaints. What had happened to teaching law students? But until now, the work hadn't affected the collegiality administrators had shown.

Wondering what was up, he leaned over and whispered a query to the administrator seated next to him. She didn't respond, though, didn't even look at him or wave him away but instead just kept listening to the others speak about something that he could not quite grasp. So he turned to the administrator seated on the other side of him but with the same disconcerting result. Puzzled, he decided to wait for a pause in the earnest conversation and then to jump in with a greeting. But no one responded, no one even looked at him, when he piped up with a cheerful apology for coming in after the meeting's start. They just continued talking as if he wasn't there. He tried interrupting, but to no effect. He cleared his throat loudly, but nothing, and then rapped the conference table, and again nothing. Finally, he rose, but no one looked up at him. And so he had walked out, more embarrassed and confused at his seeming invisibility than angry.

He shook off the memory as he rose from his office desk to make his way to teach class. The class was one that he had taught so often and knew so well, just as he also knew students, that many terms had passed since anything truly unusual or especially inspiring had happened in class. He wondered if the administrative and regulatory burdens were encroaching. Even his continual modest teaching reforms, and the newsworthy events of the day that he always brought to class, had failed to produce anything memorable recently from term to term. Nothing was improving or changing, making him feel increasingly stale, uninspired, and even out of touch—the bane of administrators everywhere, at least those who cared to teach.

This class began like every other class with his brief greetings and course housekeeping, to be followed by subject-relevant news of the day, and then a brief lecture on the day's topic, anticipating discussion, case recitation, and in-class exercises. The class began normally until he turned to the brief lecture. At that point, students began to converse among themselves, paying him absolutely no attention. At first, he paused, thinking that his news of the day may finally have generated some comment, even if peer to peer rather than directed to him and the whole class. But no, as he listened closer, he could hear that the students were simply talking as if he wasn't even there. The administrative meeting that morning briefly flashed through his mind.

He tried the usual things that professors do to get student attention. He first remained silent, expecting that one of the more-respectful students would hush the rebellious classmates. But the students, all of them, just kept gabbing. So he raised the volume and dropped the tenor of his voice authoritatively, again producing nothing. So he interjected a *here now* and a *let's get started.* Again, nothing. Moving about now in agitation, he began to realize that the students couldn't see or hear him. He tried crying out aloud, even yelling loud pleas. Again, nothing.

He couldn't help noticing a decided change in the room's tenor, though. The students had grown surly. In fact, they were sneering insults, he thought at first at one another, until he noticed that they were passing a paper among them. They were mocking a figure that the paper depicted, apparently a figure that one of them had drawn. The things that they were saying about the figure were indeed scurrilous, things that he wouldn't repeat. The students plainly disdained everything for which the figure stood. This mockery continued for a time until the students grew bored with it and began to drift out of the classroom, as the dean watched in bewilderment.

177

When the last student left, the dean studied the figure on the paper that the students had left behind. The figure hung in effigy, a disturbing sign. Law students knew better than to mock and harass a classmate or anyone else for that matter. Hmm, he thought as he studied the paper: suit, tie, black folder under the arm. He looked closer. Then it dawned on him that the figure depicted him. He steadied himself on the classroom desk, his head suddenly spinning. What had he possibly done to earn the students' ire? Was he *dreaming*, he thought? He staggered out of the classroom and back toward the faculty suite.

At her workstation at the suite's entrance, Carla said in a surprisingly deep and disturbingly mocking voice, *Done already?* The dean didn't even look her way, instead waving his hand at her and saying that he'd hold a makeup class. He thought he heard Carla give a deep, scornful laugh, completely out of character for anything he'd ever heard from her. But still severely rattled by the class event, he just shook his head as he rushed past into his office. He'd stayed out of everyone's way the rest of the day, buried in his office with administrative matters, while aghast at what to make of the class, and still dabbing at the now-modest-sized pool on his desk.

Chatter from Carla, at his office's door now with a student in tow, caught the dean's attention, thankfully ending his unsettling rumination over the day's bizarre events. Except that the dean paused, thinking for some reason that the student had addressed Carla as *Karloff,* if he'd heard the student right. The momentary mental artifact made the dean glance briefly at Carla, only then having to hide his startled look. While the figure looked like Carla, it was indeed a male, apparently Karloff.

The unknown but weirdly familiar Karloff had already launched into describing the student's problem, just as Carla would have done, the dean recognized in reluctant fascination. The dean leaned forward over his desk to listen intently to this alien but strangely familiar Karloff, while also trying to hide the growing pool on his desk. He later couldn't remember the student's peculiar problem that Karloff had described. He had only surmised that he could at least begin to address the issue with a concisely worded and thoughtfully directed email. Just his thing, he thought in reassurance.

Except that the dean now had another problem, bigger than the pool he was still hiding by hunching forward over his desk. He couldn't type the quick reassuring email. Each of his hands had a large forged nail driven through it into the fake-wood laminate surface of his desk. The dean smiled weakly at Karloff and the student, trying now to distract their attention from his nail-smitten hands. He reassured them that he would take care of things right away. He would have given the student his usual confident thumbs up or jumped from his seat for a quick handshake to send the student off, but with hands pinned to the desk, he couldn't budge.

Fortunately, the student accepted his reassurance, withdrawing without taking any notice of the now very-large pool on the dean's desk or of his nailed hands. The dean leaned back just a little in his chair, relieved at their leaving, until he noticed that his feet were nailed to the floor. The blood that had pooled around his feet made him look closer at the pool on his desk. Blood, too, he realized. The dean put his head back down on the desk, ready to weep in exasperation at his horrific situation. Fortunately, in his dramatic swoon, he lapsed back into the pastoral dream.

23

The shepherd led the dean up the path. He grew concerned when his black leather-soled dress shoes started slipping on the steeper parts of the path. Yet they soon reached a narrow, darkly shadowed valley, as foreboding as the luscious pasture, sylvan lake, and dazzling mountain vistas had been alluring. As they dropped deep down into the dark valley, the shepherd leaned more heavily on his staff, whacking aside thorny brush with the rod held in his free hand.

The shepherd soon stopped ahead in the near darkness. The dean noticed that pools of blood had formed at the shepherd's feet from deep wounds in the shepherd's hands, side, and feet. The shepherd also bled from gashes to the head and lashes to his back, now soaking the thin white robe into a deep red. The bloody sight momentarily reminded him of a motor-vehicle-accident case he'd once had in which the collision's trauma had marred the decedent nearly beyond recognition. He put the thought quickly out of his head, instead watching the mutilated shepherd stagger slowly onward.

Suddenly feeling faint, the dean sat abruptly down on what looked in the darkness to be a boulder at the side of the path, leaning heavily against a rocky ledge. The shepherd turned around to face him. Dim light from the shepherd's bloody robe illuminated the rocky ledge's wet, dark-stained surface, except that the dean now realized from the growing illumination that he leaned not against rock but his office's familiar desk. How, he wondered, had his desk appeared in this awful valley? He thought only fleetingly of checking his email. The shepherd instead held his attention.

The dean had no earthly reason to suspect what happened next. The wounded shepherd set aside his rod and staff to draw first bread and then chalice, fruit, meat, cheese, and other fine fare from somewhere deep within his robe. The shepherd set the repast ceremoniously on the dean's desk. The ornamented chalice overflowed with wine, spilling out over the desk in a large blood-red pool that the astonished dean made no attempt to stanch. The shepherd made a motion that the dean understood to mean that he was to eat and drink of the shepherd's banquet.

As the feast unfolded on the desk before the dean, the illumination from the shepherd's blood-stained white robe grew gradually brighter until the dean could see that he sat not in the dark valley but in his corner faculty-suite office. The shepherd stood regally now on the other side of the desk, arms spread wide in full offer of the fabulous feast spread across the desk. The two figures' eyes met for the first time. Looking deep in the shepherd's eyes only for an instant, the dean thought that he saw at once both the broken past and glorious future. But the shepherd's robe continued to grow so brilliant that the dean finally had to shield his eyes and then lay his head down on the desk, at which moment, he promptly fell asleep, beginning to dream.

22

In his dream, the dean sat nailed again at his desk, hands to desktop, feet to the floor. While the office was dark, the computer monitor, standing in the pool of blood, cast a sickly glow. He could see email accumulating quickly on the screen, five messages, ten, fifteen, and on. Some senders had starred their messages as urgent, while other messages poured in from the president, vice president, and even the law school's board chair. Pinned in position, though, he was powerless to address any of it. Desperate, he even thought of trying to type out replies with his chin or nose but couldn't quite reach the keyboard.

Just then, Karloff poked his head back into the office, this time with a staff member in tow. To the dean's great relief, they didn't seem to notice him skulking behind his desk where the forged nails still pinned his hands and feet. Instead, oblivious to his presence, they were picking his suit up off the floor in front of his desk, laughing and arguing over who would get to keep it. Indeed, he now seemed to have lost his clothes, making his awful situation even more grossly shameful. Panic rose in the dean's heaving breast.

As he tried somehow to remain innocuous at his desk, the dean listened to their laughter over how he had been exposed, punished, disbarred, and banished. He couldn't quite put together the details of what they shared. Apparently, he had ignored key federal regulations and accreditation standards, compromised bond and compliance audits, and failed to meet enrollment, bar-passage, and graduate-employment targets. Worse yet, he had lost the confidence of faculty members who had labeled him tyrannical for having pushed too hard for accreditor-required course outcomes. And a student had sued him for refusing to change a professor's grade. Karloff and the staff member laughed again in glee at the dean's demise.

The dean slowly put his head down on his desk, trying to remain unnoticed while silently despairing at his fatal and hopeless shame.

23

The dean lifted his head from the desk with a start, his cellphone's appointment notification having reminded him that a student was due in for career advice. As the despairing dream faded from memory, the dean turned to the emails that had come in during his brief lapse.

Ah, the registrar's daily report indicated that campus enrollment had jumped and had now at least attained last-year levels. Another email attached the finance vice president's monthly budget report showing that the campus's expense cuts had finally put the campus back into the black, even if only marginally. Another email from the dean of students indicated that she was going to handle the tangled mess on which he had been trying without success to report to the president. And one more email showed faculty progress on the accreditor-mandated course outcomes.

The dean jumped out of his chair in greeting when Carla, not Karloff, appeared at the door, student in tow. The sun shone brightly through the large office windows as the student settled into the chair across the desk. The student's problem for which she sought the dean's advice was that she had not one, not two, but three job offers and was wrestling over which one to take. As she related the happy news, the student thanked the dean profusely for her great education, marveling at how the campus's skilled faculty members and inspired programs had changed her outlook and life.

After a brief consultation that was more like simple celebration, the dean showed the glowing student out his office door. He then returned to his seat, entering his computer's security password for the umpteenth-plus time that day. Ah, no emails in the last fifteen minutes, he laughed to himself—another miracle. The email deck clear, he could finally turn to his love, which was helping students learn law, mature into creative and generative professionals, and in doing so discover the great shepherd's gorgeous green pastures. Time to teach an evening class.

The dean paused as he entered the back of the room filled with chatting students. Hadn't something alarmingly bizarre happened recently in class, or was he recalling a recent nightmare? He shook off the thought as he made his way to the technology-stuffed lectern to boot up the multiple systems, programs, and files for class. Students smiled and greeted him as he passed, their joyful glow making him think again of the great shepherd.

The class turned out to be like none prior, although he had many more like it follow. The day's legal news at the start of class triggered a flood of eager student comments in which they connected the evening's topic with their own experiences like that in the news. His brief lecture that followed was less lecture and more discussion. Indeed, student observations drew out an entirely new conceptual paradigm that organized and invigorated the evening's law into a memorable and practical new framework. He even managed somehow to capture the framework on the whiteboard as the students spoke, photographing it with his cellphone for later development into an article.

The students' tight case recitations drew out just the distinctions their organization intended but also fresh insights leavened with student humor. Excited student voices reflecting high and focused energy filled the classroom air throughout the class's peer-to-peer exercises. The dean then treated concisely the few hanging questions recorded in the whiteboard parking lot, just in time to dismiss the students into the chill late-evening air. The evening's whole effect was so fresh, its revelations so confident and even profound, that the students buzzed with positive energy as they gathered their belongings and left in happy pairs.

The dean dropped his materials off in the office, checking one last time for emails—again none, yet another miracle. As he steamed down the long, empty hallway hitting the off-light buttons as he passed toward the end-of-hall stairs, the dean smiled, thinking again, *what will another day bring?* And for an instant, he thought that he caught a glimpse of the great shepherd disappearing ahead of him up the stairway.

22-23

A faint buzzing grew into an annoying rattle. Sensing the soft light of early dawn glowing through the window, he reached for the smartphone on the nightstand, swiping its screen to stop the alarm. Rolling out of bed, he staggered down the hall toward the shower, wondering what another day of law school would bring. As he did so, he faintly recalled an odd dream—no, *two* odd dreams, somehow set against one another. How strange, he thought. What had he been dreaming?

Client Intake

Sylvia C. Herald

Here, a general practitioner who devotes herself to client service and communication, and uses technology for efficiency, illustrates those practices with a client-intake dictation exploring the impact of personal injury on family dynamics.

Hey, 'Chelle, thanks for listening to this audio file while Kingston is out. He'll run it through voice recognition and prepare the word-processed file to include in the new client's electronic shared-secure folder when he gets back next Monday from vacation. I copied him on my forward to you, and so he'll already have it and probably get right to it when he gets back. I just wanted you to get started on this significant new file right away. And by the way, it has more than the usual sensitivities, which I am sure that you'll appreciate.

To: File. From: SRM. Date: 07/28/17. Client: Ronald S. Huffman. Matter: MVA. Opposing Parties: Rudolf Jacobsen and parents Marcus and Marcella Jacobsen. Conflict Check: completed (none). Insurer: Progressive. Claim Rep.: Unknown. Incident date: 05/29/17. Referring Attorney: None.

Narrative: I met this date with new client Ronald S. Huffman in the critical-care unit of St. Joseph Mercy Hospital, after meeting with his wife Nancy Huffman in the office last week. Nancy came to the office reluctantly last week, solely to connect me with Mr. Huffman. She indicated at the time that although she recognized that Mr. Huffman suffered serious injury in the subject motor-vehicle accident, she wanted nothing to do with any legal claim. I indicated to her that if Mr. Huffman established a third-party claim, then she would have a derivative right of recovery for loss of consortium that could have a substantial value to her. She indicated that she understood so but that she still did not want the firm's representation or to pursue such a claim even if her husband did retain us to proceed. Please mark and maintain the file as for Mr. Huffman's access and review only. Do not include Mrs. Huffman, whom we do not represent in this or any other matter.

I confirmed that understanding that Mrs. Huffman does not desire representation, when I met today at the hospital with Mr. Huffman. Mr. Huffman indicated frankly and confidentially that he and his wife have had marital difficulties reflected in periodic brief separations, counseling, and discussion of divorce. They were nonetheless living together at the time of the motor-vehicle accident. Because of Mr. Huffman's now two-month-long hospitalization, Mr. Huffman was unable to contact and meet with counsel and thus enlisted Mrs. Huffman to do so, despite her reluctance. While Mrs. Huffman attributed her reluctance to not wanting to deal with lawyers and lawsuits, against which, she briefly expressed, she holds religious beliefs, Mr. Huffman confirmed to me that she has otherwise expressed an unwillingness to get involved in any of his legal, financial, administrative, or other matters, given the insecure status of their relationship. Mr. Huffman is concerned that his wife is withdrawing.

When I met with Mr. Huffman in the hospital today, he was still confined to the critical-care bed and immobilized, nearing the end of a lengthy period of immobilization to ensure the healing of his hip, rib, and spinal fractures. As Mr. Huffman put it, he was not to move or was to move as little as possible in case the comminuted fractures severed an artery and he bled out. He indicates that his most-recent imaging shows good healing, and he expects the confinement to end shortly. He is grossly uncomfortable but well cared for in his present situation. He does still exhibit marked bruising, which he indicates hospital staff have documented photographically. I nonetheless took photographs of the bruising that he showed me and will upload those photos to the file folder when available on Kingston's return.

As Mr. Huffman described it to me in the hospital today, the accident occurred at about 2 p.m. on the above-indicated date on westbound Meridian Highway just west of the Baxter Road intersection. Mr. Huffman was driving his 2009 Honda sport-utility vehicle in the right-hand lane when the nineteen-year-old Rudolf Jacobsen approached at high speed from the rear, first in the right-hand lane and then at the last moment swerving or attempting to swerve into the left-hand speed lane, which was clear. Mr. Huffman saw the Jacobsen vehicle's fast approach through his rear-view mirror and in response first moved to the right portion of his right-hand lane and then attempted last-second evasive action. The Jacobsen vehicle, a newer-model Mercedes-Benz SUV, struck the left rear of Mr. Huffman's vehicle, causing Mr. Huffman's vehicle to yaw, slide off the highway to the right, and roll in the ditch to the north/right, coming to rest on its driver's side about thirty feet off the highway. The Jacobsen vehicle ended upright in the median ditch to the highway's south/left.

Mr. Huffman's account was thus consistent with the UD-10 Official Traffic Accident report, which Mrs. Huffman dropped off at the office last week. The report attributes C-level injuries to Mr. Huffman, no injury to Rudolf Jacobsen, and hazardous-action citation to Rudolf Jacobsen with no such citation to Mr. Huffman. The report's narrative indicates that the Jacobsen vehicle was traveling at a "high rate of speed" but gives no speed estimate. The report indicates that photographs of vehicle positions and skid marks are available, as are measurements from an accident reconstruction that took place immediately following the clearing of Mr. Huffman from the scene by ambulance. The report indicates that Rudolf's parents Dr. Marcus and Mrs. Marcella Jacobsen own the Mercedes-Benz SUV, which Progressive Insurance Co. insures, giving telephone (517) 663-2813 for the claim office but no claim rep.

'Chelle, please draft a third-party complaint consistent with this information, after confirming the parents' ownership of the Jacobsen accident vehicle. Follow our complete office protocol for these cases, including especially obtaining the driving, criminal history, and any police-obtained diagnostic or lab work for the son Rudolf, and confirming whether prosecutors issued any charges against Rudolf relating to the accident. The report gives no indication of alcohol or drugs, and Mr. Huffman indicates not having heard of anything, but let's check it out closely. Officials may have shown Rudolf more grace than they might have a careless driver driving a less-expensive vehicle and having a different demographic profile. Mr. Huffman knows (what our office already well knows) that the father Dr. Jacobsen is a prominent retired physician/business owner. I do anticipate a high-limits policy and probable umbrella coverage. 'Chelle, you know the routine for learning that information pre-suit if possible. Let me know promptly if you do find out so that I can communicate it to Mr. Huffman.

Mr. and Mrs. Huffman's adult daughter Trish had obtained the UD-10 report at Mr. Huffman's request. Mr. Huffman indicates that Trish may be able to help him manage this matter until he recovers further. Mr. Huffman does not have ready access to a computer in his current circumstance, doctor's orders not permitting it, but he expects access as soon as his confinement ends. Until then, he gives Trish's email *trishwish21@aol.com* as an appropriate electronic contact for this matter, granting Trish full client access to his electronic folder in his stead. Mr. Huffman does have his flip-style cell phone (517) 661-9871 available to him and does take texts on it but not email. When he regains computer access, we are to use his personal email address *huffinron@gmail.com* for electronic contact. Mr. Huffman asks that we continue Trish's access after he gains his own direct access. He wishes to have Trish's support in this matter in the absence of his wife's participation, which he does not foresee.

My evaluation is that Mr. Huffman's injuries readily meet the serious-impairment tort threshold for a third-party claim under the current standard and would likely meet the threshold under the former standard or *a new standard like the former standard if the current supreme court were to adopt one. Mr. Huffman has multiple objective manifestations of his complete impairment in the many images of his comminuted and mildly displaced hip, rib, and spinal fractures. Using his hips and spine for sitting, standing, turning, lifting, and other mobility and function, certainly constitute important body functions, all of which have together had a general effect on his ability to lead his normal life. He has no present functional ability outside of his confinement to bed. Once released from total confinement, likely in the next couple or few weeks, his prognosis is for wheelchair, walker, motorized cart, and other mobility-assist devices for an additional recovery period of from three to six months and potentially beyond, up to throughout his life. 'Chelle, of course plead the precise medical diagnoses that you discern from the medical records, but also use some of the above language to craft the complaint's threshold allegations, as usual citing the statute.*

Mr. Huffman indicates that he has inquired of his medical-care providers, including probable orthopedic, neurologic, internal-medicine, and physical-therapy consulting providers (about whose precise qualifications Mr. Huffman was unsure) as to his longer-term prognosis. He indicates that they were all guarded as to any prediction but that they each indicated serious reservations as to his full recovery. In fact, he reports that they each indicated probable long-term or permanent partial-to-full disability that will almost surely include restriction from manual labor, lifting, carrying, running, twisting, bending, and similar activity.

These restrictions certainly implicate Mr. Huffman's work ability as a delivery driver for HLH at its Marlette hub, where Mr. Huffman has worked continuously since his high school graduation. My early prediction is no return to that employment. Mr. Huffman indicates that his motor-vehicle insurer Citizens is paying the 85% work-loss benefit so that he is receiving most, although not all, of his pre-injury compensation. We did discuss that the benefit will conclude after his return to employment or three years from the accident date, whichever occurs first. 'Chelle, please be sure to plead

188

excess economic loss, making clear that the recovery is available whether his injury meets the threshold or not. Depending on Mr. Huffman's medical recovery, we could have a high-recovery case here even without a threshold injury, if Mr. Huffman cannot regain employment in this difficult economy and without education beyond high school. At age forty-five, Mr. Huffman may have substantial opportunity for career retraining, but in his current condition he has not given substantial thought to the subject, and I didn't press him on it.

Mr. Huffman also exhibits a significant emotional overlay of mixed anger, frustration, and discouragement that may constitute clinical depression. While I haven't reviewed any medical records yet, Mr. Huffman describes that the hospital did have a "counselor" see him. He did not know whether the counselor was a psychologist but doubts that he has had formal psychiatric or psychological review. I encouraged him to ask his attending physician, who by the way is Dr. Roald Dworkin, for review for potential referral, which Mr. Huffman agreed to do. 'Chelle, please follow up with Mr. Huffman in one week to ensure that he has done so.

At the conclusion of our meeting, Mr. Huffman signed the firm's standard contingency-fee agreement and authorizations for the release of medical, employment, insurance, tax, Social Security, and education records. I left with him our firm brochure on his first- and third-party rights and also briefly explained to him his first-party benefits including the lifetime unlimited medical and the three years of replacement-service expense capped at $20 per day. 'Chelle, please investigate whether Mr. and Mrs. Huffman are hiring services at home to do what Mr. Huffman would have done for himself and for Mrs. Huffman, so that we can help Mr. Huffman make a replacement-service claim if appropriate.

'Chelle, please use the medical release only to obtain the hospital admission record, emergency record, emergency consults, evaluative consults, and, after it occurs, the discharge summary. Ask for a cost estimate just in case, although we needn't and shouldn't be cheap on this file, especially once we confirm the probable high limits and umbrella

coverage. The hospital records are going to be voluminous given the two-plus-month stay. Please also obtain the limited employment, insurance, tax, Social Security, and education records for which our office protocol for these cases provides.

I am placing a generous $25,000 expense estimate on this file because of the egregious injuries and the probable high limits, which I will review as soon as you get us the policy-limits information. I see filing the case promptly to get the resolution clock ticking, certainly if the insurer resists disclosure of insurance information but also if the insurer resists pre-suit mediation and maybe even if the limits are so high that a full-value recovery looks possible well within those limits, and the insurer will need case evaluation or other independent review to establish the case's settlement value.

When I asked Mr. Huffman his goals in this matter, he indicated that he above all wishes to preserve and improve his marital relationship with his wife. He recognizes that his pursuit of a third-party no-fault claim may to some degree further burden that relationship. Yet he simultaneously expressed that his pursuit of this claim may fulfill his strong desire to remain a provider for his wife, and what he believes to be her strong desire that he do so. He thinks of himself as the family "breadwinner" and believes that a source of the marital strain has been his recent inability to fulfill his wife's expectations in that regard. Thus, he sees a third-party recovery as consistent with his achieving an important financial-security objective toward realization of his overarching marital-security goal.

So, 'Chelle, while I ask your usual fine file work-up and associate support in this case to achieve the financial-recovery objective, I make a special request that you employ your social-work education and skills to pursue Mr. Huffman's overarching marital-security goal. Sooner rather than later, I would like you to meet with Mr. Huffman, yes, to gather additional information necessary to respond to the doubtless-coming standard discovery requests but also to explore marital counseling, career services, financial budgeting, retirement planning, and other services that

190

may help Mr. Huffman preserve his marriage. Because Mrs. Huffman expressed a religious belief against litigation, I also ask that you explore with Mr. Huffman any spiritual component to their marital strain, with the idea of exploring Mr. Huffman's referral for counseling as to that subject as well. Let's make this work in the broader sense, even while we pursue Mr. Huffman's legal claim. Thank you. Kingston, do your magic. I'd like Mr. Huffman to have electronic access when he gets out of the hospital bed and to the computer. Go get 'em, team. This one's important, like they all are.

Return on Investment

Malik Fiobehr

Here, a senior lawyer who devotes himself to ensuring the professionalism and integrity of, and opportunity for, the next generation of lawyers writes of the role of mentors and pro bono service in accomplishing those goals.

They entered the large, brightly lit day room of the homeless district's main social-service center, walking up a back stairway so old that footsteps had worn dangerously deep cups into its wide marble treads. They had waited outside in the heat, standing by the stinking curbside dumpster in a crowd of the center's patrons, until the young manager had come down to unlock the door after staff prayer. They had all then dutifully stumped up the stairs, the two lawyers to serve the patrons, and the patrons for showers, haircuts, mail, handout food, air conditioning, and rest for their weary feet.

The lawyers crossed the second-floor dayroom, to a flimsy three-sided cubicle in the corner, its low moveable walls leaning precariously. Staff had drawn tight the thin canvas blinds along the high south window wall, but the relentless summer sun suffused the blinds with bright light, in contrast to the darker spirits of the broken and downtrodden patrons. The young lawyer started to pull a chair toward the card table in the cubicle's middle, but the chair had only three legs and was holding up one wall of the cubicle. The young lawyer caught the wall just before it collapsed in on the tiny space. Tucking the three-legged chair back up against the wall to restore it to vertical, he dragged three other rusty-metal chairs into the cubicle.

The old and young lawyers took their seats at the card table, ready for their first pro-bono client. The old lawyer, a prominent name partner in a local large firm, had been doing this free work two hours a week at the center for years. The young lawyer, sharing office space at a local small firm, had recently joined him, desperate for clients and trying any way possible to get in the game. The two lawyers had hit it off immediately, although the old lawyer, well known as an outstanding mentor to new lawyers inside and outside of his corporate-services law firm, was so well-constructed of character and so gracious that he could have mentored, charmed, and reformed the devil.

The first client peeked into the cubicle. The lawyers had met with the client before in what seemed to both lawyers like a test of wills, trust, and confidence. Many clients mistrust their lawyers initially. Good lawyers dispel that mistrust quickly. Yet the process hadn't happened so quickly here.

"Hey, Petey, good to see you," the old lawyer greeted the client cheerily, waving his arm toward the open seat at the card table while adding, "come on in and rest your weary feet."

The client winced, adopting a sour look. Both lawyers silently realized the gaffe. Petey held himself apart from the other homeless and unemployed patrons of the center, indeed held himself *above* the other patrons, not in humanity, for he cared for his fellows as much as anyone else did, but in two other important respects. Petey, a community advocate, was homeless by choice, not dereliction or circumstance. He had once protested community development that was displacing low-income housing, by trying to put up a tent in the city hall's lobby and, when officers pulled down the tent, rolling out his sleeping bag and encamping anyway on the marble floor. Petey thus took pride in both his choice of homelessness and his advocacy skills.

"So how can we help today?" the young lawyer asked quickly, trying to soften Petey's suddenly sour mood and avoid the anticipated lecture.

Petey pulled papers from a worn backpack but, rather than handing them to the lawyers or laying them on the little table where all three could see, held them up only to himself like a hand of cards. He then began speaking in his usual inquisitorial style.

"What do you know about LLCs?"

"Well, depends on what you're trying to do with one," the old lawyer answered. The usual client would have started with exactly that information, what the client was trying to accomplish, but not Petey. The old lawyer knew that the game was now joined. The client continued.

"An LLC is a limited-liability company formed to conduct a business," the client answered his own question, the question that the old lawyer had deflected in gentle but unavailing effort to first discern the client's objective.

"Yes, I'd say so," the old lawyer confirmed, smiling at the pride Petey was already taking in his own acumen. "Looks like you don't need a lawyer," the old lawyer added, ready to play along.

The client ignored the old lawyer's last comment, instead continuing, "How does one form an LLC?"

The old lawyer turned to the young lawyer who answered simply, "File articles of organization with the state, and then adopt an operating agreement."

The client paused as he shuffled through his papers, still held aloft only to himself like a hand of cards. He then nodded silently in agreement, apparently confirming that he held the requisite documents.

"Can we look at those for—can we look at those *with* you?" the young lawyer tried.

The client scowled but didn't answer. Instead, he momentarily put the papers down on the table in front of him to quickly scribble a few pencil notes at the top of one of the papers, all the while shielding the papers from the lawyers' view with his hands and arms, like a test-taking student trying to hide his answers from a peeking compatriot. The lawyers smiled at one another over the client's secretiveness but said nothing. The client then scooped the papers back up into his hand of cards and continued.

"What happens after you file the articles with the state?"

"You'll get the file-stamped original articles back in a week or two, after the state assigns your LLC a number and makes an electronic copy," the old lawyer answered, adding, "Then you're good to go, as soon as you sign and adopt the operating agreement."

Satisfied with the exchange, the client crammed the papers back into the worn backpack and without thanks or further ceremony abruptly rose to go. The lawyers looked at one another with knowing smiles before the young lawyer inquired briefly, "Care to share your plans? We might have some other advice."

The client, already halfway out the cubicle, looked back at them, not pleased at the inquiry. The lawyers understood the more-than-usual need for secrecy that the homeless can have. On the street, predators wield information like a weapon, crushing hopes and dreams. Knowing so, seeing the client's irritation, and regretting his playful inquiry, the young lawyer tried adding disarmingly, "Anything you say, we will keep completely confidential."

"I'm going to own this place someday," the client shot back in anger before turning again and hurrying out.

The lawyers looked at one another without expression, not knowing whether to be satisfied at the consultation or crestfallen at the lack of warmth, civility, and trust. Finally, the old lawyer spoke, saying only, "Just watch. He probably will. Only, you'll be the only one of the two of us around to appreciate it." The old lawyer then rose slowly to peek around the cubicle's corner and shout "Next!" across the center's brightly lit dayroom.

"You'll need to go down to that old social-service center in the entertainment district, for the meeting," the administrative assistant told the old lawyer as he walked in from lunch, adding, "You know where it is?"

"Wow, is that place still there?" the old lawyer answered. "I used to provide pro bono service down there with old Bud Rice, when I was just starting out. Back in the good old days before the arena, when it was the homeless district."

"The board chair and executive director will meet you there," she answered, adding as she handed him his black-leather folder, "Just be sure to be back by four for the CEO's call on the acquisition terms.

I don't want to have to tell him that your pro bono charitable board service was more important than his billion-dollar deal."

The old lawyer smiled at the pert assistant's jab, took his folder from her with a wry "thanks," and headed back to the office tower's glass elevators for the long ride down.

"I haven't been here in years, no, *decades*," the old lawyer said as he greeted the executive director and board chair outside the center's front door. No walk up the back stairs next to the dumpster, he thought, as the manager met them at the door, showed them in, and escorted them up the staff elevator to the second-floor dayroom.

"This place hasn't changed," the old lawyer said as they stepped off the elevator into the dayroom. "We could have met in my office. Why here?"

"So, here's the deal," the board chair began. "Phil Robbins—you know him?"

"Name's familiar, but no, not really," the old lawyer replied. They stood now in the empty, brightly lit but badly worn dayroom. The floor creaked below what little remained of the cheap, industrial-spec carpet.

"Funny, but he asked us to retain you for this deal," the board chair rejoined before continuing. "Well, anyway, he's the developer who over the past couple of decades has been acquiring and flipping or holding properties around here, mostly right here in the entertainment district. Small operator—no, I shouldn't say that. He's got quite a portfolio by now, mostly of low-income housing. He knows what he's doing."

The old lawyer, on the local United Way board, occasionally did pro bono work for the organization's funded agencies, on governance, compliance, and real-property issues. His corporate practice for the largest law firm in town included that same kind of work but for national and international, rather than local, businesses. He had learned the nonprofit, tax-exempt side from board service for various charities around town. When the United Way executive director had put him in touch with this agency, he hadn't realized that the social-service center was among its programs.

"So, what's the deal with Robbins?" the old lawyer interjected, sneaking a peek at his watch, thinking of his teleconference later that afternoon.

"We've been thinking for a while about moving out of here," the executive director spoke up. "With the mission finally closing a couple of years ago—they moved to an old warehouse facility at the edge of the commercial district beyond the Southeast neighborhoods—and the restaurants and clubs all sprouting up here, it's just not a good place for our recovering patrons anymore."

The old lawyer knew what the executive director meant. When he had provided pro bono service at the center decades ago, the staff and patrons had taught him the needs and challenges of the homeless. Indeed, he could still see the faded mural on the dayroom's north wall, within which the amateur artist had embedded AA's twelve steps.

"I get it," the old lawyer chimed in, "too many temptations."

"Everything they want but don't need—drugs, alcohol, sex—is right outside that door," the executive director said, pointing to the door that led down the back stairway. "We have a hard-enough time keeping it out of the center."

"Do you have a new location?"

"The mission has offered us a free long-term lease in its warehouse," the board chair answered. "We've got a great start on a capital campaign to renovate the space to meet our own needs."

"So, where does Robbins come in?" the old lawyer asked.

Just then, the back door to the dayroom opened to a man who looked vaguely familiar to the old lawyer. The board chair leaned over to the old lawyer, whispering, "He wants to buy this place."

The old lawyer did indeed recognize Robbins, who strode quickly across the dayroom to join their group. Ignoring the old lawyer's extended hand, Robbins instead said curtly, "Let's sit over here," motioning the group toward a cubicle that the old lawyer hadn't yet noticed in the corner of the dayroom. The old lawyer smiled appreciatively while thinking, *now I know why I'm here*.

The four sat around the broken-down card table in the middle of the cubicle. Robbins pulled a sheaf of papers from his backpack, holding them up to himself like a hand of cards. Without further ceremony, he began bluntly, in inquisitorial style, addressing himself to the board chair and executive director. "Your organization owns this building free of any mortgage or liens, doesn't it?"

"Why do you ask?" the board chair replied, affronted at Robbins's indiscrete inquiry.

The old lawyer put his hand lightly on the board chair's arm, as if to say *I'll handle this*, while still looking straight at Robbins. Addressing Robbins, the old lawyer said simply but with a knowing smile, "Why don't *you* tell us, Petey? I am sure that you have made due investigation and that my client's representatives can confirm what you need."

The board chair and executive director looked at the old lawyer, surprised both at his tactic and how he had addressed Robbins. Robbins, though, was unfazed. Still addressing the board chair and executive director, Robbins resumed. "Your building is indeed free of mortgages and liens." Placing face down on the card table one of the several papers that he still held, Robbins continued, "Have you had it appraised recently?"

The old lawyer once again motioned to the board chair to let the lawyer handle it. Addressing Robbins, the lawyer said simply, "My client's representatives welcome your own appraisal, which I am sure that you have prepared."

Here, though, Robbins turned to the old lawyer, protesting, "You say that you are here representing a client that is my adversary in this matter. You, counselor, have a conflict of interest, though, don't you?"

Gently shaking his head *no,* the old lawyer smiled warmly at Robbins, saying, "I did indeed advise you long ago, right here on this spot, respecting your business startup. Yet in doing so, I was not involved with your purchasing real estate, especially not this building. And so, I have no conflict. And anyway, Petey—"

But here, Robbins interrupted the old lawyer to finish the lawyer's thought, "I waived any conflict when I told the organization to retain you." The lawyer nodded in appreciation, smiling even more broadly at Robbins. The board chair and executive director looked at one another with smiles, too, for the first time grasping the game of wits in which Robbins and the old lawyer engaged.

The old lawyer was the first to speak again, saying, "Well, my friend, let me guess that although you have an appraisal on this building—" and here Robbins laid another paper face down on the card table before the lawyer resumed, "—you do not intend to pay any amount for this building."

"What do I intend?" Robbins replied, poker faced.

"You intend a like-kind exchange." The old lawyer noticed that the board chair and executive director had puzzled expressions, and so he continued addressing Robbins. "Would you mind explaining the phrase for my client's representatives."

"A like-kind exchange allows for the replacement of one asset with another similar asset while avoiding a tax liability for the sale of the first asset," Robbins rattled off the answer.

"And I imagine the asset that you plan to offer is—"

But Robbins once again interrupted the old lawyer, finishing the lawyer's sentence, "—in the Southeast neighborhood near the mission's new warehouse home."

The old lawyer guessed that Robbins had learned of the center's interest from his contacts in the district. He suspected that Robbins would have planned the rest of things out. So, the lawyer resumed, saying, "And you believe that my client's representatives will see the benefit of a like-kind exchange when you—"

Robbins interrupted once again, finishing the lawyer's sentence, "—offer a property that requires little renovation, thus allowing the center to expend its capital on other needed projects, while substantially exceeding this building's value, giving me a charitable deduction."

The board chair and executive director, both with big smiles, clapped ceremoniously in appreciation.

"Look," the old lawyer said to all three, "Let's just get you all together for a look at the property, shall we?" He then turned to the board chair and executive director, adding, "Maybe you'd like to bring the board and staff through, too. I have a feeling that you're going to find Petey's offer to be attractive."

The meeting broke up after a little further discussion, no longer in Robbins' inquisitorial style. The board chair and executive director headed back to the elevator at the dayroom's front. Taking his leave of them, the old lawyer headed to the back staircase with Robbins.

"What are you going to do with the building?" the old lawyer asked as they headed down the stairs.

"Get rid of that stinking dumpster," Robbins shot back with a laugh. Then he paused mid-staircase, reflecting before saying, "Housing, I guess. That's my thing. With this place, though, it didn't matter. Time came to bring it full circle, to end where I started."

"What do you mean?" the old lawyer asked, not so much because he didn't know but instead to give Robbins permission to continue.

"I guess I figured that I owed it to Rice to do as I said that one day, to buy this place."

"Owed it to Rice?"

"Yeah, he meant a lot to me."

"But you never listened to him!"

"Oh, he still meant a lot. Sure, I could figure things out without him. But Rice, and then you guys, coming down here all those years gave me hope." Robbins paused, still standing on the old staircase with the cupped marble treads, looking up at the old lawyer behind him. "Staircase to heaven, huh?"

"I used to think the same thing," the old lawyer replied, "walking in that door from the stinking dumpster and trooping up these old stairs with my homeless brothers and sisters, each of us broken but climbing our way to heaven."

The two of them stood silently another moment before making their way down the last few stairs and out onto the sidewalk next to the dumpster. The old lawyer glanced again at his watch.

"You miss Rice?" Robbins asked as they turned to one another to part ways.

"I do. He stuck around just a few years after he brought me into the firm, to hand off his practice to me. Then he went *of counsel* but was gone shortly later. Left a big gap at the firm."

"No, you filled that gap, is what I hear," Robbins replied.

"Well, I don't know, but yes, he invested in both of us, didn't he?"

"He did. Let's call it *effective altruism*, and we're his *return on investment.*"

The Bar Exam

Grace Epstein

Here, a law dean takes the setting of a school-sponsored bar-exam luncheon to explore law student attitudes about the bar exam.

"So how do you feel, big fella?" Jake greeted Todd amiably, as if they'd just finished another ten-percent mid-term rather than the first morning of the bar exam. They started together the short walk to their school-sponsored luncheon.

"Are you kidding? How do you think I'm feeling?"

"Come on now, it wasn't that bad, was it?"

"No, you're right. Everything was pretty straightforward, actually. Except maybe that one on creditors' rights. I didn't know where they were going with that one."

"Straight up notice question, wasn't it? Wait, wait a minute, let's not do this. Hey, that's Penny, isn't it?" Jake was already haling a blond woman who looked like she was trying not to be seen or recognized.

"Leave her alone," Todd called to Jake, waving his little plastic bag of pencils, pens, erasers, and calculator to get Jake's attention.

Jake turned back, saying only "jeez" as he rejoined Todd. Neither wanted to spoil the two-hour break from the exam by making disparaging remarks about anything or anyone. They silently agreed that they were both going to take the high road for the next two hours, trying to draw a little excitement and esprit de corps from an otherwise unremittingly oppressive two-day exam.

As they entered the dimly lit banquet room in the hotel next to the arena where they were taking the exam, they made a bee line for the stack of boxed lunches that they could just see on the table along the far wall. Neither Jake nor Todd felt especially hungry, but their bodies knew better. They needed sustenance, and quick.

Professor Bright, one of those relentless law school saints who seem to care for nothing other than student success, let them grab boxes, drinks, and snacks from the table before she quietly glided up to them, saying with a warm smile, "Gentlemen, get settled. Enjoy your lunch. Believe it or not, the hardest part—the three straight hours of nine consecutive essays—is over."

Todd groaned, but Jake gladly took up the theme, saying, "You're right, professor. And it wasn't that bad, really. I mean, the property question was on adverse possession! What a piece of cake. And then the torts question was a straight-up third-party no-fault claim."

Todd gave another groan, to which Jake shot back good-naturedly, "Hey, listen to the guy who got every certificate of merit. Yeah, but I figured you'd be this way. You were the same before and after every final, and then you'd always ace the thing!"

Jake ended with one of his trademark giggles, the kind that made everyone around the table laugh. Pete and Holly had joined them, while Professor Bright had glided off after saying, "Hey, just take a look at the whiteboard over there, showing the essay subjects already covered and those likely remaining."

Turning to the whiteboard, Pete read down the list of subjects already covered until he got to constitutional law. "Come on, really?" he said, "Was that question about the landowner and the city a con-law question? I thought it was a property question, a land-use issue."

"I told you," Holly rejoined. She and Pete had walked in together.

"Stop, stop," Todd groaned again. "Let's not go over what's already covered. We just started this thing. Can we just get a break?"

Giggling again, Jake imitated Todd's grimace. Pete and Holly laughed at Jake's imitation. Todd just shook his head, put his head down near the plate, and took another big bite of sandwich.

"We should look at what's still coming," Pete said. He got up and, half-sandwich in one hand and a diet Coke in the other, headed toward the half-circle of students forming around the whiteboard.

"They're not going to cover comp this time," Todd mumbled.

"Huh?" Holly encouraged him.

"Comp. She's listed comp as a probable subject still to come this afternoon. But whenever they test no-fault, they don't test comp. The second torts question will be something else, like premises liability or a stupid intentional tort."

"See," Jake said with a big smile again, "He's got the whole thing figured out, and he only took a glance at the board."

"Well, I'm sure you do, too," Holly replied to Jake.

"Look," Jake replied, "none of us have to worry—I mean, you, Pete, Todd. No disrespect to anyone, but we've all done fine." Jake said no more, keeping to the tacit agreement not to say anything negative about anyone, which they all knew would be something like bad karma.

After a couple more silent sandwich bites, Holly, waving to another table, said, "I'll be back," and headed off to join other friends.

"That's what my last girlfriend said," Jake cracked to Todd, who had finished his sandwich and was downing the big chocolate-chip cookie. Todd smirked briefly in reply before resuming his typical intense, stone-faced look.

Dean Michaels joined their table, saying cheerily, "Hey guys, what're you doing after the exam."

"You mean tonight?" Jake asked with a surprised look.

"No," Dean Michaels laughed back, "*after* the exam. You know, *Thursday* and beyond."

"Oh," Jake replied, "because I thought you were going to invite us to The Who concert tonight." Jake giggled.

"No, I think you ought to miss that, Jake," Dean Michaels replied with another laugh. He turned to Todd, asking, "How about you?"

"My firm is off to a retreat on the island," Todd replied. "I could join them—I mean, they said I could come after the exam. But I don't think my wife would appreciate that. So, I'll just take a couple of days off at home and go back to work on Monday."

"Sounds good, Todd. It'll be your best couple of days in a while. You worked, when, until the last couple of weeks?"

"I took a week off. I knew the stuff stone cold, so I really didn't need to take that time off, but the firm pretty much insisted."

Jake shook his head in mock disbelief, just as Pete wandered back to the table, absentmindedly picked up the other half of his sandwich, and walked off again in the direction of Holly's new table.

Holly had joined Cara, Jenna, and Millie, who as Pete walked up was saying, "Ridiculous, that's what it is. What's being able to instantly analyze a wills question, one that you'll never face in practice because you're a public defender, got to do with law practice? If I was going to be an estate planner, then I'd know wills. The bar exam's just a racket to keep the labor supply down and wages high."

"Whoa," Pete said as he joined the table, adding a jest to try to calm down Millie. "What was it, the extra property question?"

Everyone at the table chuckled except Millie. Pete tried again, this time by changing the subject.

"So, what's left? Anybody looking forward to secured transactions?"

Moans came from all around the table. Jenna quipped, "I'm going to fake that one—just reel off something and hope it sticks. I felt good about this morning, but I'm not looking forward to secured—or creditor's rights."

"Hey, no," Cara piped up, "We already had a creditor's rights question, didn't we?"

Everyone looked down at the table at the same time, not wanting to venture an opinion that would make either Cara or Jenna queasy—or to start second-guessing themselves.

"Where are you all staying?" Pete asked, again to change the subject.

"Radisson," Cara and Millie said simultaneously, laughing at one another as they did so. "We're sharing a—" they began again together, this time laughing harder at themselves.

"You got in there?" Jenna asked. "I tried to make a reservation nine months before the exam, but they weren't taking reservations yet. So, the day after the last bar exam, I tried again, but they were booked up."

"So where'd you end up?" Cara asked.

"Gosh, out on the freeway somewhere. Never heard of the place. If I don't come back tomorrow morning, send a search team, will you?"

"Well, which is better?" Pete asked, "To be tortured and executed in a dump motel along the freeway or to show up for the second day of the bar exam?"

They all laughed.

"You know, though," Cara rejoined, "I don't think this bar exam is as bad as everyone makes it out to be. I mean, listen to us. We're just sitting here pretty much enjoying ourselves, when everyone back home thinks that the examiners are pulling our fingernails out with pliers right now—or, what do you call it?—water-surfing us."

"That's waterboarding," Jenna said, stifling a snicker. Cara gave her a sharp glance before continuing.

"Whatever. But really, it's just a bunch of questions, and we've seen most of them before. And who knows, maybe it does us some good."

"It's supposed to do the *public* some good," Millie interjected. "You know, ensuring the integrity of the… blah, blah, blah."

Everyone laughed again.

Dean Michaels had joined the table, listening quietly. "What do you think?" one of the examinees asked him. Dean Michaels looked puzzled, so the examinee repeated, "What do you think about the bar exam?"

"Sure, a good bit of the trade-union thing, making it harder for new entrants so that the old entrants get to live high off the land. But for you, it's a rite of passage."

He paused, looking around the table. As he did so, he thought how they had all changed so much, no, *grown* so much in the past few years since he had first met them at orientation. He thought that they might sense what he meant. Yet seeing that his view had convinced no one, he continued.

"I know that sounds like a load of fluff, and maybe it is. But the end of law school is certainly a passage, with the many changes that come in your lives. And what better transition than to focus on what may serve you the best—knowledge of the law—in that passage?"

No one seemed yet convinced.

"I remember how you feel," he continued. "I felt awful before, during, and after the exam. But I also felt tremendously challenged, which I needed, and then tremendously relieved, which was a great reward."

Still, no one looked especially impressed. So, he tried one last time, knowing, too, that right then was not necessarily the time to be profound. He just so badly, so *intensely* wanted them to know that they were doing something special—no, that *they* were special, not that they were any more special than a bricklayer on a fourth-floor scaffold or a hospital aid cleaning a bed pan but instead that a weight of glory right then pressed on them all.

"Look, all this preparation that you've done for the exam has *changed* you. It's made you smarter, sharper, more focused and discerning than ever before. You've integrated, condensed, expanded, and expounded on hundreds of law topics just for this exam. You've grasped and formed capacities that you did not know you even had, preparing to put them to uses that you did not even know others needed from you."

"Wow," Millie said quietly, "you sound like a preacher." The others chuckled.

"Well, in a way, you're right, Millie," Dean Michaels replied, "A well-known literary critic said something like God made things for him in you that you do not even understand. Like you all, I don't fully get the bar exam. It's unfair in respects, and I wish you didn't have to face it after all that you've earned. But many of you, it's changing for the better. Go knock it out of the park this afternoon."

The table was silent, each digesting the thought. Dean Michaels, a torts professor, turned their thoughts back to the afternoon's exam.

"So, you've had a no-fault question. What do you think about the other torts question? Premises liability? Malpractice? Governmental immunity?"

"Wait, can they ask *that* on the exam—immunity?" Jenna blurted. She immediately looked embarrassed.

Rather than correct or instruct her in front of the others, Dean Michaels rose and, motioning to Jenna in a gentle manner, said simply, "Let's go look at the whiteboard list together." Cara joined them. On the way, they discussed immunity.

"Millie! Holly! Pete!" Jake was calling and motioning to those who had remained around the table. "Come on! We're going to raid the lunch table. Todd's going to eat his way through the bar exam."

Todd, already veering toward the lunch table after having been in Jake's tow, gave a deeper scowl in Jake's direction. Jake giggled infectiously.

As the examinees filed out, Professor Bright and Dean Michaels met by the empty lunch table. "What do you think?" Dean Michaels asked her.

"I'm worried about Jenna—and Millie."

"Yes, me, too." Dean Michaels continued, "You know, I just realized that the graduates who sound like they will do well are those who sound like lawyers: feeling in control; assessing the situation both realistically and pragmatically; and expecting to do what they can to achieve their goal. But the graduates about whose bar-exam prospects I wonder sound more like clients than lawyers: reactive rather than proactive; feeling like victims rather than agents of their end; and doubting that they can achieve their goal."

"Maybe." Professor Bright sounded doubtful. Wanting to respect every examinee's effort, she changed the subject, "But the exam so far sounds fairer than the last one—the last several, actually."

"Yes, it does." Dean Michaels had picked up on Professor Bright's sensitivity. So, he added in affirmation, "My sense is that Jenna is the canary in the coal mine. If she does well, then the exam was fair. No one has worked harder preparing for the exam, and she also seemed to be working smart, not just going through the motions."

"Agreed, although you'd know better," Professor Bright replied respectfully. They stood silently together, watching the last examinees leave, heading back to the arena exam site.

"So, what's the rest of the day look like?" Dean Michaels asked good-naturedly.

"Prep for the new MBE elective," Professor Bright answered with her usual verve. "No rest. The next exam's coming. Gotta give 'em the best chance, right?!"

"Go get 'em, Penny," Dean Michaels replied. "Go get 'em."

Hearing Transcript

Mona Moss-Keegan

[Here, a small-firm practitioner with experience in probate matters explores the challenges of elder care in the context of a civil-commitment hearing.]

[ON THE RECORD at 1:48 p.m. Wednesday, June 14, 2017:]

THE COURT: Ready to go, Counsel?

MR. CIMARRON: Ready, Your Honor.

THE COURT: Case Number 17-20130, In the Matter of Susan Olivia Smith. What do we have here, Counsel?

MR. CIMMARON: Thank you, Your Honor, Neil Cimmaron for County Health and Human Services. The County committed Ms. Smith — Mrs. Smith to Pine Rest's watch facility last month after her voluntary ingestion of an overdose of painkillers – no, sleeping pills, in an acknowledged suicide attempt.

Mr. Smith, present here in the back, petitions for Ms. Smith's – Mrs. Smith's release to his care. The County –

1   THE COURT: Just a minute, Counsel. Let's get Mr. Jones – I mean,

2   Smith up here. That's right, Mr. Smith, come on forward – no, not

3   there, over here, let's put you at the other counsel table. There, right

4   there. That's good – you sit right there. Yes, that's alright, just sit

5   right there for now while we hear more from the County's counsel.

6   We'll be back to you in a moment. Yes, no, just – Bailiff, could you –

7   MR. CIMMARON: Thank you, Your Honor. While the County

8   appreciates Mr. Smith's commitment to his wife's care, the County

9   recommends continued monitoring, if not in the current watch

10   facility then in an appropriate nursing facility where Ms. Smith –

11   Mrs. Smith can have, well, Mr. Smith, too, can benefit from having

12   Mrs. Smith receive professional observation and care. Mr. Smith –

13   THE COURT: Hold on counsel, let's hear from him. I mean, I

14   appreciate what you're about to say. I've heard it before, and I know

15   it, and I trust in the County's care and in you counsel, but I've told

16   him he could speak, I mean, it's his petition, you know.

17   Mr. Smith, we won't be able to hear you, well, we won't get down

18   what you say, unless you step to the podium there. That's right – no,

19   this way, Mr. Smith, that's right, right there where Counsel was

20   speaking. Yes, speak right into the microphone loud and clear so

21   that –

22   MR. SMITH: Like this, right here? Can I –

23   THE COURT: Yes, you're good, just go ahead now and tell us –

24   MR. SMITH: Can I use my notes? Let me go –

25   THE COURT: Yes, of course, you can use your –

MR. SMITH: – get them. They're here —

THE COURT: – notes, Mr. Smith. Anything you need to be comfortable.

MR. SMITH: – somewhere. Just a minute, I can't hear what you're saying. Did you say something to me?

THE COURT: Use anything you wish, Mr. Smith.

MR. SMITH: No, I can't hear what you're saying. Just a minute. Give me a moment. [Pause while witness adjusts earpiece.] That's better, isn't it? I guess I mean, how would you know? [Witness laughs.]

THE COURT: Continue, Mr. Miller – I mean Mr. Smith.

MR. SMITH: Yeah, I'm Smith. Just a minute –

THE COURT: What's that whistling sound? Anyone else hear it?

MR. CIMMARON: It's his hearing aid, Your Honor.

THE COURT: His hearing aid? Wow, how could you hear with that going on?

Mr. Jones – I mean, Mr. Mill— Smith. Would you like to step out for a few minutes and get yourself together while we go on to another matter?

MR. SMITH: Pardon me, Your Honor? Did you say something? No? Shall I start? Well, I guess I'll just start. Susan and I – I mean, Mrs. Smith— am I to call her that?

MR. CIMMARON: Go ahead, Mr. Smith, you're fine.

1   MR. SMITH: Where do I start? Shall I tell him the whole thing?

2   Has he —

3   MR. CIMMARON: Your Honor, may I address the matter? The

4   County –

5   THE COURT: I'm sorry, I should of started with you, Counsel, let

6   you go ahead.

7   MR. SMITH: —read my request?

8   THE COURT: Counsel, let's do this. I have a feeling we're going to

9   need a little testimony anyway. Why don't we just swear Mr. Mill—

10   Smith and have you get right to it. We'll have the record we need

11   then.

12   MR. CIMMARON: Fine with me, Your Honor.

13   THE COURT: Well, let's just get to it then. Mr. Smith, would you

14   please step up here? No, right here. You'll – no, no, over here.

15   MR. SMITH: Your Honor, I haven't gotten to say anything yet. I

16   just, I just want to –

17   THE COURT: No, no, Mr. Smith, you'll have your chance. Just,

18   over here —

19   MR. SMITH: I just want my wife home again, Your Honor. She's,

20   she's, I don't how to say it, she belongs – I can –

21   THE COURT: We'll get there, Mr. Smith, no one's – well, we'll get

22   there. Hold on, you'll – Oh, Bailiff, were you trying to get my

23   attention? We have a brief criminal matter?

1 We have a brief criminal matter. Mr. Smith, would you please
2 just step – no, no, Mr. Smith, why don't you stay right there at
3 counsel table? You're fine. We'll be right back to you. You just sit
4 there. That's right, we'll be right back to you. I've got – the Court has
5 another matter –

6 [Proceedings adjourned.]

7 [ON THE RECORD at 2:32 p.m. Wednesday, June 14, 2017:]

8 THE COURT: Okay, let's call the Jones matter again.

9 MR. CIMMARON: That's Smith, isn't it, Your Honor? You mean
0 us?

1 THE COURT: Oh, right, right, sorry counsel, the Smith matter.

2 MR. SMITH: I had nothing to do with that criminal matter, Your
3 Honor. Honestly, I was just sitting here and – you told me to sit here.
4 And then they came in and –

5 THE COURT: [Laughs.] It's quite alright, Mr. Smith, you don't
6 have to – [Laughs.] Counsel, could you please help me here, I mean,
7 maybe I've been on the bench too long today, you know? Or too long
8 overall. [Laughs.] Oh my, oh my. I haven't had a good laugh like
9 that— no, no, I wasn't laughing at you, Mr. Smith, I just — Counsel,
0 could you please? Where were we?

1 MR. CIMMARON: You want him sworn, Your Honor?

2 THE COURT: We need to get started. We need to get through
3 this. I mean, I've got all these —

4 MR. SMITH: Don't I get heard? We were about to start and then –

1 THE COURT: No, no, Mr. Mill — Smith. Why do I keep doing that?

2 Mr. Smith, we're going to hear you now, you just – Counsel, could you

3 help him take the stand?

4 MR. CIMMARON: Right over here, Mr. Mill — damn – no. Oops,

5 sorry, Your Honor. I didn't mean to do that. I mean, I don't think I've

6 ever sworn on the record before.

7 THE COURT: Quite alright, Counsel. I thought it was just me. It's

8 catching, evidently. Let's hope that the court reporter doesn't catch

9 it, right, Martha? You don't have to put that – well, let's just get on

10 with it, shall we?

11 MR. CIMMARON: Right over here, Mr. Smith. It's the witness

12 stand, we'll put you right here, and I'll –

13 MR. SMITH: But I haven't done anything wrong. I'm just trying –

14 MR. CIMMARON: No, no, we know you haven't done anything

15 wrong, we're just trying –

16 MR. SMITH: – to get my wife back home. Damn it. Oops, I mean,

17 I'm not supposed to do that – say that, am I? I'm sorry, Your Honor,

18 I'm just –

19 THE COURT: Quite alright, Mr. Mill— Smith. Well, at least I'm not

20 calling you Jones anymore. And the prosecutor — I mean, Counsel,

21 already beat you to it, the swearing-on-the-record thing. So let's just

22 start over, shall we? Go ahead and sit, you're fine. You've done

23 nothing wrong. We just want to hear you better. Counsel and I will

24 just ask you some questions and it'll all come out, okay? Can you

25 hear me, Mr. Smith?

MR. SMITH: Yes, I can hear. You said I should just tell my story. I want my wife back home. She didn't –

THE COURT: No, no, Mr. Smith, we'll get to that. Swear him, Counsel? No? I agree, that could take some time, and he's already upset — already concerned. We're just proceeding to get the story out, then, Counsel, right? Not taking testimony, right? Then, would you please? Just answer his questions, Mr. Smith, and it'll all come out. We need to do it this way. Otherwise, we'll be here all afternoon. I mean, that would be fine, and I'm going to be here anyway, but we've got to, you know, well – Counsel, why don't you just take it from here?

MR. CIMMARON: Mr. Smith, we understand that you want your wife home, and I think nobody doubts that. But you realize that she tried to commit suicide and how serious that is, right?

MR. SMITH: Do we have to cover that? We were doing fine, and then she got upset again about —well, about not much of anything. That's the way she is, she's got – not Alzheimer's. Everyone calls it that, but it's not. She's got – what is it?

MR. CIMMARON: Dementia.

MR. SMITH: No, no – yes! Dementia. It's not really Alzheimer's but sort of like that, except that –

THE COURT: Counsel, could you move it – you know, he's sort of wandering there, and I've got, you know –

1   MR. SMITH: – it doesn't have the same – well, the insurance, I

2   mean, Social Security — no, Medicare, Medicaid calls it dementia

3   because –

4   MR. CIMMARON: We understand, Mr. Smith, it's not Alzheimer's

5   but dementia. But your wife tried committing suicide, and you had

6   to call 911, and the ambulance took her first to the ER and then on

7   the physician's orders to the watch facility where she's been –

8   MR. SMITH: That's a God-awful place. Can I say that, Your

9   Honor? I don't mean to –

10   THE COURT: Yes, Mr. Mill – Smith. You can say that. Counsel, I

11   mean, we've got to –

12   MR. CIMMARON: Mr. Smith? Mr. Smith. Your petition admits

13   that you've had a hard time keeping track of Mrs. Mill – darn it – Mrs.

14   Smith, isn't that right?

15   MR. SMITH: What do you mean, my petition admits? I want her

16   home. I just want her home.

17   MR. CIMMARON: But –

18   MR. SMITH: Oh, you mean her getting out of the house?

19   MR. CIMMARON: Yes, she –

20   MR. SMITH: That was just once – no twice – I mean, three times,

21   really, but just once when we had to call the police.

22   The other times she ended up just going next door, so it wasn't a

23   problem. We found her – I found her right away. And she wasn't

24   upset. I mean, the neighbors were concerned, obviously, but they

love her, they really do, like I do. Well, she's my wife of fifty years, so I suppose they don't love her like I do, but she's always been a favorite of theirs, for as long as – we've lived there now, I think, for five years.

I had the locks reversed after the first time. Did you know that you can do that, lock the house from the outside? I mean, lock yourself in? Well, not yourself but someone who needs, who needs your care.

MR. CIMMARON: And she was undressed – I mean, not undressed, but not dressed – she was wearing her night clothes when she left the house on these three occasions?

MR. SMITH: Are you talking to me? Did you say –

MR. CIMMARON: Can you answer my question, Mr. –

MR. SMITH: – she was undressed?

MR. CIMMARON: – Smith?

MR. SMITH: Now, that's a misrepresentation. She was not undressed. I don't know where you get that, and I don't think that's fair, and I don't like that. You –

MR. CIMMARON: I corrected myself, Mr. Smith. It's okay.

MR. SMITH: No, how can you say it's okay when you accuse me of –

MR. CIMMARON: No, I didn't mean anything against you, Mr. Smith.

1   MR. SMITH: – of not caring for my wife. We've been married fifty

2   years — over fifty years. And I've loved her every minutes of it. Well,

3   you know what I mean. No, maybe you don't know. That's what this

4   is about, isn't it? You don't know how beautiful she is and how much

5   –

6   THE COURT: Counsel? Could you please –

7   MR. CIMMARON: Yes, Your Honor.

8   MR. SMITH: – I love her. I brought a note that she wrote me

9   before she – well, she doesn't write anymore, you know. And she

10   doesn't tell me – could I have a moment, Your Honor. [Witness

11   cries.]

12   THE COURT: Quite alright, Mr. Mi— Smith. See, I'm getting

13   better. I'll have it all worked out by the time we're done. Quite

14   alright, Mr. Smith. Counsel, do you think we have enough?

15   MR. CIMMARON: Just one or two more, if I could, Your Honor.

16   Mr. Smith – you take a moment if need to. Mr. Smith – you ready?

17   Mr. Smith, you realize –

18   MR. SMITH: I'm ready. I think I'm ready.

19   MR. CIMMARON: Mr. Smith, you realize that this hearing isn't

20   over whether you love your wife? You understand that? We don't

21   question whether you love her.

22   MR. SMITH: You don't what? I thought – you told me last week –

23   last month, I guess it is – sometime after she tried – you told me that

1 you weren't going to let her go home. Well, the judge, I mean, the

2 judge wouldn't –

3   MR. CIMMARON: I didn't tell you what the judge was going to do

4 or not do, Mr. Smith. I told you what the County was going to

5 recommend.

6   MR. SMITH: No, no, you told me –

7   MR. CIMMARON: I didn't say what Judge Johnson or Judge Rowe

8 – Chief Judge Rowe or anyone else –

9   MR. SMITH: No, no, you said that the Court would probably –

0   MR. CIMMARON: I didn't say what any Court was going to do, Mr.

1 Smith. Let's not get worked up about –

2   MR. SMITH: I'm not getting worked up –

3   THE COURT: Hold on – How about this? Both of you address

4 yourselves to the Court. That usually works. And Mr. Cimmaron, I

5 have no concern about your private conversations with Mr. Smith –

6 there, I finally did it – got it right! – I have no concern about your

7 conversations with him or anyone else dealing with the County and

8 its counsel. You've always been upstanding to me. I mean, you've

9 always been appropriate in your demeanor and communications.

0   And Mr. Smith, I think that I understand it now. I've heard you,

1 and you've had your day in court.

2   Let's do this. Counsel, you don't want Mrs. Smith on watch

3 forever. I mean, you've already said that – what is it you said? – we

4 were just starting and you said –

1   MR. CIMMARON: That's right, Your Honor, I said that the County

2   was recommending an appropriate nursing facility. And in my

3   conversations with Mr. Smith – I really didn't say how the Court

4   would rule, Your Honor –

5   THE COURT: Quite alright, Counsel.

6   MR. CIMMARON: In my conversations with Mr. Smith, he

7   acknowledged, I think – I mean, we can ask him, but no – he knows

8   that the caseworker is working with Slyvan Glen, I think it is, and

9   with him. He's been great. I mean, Mr. Smith has been great, Your

10   Honor, and I want you to know how much he loves Mrs. Mill —

11   Smith. Can I – May I just ask him that, Your Honor? I think that it

12   might be a good way to put this to rest, so to speak?

13   THE COURT: I'll handle it, Counsel. That's a good idea. Mr.

14   Smith, would you please tell the Court for the record how you feel

15   not only about your wife Mrs. Smith but about your devotion — let's

16   say your responsibilities – to her. I want you to have that chance

17   because, you know, everything that you say, Martha here is

18   recording, and she's pretty sharp, aren't you, Martha? She doesn't

19   miss a word. Well, maybe when we start talking over –

20   MR. SMITH: Yes, Your Honor. If –

21   THE COURT: – one another. Go right ahead, Mr. Smith.

22   MR. SMITH: – I may, Your Honor. We've been married – I mean,

23   Mrs. Mill — Mrs. Smith – look at that! I don't think I've ever done

24   that before, Your Honor, called my wife anything other than her

25   name.

THE COURT: It's catching, Mr. Smith. See there, it's catching, and now you've caught it, too. Go right ahead. We've got people waiting their turn, not that your turn isn't important.

MR. SMITH: Thank you, Your Honor. We've been married for fifty years – fifty one this month. No, today, Your Honor! Today's our fifty-first anniversary! I'd completely forgotten because of this hearing.

THE COURT: Bad mistake to make, Mr. Smith, eh?! Just kidding, of course. You know what I mean. Counsel, you wouldn't want to make that mistake, would you? Mrs. Smith wouldn't have missed it, though, would she, I mean, in her condition and all? Is that right, Mr. Smith?

MR. SMITH: No, she wouldn't know. She doesn't remember much of anything really, or she can't say so. One of the two. I'm going right over there, though, if I get there in time because they only have short hours. And I'll do something. [Witness pauses, crying.]

THE COURT: That's alright, Mr. Smith. We'll get you over there straightaway.

MR. SMITH: We'll hold hands, if they let us. I just don't want her in that place, Your Honor, like she's done something awful. She didn't mean to, Your Honor. She doesn't know what she's doing. [Witness pauses.]

I didn't mean to leave the sleeping pills out. I thought I'd put them away. She never would have tried to kill herself. That was my fault. She likes candy. She still likes candy, even with her dementia.

1 It's not Alzheimer's but dementia. But she still likes candy. She likes
2 all food, really. Well, she never liked cauliflower. But everything
3 else, she liked and still likes. What was I saying? Oh! She must have
4 thought the pills were candy. It was my fault. I'll never do it again,
5 Your Honor.

6 THE COURT: It's alright, Mr. Smith. You're a good husband. It
7 wasn't your fault. I mean, anyone could do that, anyone trying to
8 care for a loved one alone. So we should get her to a home where
9 you have more help, shouldn't we? Let's just do as the
10 recommendation says, Mr. Smith. They're not going to leave here
11 there. I agree, it's not much of a place. I mean, it's perfectly
12 necessary. The County is just doing what it must. But I don't want
13 her there, either. Mr. Cimmaron doesn't even want her there, I think.
14 We just have to let the caseworker — oh good, I see it's Katie Street.
15 She's good. She'll get this done, Mr. Smith. Counsel, when do you
16 think? How quickly can we get Mrs. Smith out of there and over to –
17 did you say Sylvan Glen?

18 MR. CIMMARON: That's right, Your Honor. No promises, but
19 Katie – Ms. Street last thought it could be any day. The County wants
20 her over at Sylvan Glen – off their dime, you know –

21 THE COURT: Oh, I know. I know the County budget. They can
22 hardly pay for this courtroom. [Laughs.] Well, no, they're doing fine
23 there. I think. [Laughs again.] Judge Rowe – Chief Judge Rowe
24 wouldn't like me saying that. The County's doing fine funding these
25 courts, aren't they, Martha? We're still getting our paychecks,

anyway, although the green tile in the hallways is looking a little old, a little dated.

Where was I? Mr. Smith, how's that? I'll put right in the order that the County is to act in all reasonable haste. Would that help? I'll put it right in here. And then you'll not be to blame, right? I mean, you wouldn't want anything to happen, right? Well, that's not fair. No, nothing would happen anyway because you're a good husband.

MR. SMITH: Thank you, Your Honor.

THE COURT: And it's your anniversary, you said? Well, happy anniversary, my friend. I mean, I can call him that, Counsel, can't I, without your objection?

MR. CIMMARON: Fine by me, Your Honor. May the witness step down?

MR. SMITH: Am I done, Your Honor? I've got just time to see her before they close – before they end visiting hours.

THE COURT: You be on your way, Mr. Mill – Mr. Smith. Had to do it one last time, I guess. You be on your way, Mr. Smith. And happy anniversary. Give my best to Mrs. Smith, and soon we'll just close this file.

Counsel, do you have any other matters? Can we let you go, too?

MR. CIMMARON: All done, Your Honor. Thank you.

THE COURT: This way, Mr. Smith. No, no, over here – that's right. The door right there at the back of the courtroom. Bailiff, could you – he's got to get out of here and over to the facility to see her. That's

1   right, take him – just walk him down to his car, would you please,

2   Bailiff? I mean, the least we can do, right? That's what I like to see,

3   real service. How many places do you get that?

4   Martha, with Charlie out taking Mr. Miller down to his car, could

5   you please call the next case? What, did I call him Miller again?

6   Geez, what's wrong with me? Counsel, you did it once, too, didn't

7   you? Oh, yes you did! We'll get it right next time. No next time?

8   That's right. Martha, you're not taking this down are you?

9   [OFF THE RECORD at 3:12 Wednesday, June 14, 2017.]

Northeast, 2217

Raymond Arbiter

Here, a trial lawyer confirms the value of a justice system providing due process, through a depiction of the absence of due process in a post-apocalyptic system.

He came slowly to, listening to the murmurs around him, while being careful not to let others know that he was conscious yet. He'd learned the trick in his first pen ages ago. He could already tell where he was, from the dim artificial light and suffocating air. He just needed more information to help him get out of here. And the only way he figured to get that information was by wit and sleight.

"He's gotta be a *pre*," one cellmate grunted to another. "Look at the size of them knuckles and at his chewed ears. And they don't mark 'em like that anymore."

He guessed the cellmate was referring to the tattooed numbers on his forearms, one of the first things that he, too, had noticed when he'd last come to and been let out. That small venture in liberty hadn't lasted long, he remembered. Within minutes, a click had called him out for a 101 and then promptly anesthetized him before he could escape. The click must have dragged him back into this stinking pen, he grumbled.

"Yeah," the other cellmate agreed. "And I bet he's a colonist, probably a 'Hian or 'Chigan. A *primitive* for sure." The cellmate spit out the word primitive.

So, he mused, the Coasts had indeed finally colonized the Midwest. Labor reform—*enslavement* opponents had called it—had only been proposed when he'd.... What *had* happened to him? He still couldn't remember who he was, even where he was from, since he had last come to, before the click picked him up and tossed him back in the pen. Apparently, though, from the Midwest. Michigan, maybe? A *pre* and a primitive, too, apparently, whatever that meant.

"Shall we kill him now?" one of the cellmates grunted, adding, with a snort of humor, "Spare him his *trial?*" The cellmate had drawn out the last word with a sneer.

"Shut up," the other answered, "He's awake."

Discovered, he opened his eyes fully now to stare down his cellmates from trying any shenanigans. The word *trial* had stirred something deep inside him. Had he been... a *lawyer?!* Maybe that would explain the acuity that he seemed to possess, relative to the others whom he had encountered in his brief liberty.

"You a *pre?*" one cellmate asked, then after a pause adding, "You a snitch?"

"They ain't need no snitches to do what they gonna do," the other cellmate scoffed.

He knew he needed to say something now, or things could get dicey. "What if I am a *pre*," he finally grunted back in answer the pending question. He figured that he may as well see if he could entice his cellmates into giving away whatever *that* meant.

"Told you," one cellmate said to the other before turning back to ask him, in surprisingly sensitive voice, "What was it like before... the dark?"

The other cellmate exploded. "Shut up, man. You crazy? We'll pay with our lives for your little bedtime story."

Just then, a door opened, letting in a shaft of bright, warmer light. "See, you idiot," the cellmate sputtered under his breath as they both turned sullenly away as if to hide from the hulking entrant whose figure cast a shadow in the light.

But the entrant wasn't coming for his cellmates. The hulking figure shuffled over to him, grabbing his collar to lift him from where he sat on the edge of the low bunk. "Get going," the figure snarled at him, motioning toward the open door through which streamed the bright light.

While the light was too bright for him to tell what lay through the door, he did notice an old English D tattooed on the back of the hulking figure's thick wrist as the figure pointed toward the door. The figure jerked his hand down, letting his sleeve once again cover the tattooed wrist. Damn, he thought, the figure had seen that he had noticed the tattoo. He hated giving up information without intending to do so and admonished himself not to do so again—if he had another chance, which he doubted that he would.

Another figure, this one slight, stood casually inside the brightly lit room.

"I'm your lawyer," the slight figure said, drawing out the last word with more than a hint of humor. He looked up to see that the slight lawyer indeed wore a malevolent grin.

Saying nothing, he instead jerked his chin slightly in the direction of the lone table in the room with two chairs behind it, to see if he was to sit at the table.

"Yeah, go on," the lawyer said in response but then added, "The other one, primitive," when he had started toward the far chair rather than the near chair. Good, he thought: more information.

The lawyer had spit out *primitive* much like the cellmate. So, he figured, he was indeed a pre-apocalypse Midwestern lawyer. Things must have gone dark while he was anesthetized for some conviction that he would not, of course, remember. When fed central had directed anesthetization to save on incarceration costs, it had also commanded chemical and electro-shock memory erasure on the premise that new identity was rehabilitative. He knew, though, that fed central had not perfected the memory-wipe procedures, as his reviving memory showed.

Mimicking the lawyer's casual stance, he pulled absentmindedly at his left ear, the one that the rats had most chewed during his long-slumbering sentence, before making his way to the chair. As he did so, he looked around the courtroom. Nothing other than a small but traditional judge's bench immediately in front of the table in the small, brightly lit room.

The lawyer took the chair next to him. The hulking figure who had summoned him from the cell stood guard at the now-closed door near the back corner of the room. He noticed more clearly now that the figure held a weapon so big it appeared comical, more like an anti-aircraft gun than a firearm to quell primitives.

"Rise," the figure suddenly commanded, strangely with a tinge of fear. He could just see the old English D tattoo poking out from the figure's sleeve as the figure held the ridiculous weapon.

He turned back to the front of the room to see the judge enter through a small door that he had hardly noticed behind the bench. The judge sat without looking at him.

"Prisoner 843?" the judge said unceremoniously, again not even looking up from the desktop data display.

"Yes, Your Honor," the lawyer answered offhandedly, "It's him."

"The court finds the prisoner guilty," the judge said swiftly, almost before the lawyer had finished speaking. "Sentence is harvesting. Any objections?"

"None, Your Honor," the lawyer answered, again offhandedly and almost as promptly as the judge had found him guilty.

He looked over at the lawyer who smiled back at him with a small, mocking nod, as if to say *you're welcome*.

"Summon the jury," the judge said stiffly.

Seven small images slowly appeared in projection on the courtroom's side wall. The judge continued, "The jurors are drawn. Any objections, counselor?"

The lawyer first looked at him with another mocking smile, as if to say *watch this*, and then, turning back to the judge, answered, "Yes, Your Honor."

The judge's head snapped up. Still not looking at him, the judge stared instead in momentary disbelief at the lawyer. The lawyer smiled wryly to let the judge in on it.

"The prisoner objects to Juror Three, Your Honor, for having calculated to acquit the prior prisoner."

The judge smiled broadly back at the lawyer in appreciation. The lawyer then continued, "But the prisoner waives a jury." The lawyer turned to him once again, offering the same mocking smile and nod.

He leaned over to the lawyer, saying quietly, "Nice going, *Ace.* So much for effective assistance and due process."

Searing pain suddenly convulsed him, coming from his chair. He had just noticed the lawyer push a button under the table's edge.

"Counselor, for the record?" the judge asked, apparently about his convulsing pain.

"He called me...," the lawyer's voice trailed off, instead finishing, "101 insolence, Your Honor."

"Noted," the judge replied. He felt another surge of searing pain, although the lawyer hadn't moved again for the button. "That one's for the court, primitive," the judge added.

The judge then for the first time looked up at him from the bench-top images that he had been scrutinizing since he entered. "He's a damn *pre*, isn't he?" the judge asked the lawyer as he looked the prisoner up and down.

"Yeah. Three consecutive life sentences."

Wow, he thought. He'd lain anesthetized for over two-hundred years.

"Ah, I see it now," the judge answered. "Multiple counts of insolence, but a genetic disorder not yet remedial, so no harvesting. Lucky fella!" The judge pretended to smile at him before turning back to the lawyer. "Well, your case, counselor."

"Given the court's conviction and sentence, I will be brief," the lawyer answered. "The primitive admits to 101 insolence, fourth offense. The primitive requests harvesting to end his suffering. As the records reflect, it should've happened long ago, but his sequencing had an anomaly that fed central just resolved. We brought him back as a military sacrifice, but a click picked him up. He's irredeemable and deplorable, a true primitive, unworthy of the court's mercy."

So, he realized, that was why they'd brought him back. They'd finally found a cure for the disease that had killed his parents and sisters, leaving only him and his younger brother. Hadn't his brother followed him into law school? His mind was regaining growing glimpses of his former life.

The proceedings interrupted his brief reverie. "Did the clinic correct the disorder on the prisoner's re-arrest?" the judge asked the lawyer.

And that, he thought, explained the multiple port wounds he had noticed as he had awakened in the cell. They'd cured his condition so that they could transplant his organs after he'd died in battle as an expendable.

"Yes, he's clean and ready for harvest. Just needs the declaration." The lawyer had momentarily paused before that last word and then drawn it out, as he looked the prisoner up and down with that same malevolent smile.

He looked back at the lawyer, pointedly imitating the malevolent smile, while saying to him under his breath, "So whose side are you on, *Buddy*?" This time, the searing pain only sharpened his mind.

"Then proofs and plea accepted in support of the prior conviction and sentence," the judge answered, adding, "I find the prisoner dead. Oh, and was that a 101 again, counselor?"

The lawyer nodded and then, remembering the record, blurted out, "Yes, Your Honor."

His muscles tensed now, waiting for the exact right moment. He rehearsed the script again swiftly in his head as seconds ticked.

"Anything from the primitive?" the judge finally asked the lawyer, looking up again from the desktop data display, which appeared to have gone dark.

Before the lawyer could speak on his behalf, surely denying him any voice, he interjected boldly, "Yes, Your Honor."

He could see the lawyer pressing and holding the button again, but the searing pain meant nothing to him now as he continued.

"I raise a due-process challenge based on my counsel's ineffective assistance."

He gave the lawyer seated next to him a condescending sneer as he finished his sentence. The lawyer let go of the button, stopping the searing pain, and instead turned toward him, moving his right hand toward a weapon on his belt.

231

The judge had momentarily frozen, staring at him with a puzzled, far-off look. Noticing the change in the judge's demeanor, and suspecting that it didn't bode well, the lawyer gave a snort of disgust, saying to the judge only, "Mayor Carter."

"Shut up," the judge answered the lawyer, still seeming to search his memory for something long lost.

"That's *Magna Carta*, counselor *Ace*," he said to the lawyer in a mocking tone, this time plenty loud enough for the judge to hear. The judge smiled appreciatively both at his legal reference and his insult. The judge's smile enraged the lawyer who pulled a weapon from his belt.

Now addressing both the judge and the hulking figure in the back corner of the courtroom, he continued quickly, "I call on bailiff to defend the prisoner." Out of the corner of his eye, he could see the bailiff stiffen and raise his huge weapon.

"Good try," the judge huffed with a snort of condescension, "but like you, he's only a *pre* and *primitive*." The judge suddenly stiffened, realizing his error. He seized on the judge's error, just as he would long ago have seized on a cross-examined witness's unwitting answer.

"And so as a *pre*, bailiff knows well that law rests on justice," he nearly shouted now, as if finishing the judge's errant thought, at the same time turning to goad the lawyer further.

It worked. The lawyer stood from his seat next to him at counsel table and took a step back, raising his weapon to take aim at him, the prisoner. He steeled himself for whatever would happen next. A flash filled the room. He looked down instinctively at his torso, expecting to see his fatal wound but instead noticing nothing unusual.

A thump drew his attention back to the lawyer, now fallen in a lifeless heap. He knew what had happened. Now, he needed to see that the right thing happened next. As he looked back at the judge, out of the corner of his eye he could see the bailiff still pointing the huge weapon where the lawyer had just stood. Vapor rose from the weapon's end.

Stunned and without any protocol or script, the judge looked back at him, then at the bailiff, then back at him. He began again quickly before the judge could move or speak.

"I now call on the juror for his verdict."

"You have no jurors here, stupid prisoner," the judge replied, trying to resume his former command by spitting out the slur.

"Every courtroom has a jury, in this case, a jury of one, Your Honor." He paused, then added, "Just as the state hold's the people's authorized force, so your jury is the one holding the gun."

"What are you saying?" the judge raged back at him, adding, "*I'm* not on trial here."

"Oh, we're all on trial, everywhere," he replied. "Justice holds court for everyone."

"Justice is an illusion, you *fool.*"

"Justice is no more illusory than the working end of my brother's gun."

"He's not your *brother,*" the judge replied. "He remembers *nothing.*"

"Oh, he remembers, Your Honor." He put as much esteem as he could muster into that last honorific before continuing, "He remembers the '67 riots and the '68 Tigers with Kaline, Horton, and Cash. He remembers '84, too, with Gibby's crew."

He hadn't planned to say any such thing, indeed, hadn't thought that he had recovered any such memory. But more was making sense to him at every second and, he assumed, also to the hulking figure in the back of the courtroom.

"Nonsense, prisoner. It doesn't matter *what* he remembers," the judge snarled, although the judge was now obviously fearful of the bailiff. He stole a look at the bailiff who had indeed turned the huge gun toward the judge. The judge continued.

"He killed your lawyer. He's a *murderer,* not a juror."

"Defense of others, Your Honor," he replied, adding, "He's no murderer. He's only a good man doing justice with a great gun.

233

You'd have your lawyer bailiff defend an innocent man in your courtroom, wouldn't you, Your Honor?"

"Enough of this charade!" the judge shouted, rising and turning swiftly toward the little door behind him.

"Juror! Your verdict?!" he shouted in command, motioning grandly toward the hulking bailiff who still trained the gun on the departing judge.

The judge froze, realizing that he could not escape. He turned slowly back toward the courtroom. Reaching cautiously into a slit at the hip of his long black robe, he drew out a gun and slowly raised it toward the prisoner, saying, "*I'm* the judge here, and *I* have already pronounced *you* dead."

A flash filled the courtroom. This time, he didn't look down for a fatal wound because the judge had already fallen in a lifeless heap.

After a respectful pause, he walked over and, using his foot to roll the body over, managed to remove the long black robe. He paused for a moment, holding the black robe up before him, remembering how profound and fitting he had once felt, when appearing long ago in consequential cases before esteemed judges.

A thought then occurred to him. Donning the black robe, he marched to the bench and, still standing, turned to the bailiff, who stood proudly with his great gun across his chest.

"Bailiff, free the remaining prisoners," he said with a huge smile. "And direct them to help remove the dead for harvest. Justice here is done. Court stands adjourned."

Changes

Emily Mugerian Maltby

Here, a law student with education and experience as a mental-health care provider writes about a woman trying to manage her lawyer husband's changing persona.

Thursday

"Penny, sunrise, chair. William, can you remember those three words for me?"

"Yeah, yeah, yeah, Doc. Penny, sunrise, chair…. Are we almost done? I have to be in court at two o'clock."

Tuesday- Two Days Earlier

I walked into the office a bit on edge; it was strange going to an appointment that was all about someone else, even stranger that William didn't know I was there. Twenty-two years ago when William and I said "I do," I never would have imagined our life would take this turn, that I would be asking these questions and seeking these answers. But I guess that's life; you never know what it will bring.

The waiting room was small and simple, yet inviting, not as clinical and sterile as most physicians' office. After all, this was a different kind of physician. The room was empty, probably because it was noon. Appointments weren't normally scheduled between 12pm and 1pm, I had been told. But my many emails and helpless phone calls, a flurry of frustrated, confused, and at times panicky

235

communications, had induced Dr. Peters to agree to meet with me during his lunch hour two days before William's appointment.

"Christina Bradley, I presume." The deep voice took me out of a trance, lost in my own conflicting thoughts and self-pity. "I'm Dr. Robert Peters. It's nice to meet you."

I stood to gently shake his hand. "It's nice to meet you, too, Dr. Peters," I managed to say as I took it all in. A tall, well-dressed man in his mid-fifties with a slim but athletic figure suggesting he must run, or bike, or possibly swim, stood before me. I'm not sure what I was expecting, but Dr. Peters seemed normal. Maybe I expected him to be a bit disheveled, the idea that you must be crazy to work with crazy people?

"Christina, come with me," he directed as he held the door to an inviting hallway. The lights were dimmer, the paint color warm; comfortable furniture and beautiful artwork lined the walls. It smelled floral and clean, like lavender and lemon. I felt I was walking down the hallway to a spa, not a medical office. He led me to Room #3, where I expected an exam table and white walls, but the spa-like feeling remained. The room was well decorated with warm, earthy tones; nothing was white. Instead of an examination table, a dining-room table with four comfortable chairs filled the room. A large window brought in natural light and a wet-bar area held a mini-fridge and large clear containers with pretzel sticks, animal crackers, and fun-size candy bars.

"Can I offer you something to drink, Christina?" Dr. Peters asked as he poured a cup of coffee.

"No, I'm fine," I replied as my nerves took over and my stomach began to toss. The spa-like calmness had only helped for a few minutes. Maybe we'd be better off in a typical, sterile, exam room, I thought. I'd hate to get sick in here.

"Christina, I've received your emails expressing concern about your husband, and I commend you for being persistent about meeting." He paused, his body language relaxed slightly as he continued. "It's normal for spouses to be deeply involved in my sessions with patients. I will say, it's slightly less normal for a spouse's involvement to be separate from my patient meetings, but I understand your unique situation."

I nodded in agreement. He thinks we're crazy. The doctor who sees crazy everyday thinks we're crazy.

"I know you've expressed some of your concerns in your correspondence with the office, but I'd like you to open up with me now about those concerns, about William, about changes you've noticed. Start at the beginning," he stated as he adjusted his glasses and took out a pad of paper and pen.

"Well, we met twenty-two years ago when he was just starting law school. I was beginning my master's in teaching. We met through mutual friends, dated for a few years, and were married a month after he graduated. We moved to Northern Michigan and both took the first job that came our way, him with the firm he's still with today and me with the school district. That was our life until Collin was born."

I paused, took a deep breath, and fidgeted with my scarf, suddenly feeling claustrophobic. "I stopped working when Collin was born. William worked enough for both of us. Nicolas was born two years later, and our life continued with William as the breadwinner working seventy-five-plus hours a week and me staying home to raise the boys. It worked for us, became our normal. William's dad is a lawyer and still works to this day; work, work, work, it's what the Bradley men do; I don't think they know any different. "

"Christina, how was your marriage during this time?"

"Good?... I think...," I replied, wracking my brain for the right thing to say. "I didn't have worries like I do now."

"Tell me more about the worries you have now."

"I worry about our family, about our boys, about William's job. I worry about William's behavior, about his anger, his secrets, his lifestyle. I worry how the boys are taking it, their dad living in an apartment across town and me not having any reason why he lives there. I worry about William's safety and well-being. He doesn't seem to care about us—he's not taking care of us—I have no idea if he's taking care of himself." I blurted everything out almost in one breath, my face warming as my blood pressure rose and tears welling up in my eyes.

Dr. Peter's looked at me with warm, compassionate eyes. I felt a sense of comfort with how attentive he was. He took in every word, nodding occasionally while listening intently. "Christina, when do you recall things changing?" he asked.

"A few years ago I guess. I don't know, it's not like it happened all at once."

"Try to explain that to me" he replied.

"I think the first unusual thing was the silence. William was always friendly, always talkative, always the life of the party. At the time, I remember blaming his work, blaming stress. William stopped talking about work, so I stopped asking. Then came the anger, which I also credited to his job, to the million hours a week he was working, to the enormous case load he had."

"Christina, where did William direct this anger?"

"At first he directed it at himself. H kept to himself and didn't interact with us as a family as much. It was like he wanted to be alone in his silence. As time went on, we would see outbursts of the anger, directed at the kids or me. Anger that didn't make any sense, anger over things he never would have gotten upset about in the past."

I took a deep breath remembering Collin's tears when his dad didn't show up to his regional finals lacrosse match. "It was hard on the boys," I continued. "It was hard on me to watch William disappoint them again and again."

I started to break down. Thinking about the pain he caused the boys over the last few years, the promises he broke, the disappointment on their faces. I could be tough, I could fight through, but no mother wants to see her children hurt. "The boys don't understand what's going on.... I don't understand what's going on.... We don't know what's going on! All we know is it's not the William we know, it's not the dad we know, it's not even the attorney we know. Midlife crisis, personality disorder, I don't know.... That's why I'm here."

It was relieving to say it out loud. Throughout the last few years, I hadn't had anyone to whom to turn. I put my best face on for the boys but also for our family and friends. How do you open up to someone when you think your husband has gone crazy? I know Dr. Peters wasn't my support or therapist. He's a neurologist, and his patient is William, but I was thankful to finally be heard.

"Christina, tell me what you know of William's daily routine. Where is he spending his time? What are his current focuses?" Dr. Peters calmly asked.

"Well, he moved to an apartment across town. I found out about six months ago that he had this apartment, but who knows how long it's been. He never talked about it. He never took anything from our home for it. I've never been there. Collin stopped by in June wanting to spend time with William. It was Father's Day."

I paused wiping away a single tear. "Collin hadn't seen or heard from his dad in weeks.... So he stopped by the apartment, but it didn't go well. William is still working, but I know there have been issues there. His boss reached out to me at one point to check in. I didn't know what to tell him. I also got wind of a complaint that was filed against him by one of his clients, but I don't know the details."

I stopped, thinking of how pathetic I sounded. I know nothing about my husband, but there's no sense trying to sugar coat it now. "I don't know what he does at night or on the weekend. I got a notice from the bank that he took out another line of credit. I have no idea what the charges are but there are a lot of them. When I do talk to William it's like talking to a stranger. I'll tell him something about a close friend or relative, and he'll look at me like he has no idea who I'm talking about. He really does not care."

The room fell silent... but not an uncomfortable silence. I felt a sense of relief to say these things out loud. I had a right to bitch and complain; this was my life, and it was spiraling out of control. This mid-life crisis William was having was affecting all of us. It was selfish of him, and I was justified in my anger and utter confusion.

Dr. Peters broke the silence. "Christina, can you tell me about any incidences of domestic abuse or times you have feared for your safety or the safety of your children?"

"Just once...," I whispered, thinking back to the day I pulled Nicolas away from him, leaving William to punch a hole in the kitchen wall—the day I told him to get lost, the day I changed the locks. "Just once, William's anger turned physical. He didn't hurt any of us, but I thought he might. It wasn't William. The William I know would not hurt a fly. The William I know has patience and can keep his calm in the tensest of situations. This is one of the things that make him so effective in the courtroom; he has always been able to calmly roll with the unexpected and make it seem like everything is going to plan."

"Christina, is there anything else I should know?"

"I just want answers," I replied strongly, feeling the need to stand up for myself and stand up for Nicolas and Collin. "I want communication with William, even if it's bad news. Even if he's got another family across town, or is losing his job, or lost all our money. I just want answers."

"Christina, you know William has an appointment with me later this week, and I appreciate you opening up with me about your concerns. I'm sure you're aware I will not be able to discuss Robert's appointment with you unless he gives me permission."

"Yes, I understand. Thank you, Dr. Peters."

Dr. Peter's continued, "In the meantime, please keep in contact with me. Your priority needs to be taking care of yourself and your children. If you need access to any resources please don't hesitate to contact our office."

A phone call was distracting the receptionist as I made my way back through the lobby to the front door; the lunch hour was over. I started the car and drove home in a daze, functioning on autopilot. I replayed my conversation with Dr. Peter's over and over. It was a start. Getting William to agree to see a neurologist was a victory in itself. Being able to meet with the doctor privately before William's appointment was its own feat. I said a quick prayer that William would show up to the appointment on Thursday. I couldn't make him go. Nobody could.

Thursday

"William, today I have performed what is called a Mini-Mental Exam." Dr. Peters explained, "I don't know if you are familiar with the exam but it checks an individual's problem-solving skills, attention span, counting skills, and memory...."

"So what are you saying?" William interrupted with frustration. "I have a short attention span. I have adult ADD, so of course I have a short attention span. I don't have time for this."

"Looking at learning, memory, thinking, and planning can help determine if you have problems in those areas of the brain," Dr. Peters said, taking a colorful rendering of a human brain from the top drawer of his massive desk. "The tasks I asked of you today are all scored to help determine any deficiencies. Any deficiencies found are not the result of ADHD or another conduct disorder; any deficiencies found are a factor in a potential diagnosis of Alzheimer's disease, specifically early-onset Alzheimer's disease. "

William felt the world stop around him. Dr. Peters may have continued speaking, but William's mind wandered. His stomach churned, and a large lump formed in his throat. He felt a strange combination of disbelief, shock, and anger; he wanted to both scream and cry at the same time. Yet he also had a strange feeling of relief. Maybe this was something he knew all along; maybe he needed someone else to bring it up first; maybe he could finally have an answer to why he was doing what he was doing. Who could be mad at him then? Who can be angry at someone with Alzheimer's disease? But Alzheimer's disease? At forty-eight years old?

"William.... William...." Dr. Peters' authoritative yet compassionate voice finally brought him back to their conversation. "William, at the beginning of our session today I asked you to remember something. Can you tell me those three words?"

"No doctor," William whispered, holding back tears. "I can't remember."

Epilogue

The winter sun's reflection shined on the snow-covered ground as we made our way from the parking lot into the assisted-living center. It was one of those December days that felt warm, although the temperature had barely reached 15 degrees. The sunshine brought a smile to my face. The now-familiar staff greeted us as we made our way through the living room towards William's apartment. The community was beautifully decorated. Wreathes and lights complemented the magnificent Douglas fir towering toward the vaulted ceiling. Staff members were preparing a large buffet and setting tables, as a gentleman sat on a tall stool in the corner of the dining room, quietly tuning his acoustic guitar.

Nicolas led the way down the hallway, gently knocking on Room 126 before entering the small apartment. "Hi Dad!" he called, announcing our presence. I stepped into the room, removing my coat and scarf. Collin brought up the rear, a large box of gifts in his arms. William smiled warmly. He was genuinely happy to see us. He looked handsome, wearing a new sweater I had dropped off the day before especially for the Christmas party. His hair had recently been cut, and the staff had helped him shave. He looked good; he looked happy, no more anger in his eyes. William's room reminded me of home. We had been encouraged by the community to bring in pieces that familiar to him. Family pictures filled the walls, along with his degrees in handsome mahogany frames. A dresser from our bedroom set filled one wall, and a beautiful Oriental rug we held onto from William's childhood home covered the floor. William was seated in his prized Herman-Miller Eames chair, purchased after receiving his first paycheck out at the law firm.

After William's diagnosis, the disease progressed quickly. Of the estimated five-million American's suffering from Alzheimer's disease, William is in the five percent experiencing early-onset Alzheimer's disease, affecting individuals under age 65. His diagnosis was tough to understand; life as we knew it was over, and we had nothing we could do to reverse it. I learned a lot, researched for hours, joined a support group, and tried to plan for the journey ahead. What I quickly learned was as soon as you think things are under control, the other shoe drops, and you once again have more questions than answers. Someone at the support group told me, "When you've seen one case of Alzheimer's, you've seen one case," getting at the fact that each individual experiences the heartbreaking disease uniquely. Alzheimer's offers no normal.

William's placement to assisted living was the best decision we made. Placement ensured his safety and our peace of mind. Placement ensured routine observation and proper medication management. William's anger didn't last forever; as the disease progressed, he found a sense of calm. Assisted living simplified his world to a small, specialized community that knew and could provide for his needs. The facility facilitated activities with the residents' needs in mind and with the goal of resident success.

For me, support from others has been critical; I've become close with families of other residents, relied on the support of the community's staff, and bonded with others at the support-group meetings. Alzheimer's is a disease that takes away everything, including who you are and what you do. We have so many unanswered questions about this terrible disease, and I pray that breakthroughs come soon. They may be too late for William, but nobody should live through this pain. Things may have not gone as expected for us, but we are family, and family sticks together.

Draft Complaint

Priscilla Van Ost

> *Here, a civil litigator employs the unusual format of a draft complaint to tell the story of a typically difficult small-business breakup, said by some lawyers to be more difficult than a literal divorce.*

Plaintiffs William F. Burger and Burger-Trost Corp. complain against defendant Jeffrey C. Trost as follows:

PARTIES, JURISDICTION, AND VENUE

1.   Mr. Burger is an individual residing in Marion, Lake County, Michigan.

2.   Mr. Trost is an individual residing in Whitehurst, Lake County, Michigan.

3.   Burger-Trost Corp. is a Michigan corporation headquartered and doing business in Marion, Lake County, Michigan, that Mr. Burger and Mr. Trost together incorporated and in which they remain the sole and equal shareholders exclusive of any other shareholder or interest.

4.   This case is for more than $25,000 in damages exclusive of interest and costs, and for declaratory and injunctive relief.

5.   This Circuit Court has personal jurisdiction over the parties and subject-matter jurisdiction over the case.

6. Venue is proper and convenient in this Circuit Court.

FACTUAL ALLEGATIONS

7. Mr. Burger and Mr. Trost were until recently lifelong friends in whom each confided their mutual confidence and trust, and whose families and children were close, to the point that they frequently took family vacations together.

8. Mr. Burger and Mr. Trost together formed and incorporated Burger-Trost Corp. twenty years ago, in 1997, to conduct maintenance, repair, renovation, security, and other services together and through their employees, drawing on their shared skills and mutual interests.

9. Up until early this year, Mr. Burger and Mr. Trost devoted substantially their full time to Burger-Trost Corp. business, sharing in wages, benefits, dividends, capital accumulation, goodwill, and other business benefits, without substantial dispute or division.

10. Beginning in about January of this year, Mr. Trost made substantial unauthorized withdrawals from the Burger-Trost Corp. accounts, without Mr. Burger's consent or contemporaneous knowledge, for personal use unrelated in any way to the corporation's business.

11. On information and belief, Mr. Trost made those unauthorized, personal withdrawals to pay gambling debt, debts in connection with the use and abuse of illegal drugs, and debts or other obligations in connection with the theft and resale of the personal property of others.

12. Despite his reasonable care, diligence, and caution in the conduct of Burger-Trost Corp. affairs, Mr. Burger remained unaware of these unauthorized and illegal activities of Mr. Trost until Mr. Trost's arrest and the public disclosure of charges relating to those illegal activities.

13. On information and belief, Mr. Trost prepared false Burger-Trost Corp. financial statements, records of account, and other documents to conceal his unauthorized withdrawals from Mr. Burger until Mr. Trost's arrest, with the intent that Mr. Burger rely on them to his detriment.

14. Mr. Burger is still investigating the extent of Mr. Trost's unauthorized withdrawals, but the amounts appear now to total more than $275,000 and may end up being substantially more than that amount, depending on the release and recovery of certain frozen funds.

15. Mr. Trost's unauthorized withdrawals and associated criminal misconduct have destroyed and burdened, and threaten to continue to destroy and burden, not only the financial, legal, and other business affairs of Burger-Trost Corp. but also Mr. Burger's individual financial and legal affairs and those of Mr. Burger's family, while causing extreme mental and emotional distress, social humiliation and embarrassment, and reputation loss.

16. On information and belief, Mr. Trost, who remains incarcerated under criminal charges relating to this matter in this Circuit Court's case of *People v Jeffrey Trost, Case No. 17-000658-CJ*, has not cooperated with law-enforcement or other public officials, and certainly has not cooperated with Mr. Burger or his representatives, in the recovery of misused funds.

17. To the contrary, Mr. Trost has continued to actively undermine public and private trust and confidence in Mr. Burger and Burger-Trost Corp. by falsely alleging that Mr. Burger has engaged in the very criminal misconduct for which prosecutors now charge Mr. Trost in the just-referenced criminal case in this Court.

18. Mr. Burger is not a gambler, has no gambling debts, is not a drug abuser, has no drug-purchase or drug-dealing debt, has not misappropriated and converted corporate funds, and has to the

contrary at all times acted lawfully, diligently, loyally, and in good faith and fair dealing with respect to Mr. Trost and the corporate affairs of Burger-Trost Corp.

19. Thus, Mr. Burger, who since Mr. Trost's arrest has exclusively controlled the funds, property, and affairs of Burger-Trost Corp., brings this action on his own behalf as an officer, employee, and shareholder of the corporation, for the corporation itself, and for the indirect benefit of the corporation's suppliers and customers whose interests Mr. Trost's misconduct may have adversely affected and may continue to adversely affect.

20. While Mr. Trost's criminal charges are not set for trial for some time yet, and no guilty plea or other conviction has entered as of this date, no reasonable likelihood remains that Mr. Burger may rely on Mr. Trost for the conduct of any Burger-Trost Corp. matters.

21. Mr. Burger and Burger-Trost Corp. further require the court's protection against any control of corporate funds, property, or affairs by Mr. Trost or his family, representatives, or those under Mr. Trost's control or influence, until this case establishes the rights of Mr. Burger and Burger-Trost Corp., and liability of Mr. Trost.

This reference incorporates the above paragraphs into the following counts.

Count I: Conversion

22. Mr. Trost's above actions constitute the intentional unauthorized total deprivation of Mr. Burger's and Burger-Trost Corp.'s funds, property, and interests, causing Mr. Burger and Burger-Trost Corp. the above loss, expense, and damages, for which Mr. Trost is liable to them in conversion.

Count II: Breach of Fiduciary Duty

23. As a Burger-Trost Corp. officer, director, and equal shareholder, Mr. Trost owed Mr. Burger and Burger-Trost Corp. duties of loyalty and due care, and the duties of a fiduciary, which Mr. Trost intentionally, recklessly, and carelessly breached in the above ways, causing Mr. Burger and the corporation the above loss, expense, and damages, for which Mr. Trost is liable to Mr. Burger and Burger-Trost Corp. in breach of fiduciary duty.

Count III: Declaratory and Injunctive Relief

24. This complaint alleges an actual and justiciable controversy between Mr. Burger and Burger-Trost Corp. on one side and Mr. Trost on the other side, in which Mr. Burger and Burger-Trost Corp. have suffered irreparable harm and will suffer further irreparable harm unless the court declares the rights of Mr. Burger and Burger-Trost Corp. while dissolving the interests of Mr. Trost, and enjoins Mr. Trost and his family, representatives, and those under his control or influence from interfering with the affairs of the corporation.

Count IV: Intentional Infliction of Emotional Distress

25. Mr. Trost's conduct in this matter has been beyond outrageous and beyond all bounds of decency in civil society, with the purpose and effect of causing Mr. Burger severe mental and emotional distress, manifested in weight loss, anxiety, sleeplessness, and other physical manifestation of distress, or with knowledge to a substantial certainty that it would do so, for which Mr. Trost is liable to Mr. Burger for intentional infliction of emotional distress.

ON THESE GROUNDS, William F. Burger and Burger-Trost Corp. pray that the Court grant judgment in their favor and against defendant Jeffrey C. Trost for all money damages, fees, costs, interest, and other amounts to which the Court finds them entitled, together with declaratory relief approving the dissolution of Mr. Trost's corporate roles and divesting of his entire interest, and exclusive grant of all such control interest to Mr. Burger including approving that Mr. Burger change the corporate name, and an order enjoining Mr. Trost and his family, representatives, and others under his control or influence from interfering or attempting to interfere in Mr. Burger's sole and exclusive conduct of the corporation's affairs.

Tomorrow

Victoria Faustin

Here, a law student with a passion to benefit her community, following in the footsteps of her courageous mother, uses a powerful analogy to tell of her community's need for law reform.

Peace

Wind roared and tree branches slapped the Walker home's windows, as the severe-weather cell approached. With television and radio weather alerts, and a warning from the mayor, Mayflower, Arkansas, had prepared for the coming storm, just as it prepared for so many other storms. Although Mayflower didn't know that it was about to experience an unprecedented tornado, somehow Travis Walker sensed it.

Inside the home, Travis and his wife Leah were enjoying the evening with their children Abraham and Michelle. The smell of a flavorful home-cooked meal lingered as Travis helped Leah clean up the kitchen. He then went into the children's bedroom to play video games with them, yet knowing that the weather outside was worsening. Leah joined them until the children tired, Travis lifting tiny Michelle and Leah small Abraham into their beds.

Travis and Leah had met and married while in college. In one respect, they were as different as night and day, Travis a studious meteorology major while Leah a political-science major with a passion for justice. But in another respect, they were as alike as life partners could be, both committed to faith, family, and community, each with a huge servant's heart. After graduation, Travis had taken an entry-level job with the National Severe Storms Laboratory, while

250

Leah entered law school. The up-and-coming young couple had one of their darling children with Leah still in law school and the other after Leah graduated and entered a small-firm law practice.

On this stormy evening, other couples might have cuddled together inside, sipping hot chocolate, but Travis instead prepared to meet the storm head on. If tornado conditions grew acute, then he couldn't stay home. His job would require him to leave his warm home and family to chase the storm. So, he asked Leah to monitor the worsening weather through the late evening, while he grabbed a little sleep, before the storm hit full force. But first they would share a few private minutes together, discussing Leah's day.

Leah was now a state senator. She had gone to law school to make a difference. Politics drew her. A few short years of law practice had taught her the limits of working within current laws. She wanted to use law reform to make a greater difference and drafted an education bill to foster a stronger local education system. Together, Leah and Travis were passionate about fighting the great fight for better tomorrows.

"Today I was on the floor during session speaking on the education bill," began Leah. She then filled Travis in on all her day's details.

Travis and Leah knew that black communities face special educational issues. Adequate and equitable school funding is critical for children from families in poverty including many of Mayflower's black students. School-funding measures still leave some schools without adequate and equitable resources, widening student-achievement gaps.

Leah wanted to close funding gaps to ensure that all students have access to a quality education. Leah knew the problems firsthand. She knew local schools that had more students than books and desks, with poor student attendance, low test scores and morale, and high student and teacher attrition. Leah blamed politics—inequitable funding in particular—more than the local school system.

And so, Leah's education bill aggressively addressed funding issues to close the achievement gaps. Leah told Travis again that "decreasing gaps in student achievement requires public policies and

251

legislation ensuring public support of teachers and students in their educational efforts." The passion in his wife's voice flamed Travis's own passion to attack the coming tornado. He, too, wanted to change his community for the better.

Leah and Travis lived in a predominantly black neighborhood in their town, exactly the kind of location that seemed always to have the worst educational system, in which the children seemed least likely to achieve. Leah spoke passionately about how their dream for their children depended on a good education, which she felt was a basic human right.

"When do you vote on your bill?" Travis asked Leah.

"Tomorrow morning," she replied, adding, "I hope the storm doesn't delay a vote."

"It won't," Travis replied firmly. "We'll see that you get there."

"I believe you, Honey," Leah replied, adding, "but you still have to make it home from the storm in one piece."

"Goodnight, Sweetheart," Travis replied.

Leah smiled sweetly at him for a moment before turning back to studying her bill. Leah studied late into the night. Tomorrow would be her crowning day to advocate for her community. Using her lawyer skills, she prepared her argument, anticipating every question that any senator might have. While the bill was important to her constituents, she, too, needed this bill to pass. Her own children needed a fair chance to succeed.

Love

Soon, Leah called gently to her husband who slept lightly in their bedroom. The weather had worsened. He must get up, even while she went to bed to get some rest for her big legislative session. Travis rose, dressed in his storm-chasing gear, and slipped quietly out into the night.

Travis ran through the dark to his car with his Totable Tornado Observatory, or TOTO, in hand. TOTO was one of the first tornado observation devices that the National Severe Storms Laboratory had built, a small drum packed with scientific instruments. Place the TOTO in an oncoming tornado's path, and it would collect information about conditions as the tornado passed over or even picked up the small drum. Information could save lives.

Travis enjoyed being a storm chaser. With his kids growing up in a city having the second-highest tornado risk in the country, he was willing to face the job's dangers in exchange for the hope of a safer and better tomorrow. So, he left his house determined to place the TOTO in the right spot to gather the best information. Lives were at stake. Although the wind blew stronger outside his car, Travis was at peace inside. Love would bring him home.

Other storm chasers joined Travis as they drove through the dark, at times through pouring rain, trying to anticipate where a tornado might touch down. The storm chasers shared a mission, knowing what they needed to get it done.

Sometime in the middle of the night, Travis heard the classic James Blunt refrain, "You're beautiful, you're beautiful to me"—the ringtone he had chosen for cellphone calls from his beloved wife. Travis touched the hands-free indicator on his car's console screen. Yes, he told Leah, he was alright, and no, she shouldn't worry about him. "Back to sleep, my love," he ended, "You've got a big day tomorrow."

Leah's call made Travis more determined than ever to go after this tornado. Travis thought again about how tornadoes form, when thunderstorm updrafts and downdrafts combine to form the viciously circling winds. Dry, cool air from Canada seemed to meet the warm, moist air from the Gulf of Mexico right over Mayflower every spring and summer, giving the area the highest number of tornadoes every year.

Travis thus knew that his fight against tornadoes had a lot to do with a history of severe storms right in his location, just as Leah knew that her fight for education involved a history of racism embedded in segregated location. Travis again resolved to place the TOTO in a tornado's path to gather the data needed to avoid or protect against tornadoes. He also wanted to show Leah and his children that the seemingly impossible—fighting the fiercest natural force on the planet—was possible.

Faint light now showed in the early morning sky, but Travis still chased the storm across the region, with other chasers following behind. The chasers had spotted a tornado forming, and not just any tornado but a fierce Fujita-scale 4, possibly even an F5. An F4 tornado would cause devastating damage, leveling even well-constructed houses, while carrying away vehicles and houses with weak foundations. An F5? Who knew what damage it could wreak?

Travis was by now exhausted and his nerves shot, but he was determined to make a difference for his wife, children, and community. Using his onboard computerized weather system, he could now plot where the tornado would approach a road up ahead. Driving furiously over bumpy back roads, Travis made his way to the spot, with other chasers in tow.

Yet when he reached the point on the road nearest where the tornado would pass, Travis pulled his car off the road and onto a beaten two-track heading right into the tornado's path. The other chasers did not realize until then that Travis would drive directly into the tornado to place the TOTO inside the tornado, determined to gather the needed data. He didn't want to risk the others' lives, and so he knew that he couldn't inform them.

As the other chasers watched from afar, Travis's car plunged into the tornado's base along the bumpy two-track. Travis had expected the worst, and indeed, the tornado seemed to grab and spin his car. But suddenly, the violently twisting air fell into a brief and strange calm. Almost unbelievably, Travis had pierced the massive tornado's wall to reach its small eye, as only a handful of others had ever done before, and none with such a massive storm.

Travis knew what to do next. Grabbing the TOTO and a coil of rope from the floor of the passenger seat, he threw open his car door, jumped out, and lashed the TOTO to a nearby twisted stump. He had just enough rope left to start to lash himself to the same stump, when the far wall of the tornado closed over him. He gripped the stump and rope as hard as he could.

Hope

As soon as the tornado had passed, the other chasers drove through the field toward where they had seen Travis's car enter the

254

tornado. They found his car tumbled over into a nearby drainage ditch. After more searching, one of the chasers called the others that he had found the TOTO lashed to a stump. They found no sign of Travis.

Robert, one of the chasers who had become a good friend of Travis, unlashed the TOTO and loaded it in his vehicle to return it to the weather station with its precious data. Driving back to the station, Robert called Leah to try to tell her of her husband's bravery, but Leah didn't answer.

The morning skies were clear and calm as the storm dissipated. Hoping for one last bit of encouragement from her sweetheart husband, Leah dialed Travis just before she took the Senate Floor to advocate for her bill. No answer. After a few rings, the call went to the message that Leah always loved to here because of her husband's sweet voice.

"Love you, dear. About to take the floor. Hope to see you tonight."

When her turn came, Leah took the podium to speak for her education bill. Thinking right then of her husband's doubtless bravery, she summoned all her courage and energy to deliver the speech of her life.

"As the distinguished members of this august body well know, I earned a law degree to advocate for those who cannot speak for themselves. And, like many of you, I pursued this career as a representative of the people for the same reason, to place myself in their position and to speak for them when they are unable to speak for themselves."

"Many of my constituents," Leah continued, "live in the center of a veritable storm. Global gusts carry their jobs offshore. Deluges of crime drown their young men and youths. De facto discrimination, vestiges of debilitating de jure segregation, press them into subordinate roles and decaying neighborhoods. And a sodden popular culture rots their morals and relationships. They have so few places to turn."

"Our public schools were once a place of shelter and a stepping stone of opportunity for my constituents who struggle to stay afloat in a raging river of poverty. But now those schools are the center of the storm. Rather than educating and uplifting our youth, failing and violent schools rob them of their last sense of peace, stability, hope, and order. The storm's devastation has overwhelmed the schools and now reached the last bastion of the home front."

"As most of you know, I have a devoted husband to whom to return each night, one whose courage and commitment help me shelter our own children from the storm. My husband is a hero whose literal work is to chase, wrangle, and quell storms. Here in the state's Senate, I am only a figurative storm chaser. But know, my distinguished colleagues, that a severe storm batters my people nonetheless, a storm that my education bill chases."

Leah continued her speech, advocating point by point for her education bill. After a lengthy and rousing speech, she ended, "This education bill will bring beneficial change for the next generation. It will not only stem the storm tide that floods our schools but also generate the data that will open new opportunities for learning and advancement. Chase storms with me and my husband. Let us together make a better tomorrow in the schools and classrooms for the next generation."

As soon as Leah had finished to strong applause from her Senate colleagues, she stepped from the chamber to call Travis in excitement. And somewhere in a ditch in the distant field, a lonely cell phone rang: "You're beautiful, you're beautiful to me."

The Game

Emily Dykhuizen

Here, a law student and judicial law clerk with an interest in homeland security, prosecution, and government work spins a tense tale of implied homicide that leaves just the right degree of uncertainty as to the circumstances and outcome.

She squinted her eyes hard, trying to focus on the figure lying next to her in the dark.

Olivia was straining with everything she had to pierce the black in the room. She could see the shadows and silhouettes of the objects in the room. She saw the monsters she feared in her childhood, the monsters that were waiting for her just out of reach in the darkness. As her breath quickened at the thought of the monsters reaching for her, she blindly felt for her phone, to ward them off using the display as a flashlight.

The phone screen stung her eyes as she read *2:08 a.m.* She had only been asleep for about an hour, even though her grogginess left her feeling as if she had slept for days. Her mouth was dry. Her eyes were fighting against her as she tried to keep them open. She shifted the direction of her phone's lit-up screen to view the room.

The small room, barely able to fit the over-sized furniture that cluttered it, was the make-shift master bedroom of the house, containing a king-sized bed, two wooden dressers, and a matching night stand that wasn't even next to the bed. The huge bed left just enough room on one side and at the foot of the bed to walk. Small windows, with chocolate-colored darkening shades drawn, adorned two of the room's four walls.

257

The room had no space for knick-knacks and trinkets, but Olivia proudly displayed their wedding photo on the shorter dresser at the foot of the bed. The photo sat just to the left of a lamp they bought at a garage sale, the kind that had a lightbulb with three different brightness levels. To the right of the photo was a large fan that pitifully circulated air in the room. They mostly used the fan to drown out the background sound of traffic and the neighbors, as they tried to sleep.

That night was overly hot and sticky, not that anyone would really notice a difference in the cramped room. Dried sweat caused Olivia's clothes to cling to her body. She silently begged the fan, just visible in her phone's display light, to relieve her from the heat. She hated the heat, and that hatred was increased tonight. She sighed and tossed her head back as she tried to cool down, knowing the fan wouldn't bring much relief.

With the fan not giving an ounce of extra effort, Olivia resumed surveying the room in the dim light of her phone display. That's when the light fell on Elliot. He just lay there, appearing so lifeless, as though he was holding his breath. No movement at all. She realized, with surprising disappointment, that the heat wasn't affecting him.

When her phone-display light first illuminated Elliott's face, Olivia said to herself that it was *always just a game*. The game had never been real. They never intended to follow through on it. The game had always just been something they did to pick on one another. She loved her husband. She really did. This moment was not an exception, even as she stared at him, waiting for him to release his breath. Making bets with herself on when he would move. But he didn't. He just lay there, still as death.

She had watched enough *Law and Order* to know that people didn't get away with murder. They always made mistakes. They always got caught. She and Elliot had discussed how they would do it. Their playfully morbid humor had got it started. They shared with one another how they would do it, but the other would always point out the obvious defects in the plan.

The game had started when shortly after they married, they had watched a murder mystery involving a husband killing his wife. The husband had believed that he would get away with it, but he got caught. They always got caught. Olivia and Elliott had played the game for the entirety of their ten-year marriage.

They had an unusual start to their marriage. When they met, Olivia had just recently ended an engagement. Her fiancé had called it off just two months before the wedding date. She had buried herself in work at the hospital where Elliot had just started working. They ran into each other quite often, neither looking for a relationship. But their humor and personalities meshed so well that they couldn't avoid the inevitable.

After knowing one another for six months, they had moved in together. Three short months later, while lying in bed watching a movie, Olivia had asked Elliot if he wanted to get married next week. He said sure. One week later, after getting the license, they visited the courthouse and got married in front of their families and a few close friends.

The game started playfully enough. Elliot started by saying he would suffocate Olivia with a pillow. She laughed, saying that that was a rookie mistake. Law school had taught Olivia a few things they would look for when investigating a murder. Spouses were always the first suspect. They would find fibers in her throat, and maybe bruises from her fighting back, and he would have a body on his hands.

Olivia would joke about how she would poison Elliot, if she could get her hands on the poison without investigators being able to trace it back to her. He said that procuring the poison without leaving tracks would be nearly impossible. The played the game any time that they would watch a horror movie or see a thriller on television, or if either of them were reading a mystery novel.

It was just a game. It was always just a game. Then they began to play the game when one of them made a mistake that affected the other. Except then, it didn't feel so much like a game. They would argue, and then one of them would start the game in the heat of the moment. But it was still just a game.

Olivia had told herself that she would never actually do it. She knew that even if she wanted to do it, she wouldn't because she would get caught. Too many people now knew about the game. They had begun to play the game in front of others, friends and family mostly. It would never look like an accident. It would always look malicious, intentional, deliberate, an execution of the game that they had played in front of others.

But he was just lying there. Not moving. What would people say? The neighbors had heard them fighting earlier that night. What was the fight even about? She couldn't quite remember. They had spent so much time fighting lately. About work, money, kids, movie plots. A night didn't go by where they didn't fight about something. Usually trivial things.

She tried to take herself back to when the fight started that night. That's right: it was over that woman. The one who had been texting him. The one to whom she had begged him to stop talking. *That* woman. The woman worked with Elliot at the hospital and had once been Olivia's close friend. They were all close. But then her Facebook messages to Elliot became more frequent and personal. The woman wrote about marital issues and her husband's pornography, sometimes fishing for compliments.

Then the Facebook messages spread to text messages and late-night phone calls just to chat—like a boyfriend and girlfriend would do in high school. The woman called him one night out of the blue to talk about a man who was threatening and harassing her at work. When Olivia confronted the woman at work about the phone call, the woman claimed that she had called Elliot because he was a part of the hospital's Safety Team and would know what to do. But she could have met with the Safety Team during work hours.

Olivia knew better. She had that feeling of something not being right. Her feeling of something amiss grew as the calls and messages increased. Her women's intuition, or maybe her own insecurities, nagged at her that the woman and Elliot had more to their relationship than just work or even friendship.

Then it had come out that the two were spending so much time together at work during their shifts that they weren't getting their work done. Several people had approached Elliot to warn him that he was not doing his job. A supervisor had already reprimanded the woman for spending too much time chatting with Elliot at his station rather than helping patients.

Elliot had then left work twice to drive her home at 2 a.m. The first time was at the end of his shift and supposedly her car wouldn't start. She couldn't reach her husband to come and get her. So, Elliot offered to drive her home, knowing full well that Olivia would not approve. The second time, he left in the middle of his shift, again at 2 a.m. This time, though, she was no longer in work clothes and instead in clothes fit for a bar scene. Again, he knew full well that Olivia would not approve and that his conduct would hurt her.

As she lay there, watching him motionless beside her in the hot night, Olivia recalled that Elliot had tried to hide much of what he and the woman were doing. He had lied that the Safety Team had asked him to take her home when it hadn't, and he had lied that her car was broken when it wasn't. He had even deleted messages from her on his phone. Elliot knew that Olivia was upset. His relationship with the woman had caused so many of their fights.

As Olivia lay suffering in the heat, she remembered that the woman's best friend from work had even got involved, telling the woman that she needed to back off. Olivia remembered the rumors surrounding the two, about them having an intimate relationship. Olivia had heard that when another co-worker asked the woman about it, the woman hadn't denied it, either. She had just stated that it was nobody's business. Olivia had already once endured an abusive relationship with someone who cheated on her on a regular basis. It was then that Olivia broke, when she finally found out everything that had been going on.

Olivia recalled how when she finally broke, everything that she had known seemed to fall apart. She had thought that in Elliot, she had finally found someone whom she could trust. Olivia had believed that he would be honest with her and do everything he could to keep her secure, well, and safe. Yet at that moment when she had broken, she had promptly fallen into a deep depression, became suicidal, and just lost herself completely.

Six months had passed since then. Six months had passed since Elliot had vowed to Olivia that he would cut off all ties to that woman. For six months, Olivia had lived in a constant state of doubt, paranoia, and insecurity. And then, a single short text from the woman, "Are you working tonight?" had validated all Olivia's fears that night.

Elliot and that woman were still in contact! They were still talking! Elliot had confessed it all. He had tried to explain to Olivia that it was nothing more than friendship, but she couldn't hear anything other than noise. His words were unintelligible to her, as if he was speaking a different language. All she could hear was betrayal and lies. And the game nagged at her mind. It screamed at her: if ever there was a time, now would be it.

Could she claim provocation? As she lay in the suffocating heat, she tried to recall what she had learned from one of her professors about the law of provocation, when she had gone to his office for him to explain things to her. She remembered that it could be used as a defense for someone who had lost complete control and lost the premeditated state of mind in response to someone's action. Would this information be adequate provocation?

Even if it was, Olivia thought, it would only reduce a murder charge to manslaughter. Thus, she would still face incarceration. Could she at this moment disprove that she had weighed the pros and cons of her actions? Her anger had blinded her. She could only see red. But here she was having an internal debate about what was provocation and what wasn't. Clearly, she was in the right frame of mind to weigh her options.

What about an accident? Olivia wondered. Is there any way to make it look like an accident? Or even self-defense? Her anger grew as she recalled how he had continued that evening to try and justify his deceitful actions. She felt the stinging of tears in her eyes and the pain from her nails digging into her palms. Why hadn't he just shut up? Couldn't he see that he was achieving nothing here?

Olivia had let the tears fall. She had let the words escape her mouth. They had flown across the room like bullets. Even with all the hurt swelling inside her, her love for him was apparent, which was why his secrets had hurt her so badly.

She looked down at her palms now and saw the tiny cuts she had made with her nails during their exchange. Small amounts of dried blood made them stand out in the dim light of her phone. They didn't hurt much, but an annoying pain sat just below the surface.

As she reflected, thinking about the fight and that woman, Olivia's rage started to swell again. She could feel her face getting hot, feel the sweat on her nose and upper lip start to surface. She could feel the tightness from the dried tears on her cheeks. Her heart was broken. Her sanity was swaying. She broke into an even deeper sweat than just from the heat of the night. She was soaked. The bed around her was soaking it up like a sponge.

She looked back to Elliot. She didn't know if she would even heal from the heartbreak he caused her. She didn't know if she could overcome the betrayal of yet another person. She didn't know if she could ever forgive him for his lies and cover-ups. She didn't know if she would be able to move forward from this night. She didn't even know if what she had done made up for it, if it made them equal. Did he owe her more? She couldn't decide if she was whole now.

The game sat in the forefront of her mind. She reminisced on all their silly plots. Poison hadn't been the only way she discussed murdering her husband. She just didn't think she could bring herself to kill him with anything that took physical effort. She didn't care for blood. She didn't own weapons. She could never overpower him.

Olivia turned away from her hands and back to Elliot. She stared over at him, next to her in their bed. He just lay there. So seemingly lifeless. Looking as if he was holding his breath. No movement at all. She squinted through the darkness, barely able to make out his still expression, waiting for him to release his breath. Making bets with herself on when he would move. But he didn't. He just lay there.

Still as death.

The Repair Shop

Christine Doxey

Here, a law student with real-estate experience shows, in an edited and abbreviated version of a longer story, how the history of a single property can reflect a community's economic health and social relationships.

The sleek black cat with a long thin tail and empty belly peered across the dark repair shop from her perch on the workbench. Her narrow, pointed face and large ears exposed Siamese lineage. She observed the body lying face down on the cement floor for a moment before jumping gracefully from the work bench to the floor. Padding up to the body, the cat stopped when its paws touched the pool of blood. The cat shook the blood from its paws, first the left, then the right, while sniffing at the congealing liquid. Stepping around the dark stain with an air of indifference, the cat trotted off toward the weathered pet door, leaving paw prints on the cement floor. The dry ache of winter had not yet passed, and the cement floor not yet saturated with summer's humidity. The floor sucked the moisture from each paw print, drying them to permanency within minutes.

The cat pushed her head against the hinged, wooden flap, jumping through the opening to the outside, the door swinging back with a soft *swish, thump thump*. She trotted across the crumbling asphalt of the parking lot and slipped into the dark morning's shadows, still silent of the first bird call announcing the new day.

The repair shop stood bleak, years of neglect and abandonment having tugged at its worn siding and weather-torn roof. The shop held two bays, each with a heavy wooden overhead door hanging unevenly. The roof should have collapsed years earlier, but the shop railed against its abandonment, refusing to release any piece of its structure—until today.

Today, John Geddert, thin and short with pale skin and watery eyes, would try to set fire to the shop. A conniving property investor who had flunked out of law school, Geddert didn't want to be a landlord of dilapidated two-story homes crowding the downtrodden neighborhood. He had bigger plans. He wanted the repairs shop's lot and commercial zoning to build a three-story, mixed-use structure including subsidized apartments, a great tax shelter.

The city, though, refused to permit the shop's demolition. The local preservation society had registered the repair shop as a historical building. So, Geddert figured that the shop had to suffer destruction in a natural disaster. Geddert discovered the shop's commercial zoning during the city's neighborhood revaluation. e found that developers over several decades had purchased chunks of land from the farmer who owned the land before the city platted the neighborhood. The city zoned the entire area residential, except for the repair shop and the old two-story farm house sitting about thirty feet away, zoned commercial because of the farmer's small business in the shop.

While the farmer owned both buildings, the city taxed only one lot. Geddert brought the oversight to the city's attention, the city promptly giving the repair shop a separate address and sending a tax bill, to which the city received no response. Geddert paid the delinquent tax bill, and eventually purchased the lien and some title insurance.

So, on this day, when he snuck into the repair shop to start a fire that would result in a brief but uninterested investigation by the fire marshal, Geddert believed that he owned and controlled the shop. Fires happened all the time in this part of town, provoking promises from the mayor and local law enforcement, but were quickly forgotten as everyone turned to more pressing hardships.

In the early April morning, a few hours before dawn, Geddert, dressed in soft black sweatpants, a heavy dark coat, and dark sneakers, walked silently along the neighborhood's crumbling sidewalks. The only sound was the cold wind pushing against the trees' bare skeletons. His puffs of breath hung briefly in the frozen air before the wind sucked away the white wisps. The dim glow from the streetlights barely lit the dark streets. Geddert walked up to the shop's small parking lot and peered into the gloom. The dark silhouette of the repair shop stood silent against the backdrop of trees swaying in the wind. He picked up his pace slightly as he stumbled across the crumbling sea of asphalt, glancing around for any observers. He slid softly to the side of the building to force open the side door, which groaned slightly as he pushed on it. He slid into the shop, flicking on his flashlight and leaving the door slightly ajar.

His ears strained, listening for any sound of his discovery. He then shuffled cautiously across the leaves, dirt, and debris that covered the floor. The wind was strong tonight, lashing the branches of the trees back and forth causing eerie groans and angry scrapes. Hearing a soft movement, Geddert whipped his flashlight across the dark interior's cavity, meeting the reflection of a cat's eyes. It hissed before jumping up on the workbench, knocking an old pipe to the floor. The pipe landed with loud clank and rattle. Startled, Geddert dropped the flashlight, which cracked and broke when it hit the floor, plunging him into blackness.

Geddert froze and cursed silently, blood pounding in his ears. He knelt to his hands and knees, patting around on the cold cement floor, as an ancient cobweb slipped across his face. He was about to give up when his knee felt a pile of leaves, dry bits of twigs, and pieces of crumbled paper. As the wind pounded against the repair shop, he pulled together a pile of dried tinder and reached into his pocket to pull out a yellow plastic lighter, flicking it once to make sure it worked. Flicking it again, he held up the light, once again seeing the cat sitting on the bench, watching him. Pushing his pile of dry leaves, paper, and twigs against the workbench, he said quietly to the cat, "Let's see what you do now."

Geddert stood up and held out the flame of the lighter so he could calculate his escape one last time before he lit the tinder. The wind picked up strength, howling. The repair shop groaned under the wind's pressure. Just as Geddert leaned to light the pile, a support beam, weakened by years of rot, snapped in final desperation. With the roar of the wind and the repair shop groaning in defiance, the beam landed on Geddert's head, ending his life as he collapsed in a heap.

Geddert's body might have remained therefor years, except for a mischievous excursion of two fourth-grade boys Daquan Baily and Louis Garza. The pair of them conspired to skip school that day, stashing sandwiches and flashlights in their backpack in anticipation of their adventure. While the two were absent from the group of children huddled at the bus stop, they weren't missed. The tired neighborhood didn't pay attention to who made it to school. Most of the children got themselves up and off to school, not eager to learn but rather because the schools fed them both breakfast and lunch.

Daquan and Louis hid behind a large oak tree, the April mornings still dark. They watched the bus roll away, shrieking in excitement that it had left them behind. They sped towards the repair shop, racing across the crumbling asphalt, and flung themselves breathlessly against the shop's peeling, weathered side, each claiming victory. "I can get...in...through...there," Daquan panted, pointing to the ancient, hinged pet door, "and...find a way for you." Louis just nodded, slightly pudgy and not used to exercise, he had not fully recovered. Daquan was skinny and small for a ten-year-old. He squeezed through the opening and shimmied his body into the shop.

He stood up and peered into the dark interior. Looking across the dark expanse, he saw a dim sliver of light from the crack of the slightly opened side door. Walking through the darkness, he slipped on something gooey, falling hard on the cement. While his hands pressed into the dark goo, cobwebs shrouded his face. He wiped his face in annoyance and then cleaned his hands off on his pants. He then walked more gingerly in the dim light towards the open side door. "Hey!" he yelled to Louis, "We're in." Louis jogged quickly to the side of the building but when he saw Daquan, his face froze in ashen horror. "Dude! What happened?" he sputtered. Daquan looked down at himself and saw he was covered in blood. They grabbed their flashlights, pointing the beams of light into the darkness where they could see the body on the floor. The boys raced home to their mothers in two minutes. Investigating police quickly concluded Geddert's intent.

Brad Randall, a tall black man with a thick mustache, watched the excitement from his second-floor apartment of the dirty two-story house next to the repair shop. Brad lived in the upper apartment while his landlord Sam Shepard lived below. Brad had moved back to the neighborhood a few years ago after having left his home town for college and law school. After becoming a successful attorney in the mortgage industry, he had invested heavily in real estate, losing everything when the bubble burst. He had returned to his hometown a broken man, finding an apartment for rent in the house next to the repair shop. Sam, a stout black man with a thick stomach and a quick smile, and Brad often sat on the porch sharing stories and watching the neighborhood.

Sam came home from the Vietnam war mentally scarred and on disability. He would have nightmares, and Brad would sometime wake at night, hearing Sam yelling out in the apartment below. Sam had once rented the apartment that Brad now had, from the previous owner. The owner was about eighty years old, his wife already having died. Sam's rent was cheap. The owner had several bad experiences with past tenants leaving behind high utility bills. In exchange for rent, the owner wanted Sam to put the utilities in Sam's name, pay property taxes, and help around the house. Sam agreed. The owner refused to hook up to city water and sewage. "I have a two hundred foot well. If that water ain't good, no water is," said the defiant owner. Since the owner never hooked the house up to city sewage and water, Sam also paid to have the septic pumped periodically. It was a fair deal on both sides.

The utilities were higher in the winter because the furnace was electric. The owner qualified for an assistance program, and the city replaced the old oil furnace with a new electric furnace. Sam and the owner watched as the workers cussed and sweated when pulling the steel, octopus furnace and oil tank out of the Michigan basement. With the cost of electricity slowly increasing over the years, Sam got on the electric company's yearly plan. It was the same every month and reevaluated yearly, making it easier to budget.

Sam and the owner hit it off right from the start. Both were war veterans, the owner from World War II and Sam from Vietnam. The owner's wife was buried at Fort Custard, a a plot the owner would share when he died. After the owner died, Sam buried him at Fort Custard in a quiet ceremony. Sam was surprised that he was crying as the coffin descended into the ground.

Sam stayed at the house, kept paying the utilities, paid the taxes when the bill showed up, and had the septic pumped as needed. He rented out the upstairs apartment. Using the little rent that he collected, Sam maintained the old house, replacing windows one at a time while mowing the small lawn surrounding the house and the repair shop.

After Brad moved in, Sam decided to update the plumbing, and redo the electricity. Brad helped open the walls, working with Sam to replace the old pipes and knob-and-tube wiring. Then, after the final drywall, plaster, and paint, the two men sat on the front porch and celebrated with a pint of black-label whiskey.

As the weather started getting warmer, Sam and Brad sat outside more often. Sitting on the front porch, sharing stories, they watched the commotion going on next door at the repair shop. The repair shop used to be focal point when he was growing up, a place where men would gather and discuss the maladies of their lives. Brad had lived here, watching the neighborhood change.

The repair shop used to be an old blacksmith shop. At a time when horses instead of cars were the transportation, travelers would journey the dirt-packed road, past the farm and toward town. Travelers often stopped to water and feed horses and find out what was going on in town. Locals would stop by the shop, then a three-sided shed, to share stories or use the blacksmith services. Eventually, cars replaced horses, the dirt road was paved in asphalt, and the three-sided shed was enclosed. To keep visitors out of the house, the farmer added a small bathroom with a toilet and sink to the shop

As cars replaced horses, men continued to gather at the shop to discuss how to fix things. They discussed home projects, , cars, marriages, and politics. Coffee was always brewing. Sometimes, something stronger passed around. The neighborhood grew around the farmhouse and the repair shop. The town became a city and adopted a master plan that left the shop a nonconforming use in a residential district.

The neighborhood was never the best in the city but was a good blue-collar neighborhood. While not segregated by law or covenant, families still lived among their own. Blacks built their dreams together, while Hispanics switched from migrant work to factory work, fighting to gain status, while whites tried to prevent their daughters from dating anyone. The repair shop was in the black part of town.

While Brad was growing up, the repair shop was owned by Paul Duncan, a weathered, gray-haired black man. When Brad was about eight, he followed his dad across the street, While the men sat in metal lawn chairs discussing President Truman and the Korean War, Brad slipped into the small waiting room. The room held a soda dispenser and a wire display with a variety of candy and gum at the bottom. Brad glanced over at the men who were in a lively discussion. He picked out a candy bar and slipped it into his pocket. As he started to turn around, a firm black hand landed on his shoulder. "You know," said Duncan, "a person should always pay for what is important to him." Brad was immediately reduced to tears of shame. "I could use someone to help sweep up around here," said Duncan. "Pay isn't great but we could work something out, say a candy bar to start?" Brad nodded in relief and agreement. Duncan handed him a broom and showed him where to start. Over the years, Brad saw a lot of kids in the neighborhood sweeping out that repair shop.

For nearly one-hundred years, the men worked, gathered at the shop, and went home to their families. The women fussed over the men, children, and their homes. Even in the 1930's when everyone was broke, the neighborhood pulled together, and by the 1950's everyone was back to work.

However, the 1980's broke everyone's spirit. One by one the mills and factories closed and left town. Women were cranky, and men gave up and left, abandoning their children. When the men left, nobody trained the boys. With no work available, young men wandered the streets looking for acceptance from the gangs that came from distant cities. The repair shop was closed and abandoned. The men stopped gathering together. Women struggled to support their families, taking low paying jobs while working long hours. Fast food replaced home-cooked meals.

Home values dropped dramatically. Taxes went unpaid, and investors bought house after house, converting the two-story homes into rental units. As low-income renters moved out after not paying rent, many landlords gave up, and the city took over properties, selling them repeatedly. Nobody fixed anything. Windows were boarded up, paint peeled off the side of most houses, and orange extension cords ran from house to house. Brad was saddened because he could remember when the people were proud of who they were and where they lived. He told Sam stories about how it used to be and how the repair shop seemed to pull the neighborhood together.

As spring warmed the air, and the investigation next door at the repair shop ended, Geddert's relatives appeared. They demanded that Sam stop mowing the grass and walking across their land. Sam told Brad that he was worried he would be forced to leave and that he would end up in the mission again.

Brad asked Sam, "When did you buy this house." So, Sam shared a secret. "I came here about thirty-five years ago. I could never stay anywhere for very long and the landlords would ask me to leave," he said softly, "because of my nightmares, they scared other tenants. I stayed at the mission house across from the bus station. You have to leave the mission during the day by 7 a.m.," he explained. "So, I would walk around the neighborhood. Every day there was this old man who would be out walking. We got to know each other over the summer," Sam continued. "The old man offered to rent the apartment to me." Brad listened intently to Sam's story.

Sam then revealed that he had never bought the house. After he buried the owner, he just kept paying all the bills and taking care of the place. Since he had been here for over thirty-five years, everyone thought he owned the place. He managed to save about eight thousand dollars from the rent he charged. After Sam shared his story, both men finished off the whiskey and headed to their own apartments. Brad went upstairs and thought about what Sam told him. He went to sleep making plans for the next day.

The following morning, Brad took a bus to the library and went to the law-book section. He pulled out statutes on land possession. "Sure enough," Brad thought to himself, "I was right!" Sam could be an adverse possessor. Sam met all the requirements that his possession be hostile, actual, exclusive, open and notorious, and continuous for the statutory period of 15 years. Brad was elated but cautious. He wanted to do a title search. He called the mortgage title company to run a title check. Brad took a bus back to his apartment where he found Sam sitting on the porch.

Brad sat on the porch with Sam and explained, "I found some interesting things about the house and the repair shop. The city divided the lots about five or six years ago during revaluation, relying on Geddert's opinion and suggestions." Brad continued, "It will be a fight, but you may be able to keep the house and repair shop." Sam asked Brad, "Would you be willing to represent me, since you're a lawyer? I can pay." Brad refused, asking instead if he could open the repair shop up and work in it. Sam thought that was a good idea and the two of them started making plans.

After Brad filed the paperwork with the courts, things got messy. Brad found that the reason Sam never knew about the taxes on the repair shop was because the city gave the shop its own address. Because the repair shop didn't have a mail box and the postal carrier didn't recognize the name Duncan, the tax bill was returned. That aside, Geddert's estate still needed compensation for the investment. While the statutory time frame is different state-to-state, if you lose a property due to unpaid taxes and somebody purchases the lien, you still have some time to repay the taxes plus interest.

Geddert's family wanted anything Geddert might have owned. The title insurance that Geddert had purchased was in dispute because the insurance company felt there was fraud on Geddert's part. Brad convinced the judge that this was a separate issue from Sam's adverse-possession claim, leaving Geddert's family to battle the title-insurance company. While the company and estate litigated, the court agreed to let Sam use the repair shop at his discretion, after the parties agreed that using and caring for it would only increase property value if it was later sold.

The most positive thing about Sam's situation was that he was paying a higher tax rate even though the repair shop lot was separated from the home lot. Once the government gets money, it doesn't want to give it back. Brad negotiated a settlement for Sam. The lots remained separate for tax purposes and the city lowered the taxes on the house. It adjusted Sam's account, which included a veteran exemption, all of which resulted in overpayment for the last five years. The city sent Sam a check, which helped his depleted bank account. However, Sam had to agree to hook up to city water and sewage. Sam balked at first, but Brad convinced him that since the city was connecting for free, Sam would be saving this cost. Sam grudgingly agreed saying, "I sure hate to give up good water."

However, Sam signed all the paperwork and felt a great weight being lifted from his shoulders.

Brad walked over to the repair shop, opened the side door, and saw the cat. He went back to the house where he opened a can of tuna fish and emptied the whole can on a paper plate. He took it over to the shop, sat it on the floor, and walked away. As he looked back, he saw the cat approach the plate hesitantly, sniff it, then gobble the food down. Feeling content, the sleek black cat with a long thin tail and full belly, stretched and walked over to the work bench. She jumped up and laid down to watch Brad work on sweeping out the repair shop.

He opened the repair shop every morning and fed the cat. Although leery at first, the cat finally allowed him to pet her. Brad took inventory of tools he thought were in good shape and then purchased a variety of tools at the local store. He and Sam started working on an old car Brad bought. One by one the men, young and old, would stop by to talk and see what was going on. They asked if they could bring their car by and see if Sam or Brad could help them fix it. The men in the neighborhood stopped by, glad to see the shop wasn't closed. The men who stopped by would bring a tool to leave at the shop.

Brad cleaned out the old waiting room, sanded and painted the wire floor display with silver spray paint, and filled the display with packaged donuts and candy. He bought a drip coffee maker and every morning he would begin the day with fresh coffee. During the hot summer, men sat in lawn chairs, gathering in the shade of the open garage doors, drinking coffee (and sometimes something stronger), and talked about cars, politics, and women. Many of the men would bring by a car that belonged to a woman from the neighborhood. They would fix it and take it back proudly to the object of their affection resulting in a homemade meal or something more intimate. The people began calling Brad "the lawyer" and would come to him seeking advice. He accepted the title and considered the repair shop his informal law office. He felt a regained sense of value here. He knew he wouldn't stay forever, but he enjoyed helping his neighbors. He sat in the lawn chair in the morning shade of the repair shop and reached down to pet the sleek black cat with a long thin tail and an expanding belly.

The neighborhood was slowly changing. Brad thought about the programs that could help the lower-income residents purchase a home and rebuild pride in the community. It was still rough and gangs wandered in and out of houses, and the police were frequently patrolling the streets. However, the men stayed with the women longer instead of moving on. The houses started displaying thin bands of bright flowers. When the school bus picked up the children for the first days of school, the driver noticed that a lot of the kids seemed less groggy and disheveled. He could see a difference this year. "The kids smelled better too," he thought to himself. He was surprised to see mothers and a few dads gathered at the stops to send their kids off.

As summer slipped into fall, the days grew shorter, the men came by later and left earlier. Some of the men left early to go to recently acquired jobs. While the jobs didn't pay as well as factory work did in the past, the lower rent in the neighborhood made it possible to keep a stable place to live and stay with a woman. Brad would talk to his neighbors about home-ownership programs for lower-income families. A new home owner would beam in pride and show Brad their house keys when they qualified under a program.

One Saturday, Daquan, the fourth grader who had found Geddert's body back in April, followed the man who was spending a lot of time with Daquan's mom. He looked around the shop, eyeing where his adventure ended last spring. Daquan slid into the waiting room. Peeking over at the men discussing politics, he reached for a candy bar and slipped it into his pocket. As he started to turn around, a firm black hand landed on his shoulder. "You know," said Sam, "a person should always pay for what is important to him." Daquan looked down at the floor in shame. "I could use someone to help sweeping up around here," said Sam. "Pay isn't great but we could work something out, say a candy bar to start?" He handed Daquan a broom. Watching the boy sweep, Sam's eyes met Brad's eyes. They gave each other a wink and a small smile. Brad knew his job here was coming to an end.

In the corner of the of the waiting room, away from all the commotion, a gentle purring came from inside a cardboard box. A small girl with braided black hair peeked into the box, where she saw the sleek black cat with a long thin tail and new-born kittens at her belly.

Editor's Conclusion

Wow. If nothing else, then the above collected short stories should remove any impression that you may have had that law students, lawyers, and law professors are staid and stale thinkers. To the contrary, those whom the law attracts often have a fascination for all things social, human, and real. Lawyers do not wear rose-colored glasses. We deal with the real and, by extension, how the real relates to the unreal. Lawyers must know not only their clients' realities but also the illusions under which and through which their clients deal. Lawyers must know both the possible and impossible, the authentic along with the imagined. Indeed, lawyers depend on their ability to distinguish the comedic from the dramatic, the ordinary from the extraordinary, and the common from the holy. Lawyers must at once have a sense of both the profound and prosaic, seeing the possibility of order in a definitively disordered world. When lawyers tell stories, they engage in what one of our workshop participants Anna Rapa, who practices federal defense, calls their *sacred task*, humanizing participants in a dehumanizing justice system.

The above stories reveal the imaginative, creative, and yet at the same time *grounded* capacity of lawyers. The myth is that to write strong fiction, the author must live in a rich fantasy world. The opposite may well be true. To write strong fiction, the author must be especially able to differentiate between fact and fiction, to walk that fine line between the believable and arresting, the plausible but nevertheless entertaining. Clients don't hire lawyers who live in their own fantasy world. Clients instead hire lawyers who know how the authentic world works. Yet clients also hire lawyers who have appropriate literary, dramatic, comedic, and even theatrical skill. Johnnie Cochran, F. Lee Bailey, and Clarence Darrow didn't become famous trial lawyers for their buttoned-down approaches. They knew instead how to seize the moment, turning dry and barely intelligible facts into meaningful life and to some degree even into art—depending on whom you ask. With too much art, the trial lawyer loses. An advocate needs to mix indisputable fact with just the right quantity and quality of emotion, setting both within the full range of human capacity for both perfection and perversion. Persons are not saints. Their art and literature shouldn't depict them only as such, and nor should their advocates.

One also sees the broad sensitivities of the authors. Although the public might think otherwise, lawyers are not, by and large, crass. They are instead often exquisitely attuned to individuals and situations. Because lawyers make their living by reading people and their circumstances, lawyers tend to be good readers of life's subtle stimuli. A twitch of the corner of the claim representative's mouth, a very brief pause as the representative shares the settlement figure, and the lawyer knows that the offer is only about three-fourths of where the offer will soon go. Lawyers are also not greedy and materialistic, although again, the public may assume otherwise. Lawyers spend more time pulling back on their clients' reins than spurring them on. They see both sides, indeed *all* sides including the side of cosmic justice. And so, lawyers should make good story tellers, as indeed they do.

Of course, Abraham Lincoln was the greatest of lawyer storytellers, although Cicero and Aesop would also do. Some biographers construe the freed slave Aesop, if he existed, to have included lawyer-like advocacy services among his traveling offerings. The lawyer-statesman Cicero wasn't so much a storyteller as a discerning relator of historic events and a truth teller, but his dramatic skills were so compelling as to have cost him his head and hands, nailed to the Roman Senate's rostrum. In a way, Lincoln's storytelling skill also cost him his life. Lincoln told the story of a nation that did not yet exist, which would be a nation both freed of slavery and healed of its awful effects. Assassin Booth found Lincoln's vision so singularly compelling, even if in Booth's deranged sense appalling, as to end Lincoln's life, in a theater of all places. Life mimics art mimics life.

The above entries also show that good storytelling requires character, theme, and plot. If a lawyer cannot represent and depict a

276

client as an authentic individual holding genuine commitments and pursuing legitimate interests and ends, then the lawyer is not likely to be effective as the client's advocate. If a lawyer cannot portray the character of the client's adversaries, then the lawyer is not likely to be effective in advocating the justice of the client's claims. If the lawyer cannot articulate the tension in relationships, then the lawyer is not likely to be effective in resolving the client's disputes. If the lawyer cannot piece together into intelligible whole the seemingly discrete parts of a client's history and experience, then the lawyer is not likely to be able to hold the attention and gain the trust and confidence of the decisionmaker. Lawyers must know the rudiments of storytelling to be effective.

The above entries also show that good storytelling requires more than character, theme, and plot. Lawyers must be able to supply contextual detail. Clients live, think, work, and act in discrete contexts rich in detail. Unless one walks a mile in another's shoes, one has little chance of relating to the other whom the courts have called on one to judge. Justice requires exercising a degree of compassion, understanding, and affinity. Lawyers must help judges, jurors, insurers, and others *see, hear,* and *feel* what the client experiences. The devil is in the details, or more accurately, the devil works when the lawyer leaves out the details. Good storytelling involves helping the reader or listener live within the story, experiencing its smells, sounds, touches, and sights. My law school campus has helped criminal-defense lawyers reenact scenes around the charged crimes, simply to help the lawyer discover the significance of tiny details. Good storytelling evokes the senses through such detail.

The above stories also remind us that we live and work, and study and practice law, within rich and intersecting personal stories. Our lives are not a series of disconnected happenstances. Instead, our character, commitments, and pursuits shape our environments and experiences. We don't so much *tell stories* as our stories *tell us.* Even as we shape our own stories, the stories out which we live simultaneously shape us. Experience refines character, just as character builds experience. What we live makes us who we are. And so, we should *know* our stories, *tell* our stories, so that we know and to a greater degree can control or at least influence and shape how our stories shape us. Character lies somewhere between

277

genetics and environment, between biology and sociology, between organism and experience. Storytelling distinguishes humans from non-human animals. Storytelling makes us human. Storytelling also makes us divine.

I hope that you enjoyed these short stories. I also hope that you take a few more moments to review the authors' brief biographies. Every law student carries a precious ambition to weave their personal story into the stories of those around them in ways that cultivate human flourishing and promote divine glory. Every lawyer holds a precious trust, indeed has taken a precarious oath, to carry out those ambitions. Every law professor bridges the chasm from a law student's ambition to a lawyer's service. Law professors for the most part build those bridges using casebooks, treatises, learning-management systems, role plays, and Socratic examination. Sometimes, though, fiction also does the trick of setting a social servant afire with the profound possibilities of human life, aspiration, and interaction. I hope that you found something of that inspiration in the above stories.

About the Authors

Raymond Arbiter is a pseudonymous trial lawyer who in fact has practiced law for decades in state and federal trial and appellate courts. He has represented mostly individual clients, most often against corporate and government parties, and frequently in litigation over First, Fourth, Fifth, Eighth, and Fourteenth Amendment rights, and other constitutional and civil rights. His cases have included representing prisoners in cruel-and-unusual-punishment claims, citizens in excessive-force claims, and jail guards in civil and employment-rights claims against state and local government. He has also represented lawyers defending bar-official efforts to suspend rights of law practice. He also writes and publishes in defense of common-law and natural rights of justice, against overreaching central commands.

Curt Benson is a senior emeritus law professor at Western Michigan University Thomas M. Cooley Law School and a longtime practitioner with substantial experience in both civil and criminal cases, with a specialty in arson and other insurance cases. His longtime law teaching has primarily been in the subjects of evidence and civil procedure. He has also long co-hosted a syndicated radio show *The Lawyers*. As a trial lawyer and radio host, Professor Benson is an accomplished storyteller, as was his esteemed father, a longtime circuit-court judge. His one great unfilled ambition remains, like so many other trial lawyers, to write the next great lawyer novel.

Mark Cooney is a longtime law professor at Western Michigan University Thomas M. Cooley Law School, teaching research and writing courses while leading the school's writing department. Professor Cooney is the author of the acclaimed book *Sketches on Legal Style* and many articles on legal writing, notably as a frequent contributor to the Michigan Bar Journal's Plain Language column. He is also the editor in chief of *The Scribes Journal of Legal Writing*, has chaired the State Bar of Michigan's Appellate Practice Section, and served as a plain-language consultant for the State Bar's Standing Committee on Standard Criminal Jury Instructions. An award-winning legal writer, Professor Cooney frequently moderates programs on legal writing. Before joining the school's law faculty, Professor Cooney practiced civil litigation for ten years, defending medical-malpractice and other tort cases.

Bart Demeter is a graduate of Western Michigan University Thomas M. Cooley Law School. After law school, he turned his attention to education, serving as an instructor and a dean. He also produced several curricula for national educational publishers. Before law school, he operated an independent paralegal real estate service for fifteen years. In that time, he and his staff performed title searches in five states and more than one-hundred-and-fifty counties. Currently, he is a college professor teaching writing, college success, and legal courses. Additionally, he is developing a series of websites and companion books designed to aid students and new job seekers. He also serves on the Campfire / 4C of West Michigan board of directors.

Christine Doxey is a third-year law student at Western Michigan University Thomas M. Cooley Law School who held a real-estate license and had substantial real-estate experience before beginning her law studies. She expects to enter a general law practice that includes real-property transactions and litigation, drawing on her prior experience. Her husband, also a law student after retiring from the postal service, has similar real-estate experience and law-practice interests, such that Christine and her husband may practice law together or join firms where they can draw on their experiences in the real-estate field to build private transactional practices.

Emily Dykhuizen is a third-year law student at Western Michigan University Thomas M. Cooley Law School who has served as a judicial law clerk, plans on completing a master's degree in homeland-security law in addition to her juris-doctor degree, and would like to work in prosecution or other roles for federal or state government. Even while completing law school on an accelerated schedule, Emily runs a home business, cares for her husband and young children, and remains an avid reader and writer. Emily loves storytelling, for which she has an obvious gift.

Grace Epstein is a pseudonymous law dean who has served her school in that capacity for over a decade. She was a professor before becoming a dean and a practitioner before becoming a professor. She published many articles, most of them on doctrinal law subjects, while in law practice, which helped lead her to teaching. She has also served her state bar in various elected and appointed roles, both while a practitioner and since joining her law school. Her spouse is not connected with the law, but one of their adult children is a lawyer in practice. She hopes to find more time to write fiction, having enjoyed crafting a story about law school and the bar exam that, for most students, follows it.

Victoria Faustin is a third-year law student at Western Michigan University Thomas M. Cooley Law School. Her mother, a firm believer in always giving back no matter what the world hands you, named Victoria after the courageous Christian song *Victory is Mine*. Victoria grew up helping her mother serve the sick and shut-in, putting smiles on their faces with home-cooked meals and a story that would make them laugh and ponder. She also regularly visited nursing homes with her family to fill the lonely and sad with joyful songs and hope-filled scripture. Victoria strives to carry on her mother's spirit and the virtues she has instilled in her. Victoria's hope is that the seeds of love and service that her mother planted in her will blossom to benefit the community as a human-rights attorney.

Mo Fawaz is a Michigan-licensed lawyer holding a paralegal position at a governmental agency in the Washington, D.C. area. He works in the field of labor and employment law. As a law student, he interned at the Access to Justice Clinic at Western Michigan University Thomas M. Cooley Law School, representing the underserved in family law matters. He then did a law school internship at the Equal Employment Opportunity Commission in Dallas, Texas, before moving to the D.C. area to work for the government. His short story puts the drama and stress of family law practice in a comic perspective. In addition to his law degree, he holds a bachelor's degree in creative writing.

Malik Fiobehr is a pseudonymous senior lawyer who in fact has solo and small firm, individual and corporate, and government and institutional, practice experience. He has created and participated in mentor programs for new lawyers, and participates in and promotes pro bono practice including through the American Bar Association's Law Practice Management section. He writes for publication on law-practice management matters including personal and law-firm finances, design and marketing of law products and services, and business development. He also speaks at lawyer conferences on mentoring and professionalism including through the American Inns of Court. He remains active in the local and statewide bars.

Sylvia C. Herald is a pseudonymous general practitioner who includes in her suburban-metropolitan practice the representation of individuals injured in motor-vehicle accidents. While having maintained a functional office in an elegant mixed retail-office destination facility, she often travels around her metropolitan region meeting with her consumer and mostly middle-class clients at residences, coffee shops, conference facilities, medical-care facilities, and other locations more convenient to them. Prompt service and transparent communication are her mixed practice's hallmark attributes, pursued and perfected through innovative technology and disciplined management practices. She writes and occasionally speaks at professional conferences on practice-management issues.

Kris Johnson is a law student at Western Michigan University Thomas M. Cooley Law School. A former high school English teacher and marketing professional in the book-publishing industry, Kris decided to attend law school after she trained as a Michigan general civil mediator in 2015. She is an honors scholarship recipient who represents the law school on its National Mock Trial Team and has served her campus as a teaching assistant, the Mock Trial Competition chair, and a mentor for new students. She resides in Grand Rapids, Michigan, with her husband and four children.

Tonya Krause-Phelan is a law professor and auxiliary dean at Western Michigan University Thomas M. Cooley Law School, where she teaches Criminal Law, Criminal Procedure, Defending Battered Women, Criminal Sentencing, and Ethics in Criminal Cases. She also co-directs the Public Defender Clinic, teaches trial-advocacy skills, and coaches national trial-competition teams at the law school. Before joining the law school, Dean Krause-Phelan represented individuals charged with serious crimes, including homicide crimes, both in private practice and as an assistant public defender. She also speaks frequently at conferences and events, and to the media, on matters relating to the criminal justice system, has trained other trial lawyers in advocacy programs, and edited practitioner journals relating to criminal defense.

Matthew J. Levin, currently a student at Western Michigan University Thomas M. Cooley Law School, has published two fiction books *Sine Die* and *Unequal Protection* on legislative politics and many short stories on a wide range of subjects. His career has included legislative-staff and nonprofit-leadership positions with an emphasis on policy development. He has won multiple Certificates of Merit as the top student in his courses, serves his law school as a teaching assistant, and helped to develop and implement the storytelling workshops that led to this publication. He is considering re-entering government work in policy development after graduation and licensure.

Emily Mugerian Maltby is a law student at Western Michigan University Thomas M. Cooley Law School. After graduating from Michigan State University with a bachelor's degree in human biology she continued her studies with a master's degree in healthcare management with a focus on geriatrics. Emily did private dementia care before becoming the Director of Memory Care at an assisted-living facility, where she worked with residents and families during the difficult time of diagnosis, placement, and disease progression. Many residents and families did not have proper legal documents in place, sparking Emily's interest in elder law. She hopes to assist families with wills, trusts, estate plans, and asset protection, and to provide other law counseling and services. Emily is a volunteer with the Alzheimer's Association and co-facilitates a monthly support group for the caregivers of individuals affected by early-onset Alzheimer's disease. Emily is married and recently had a baby girl.

Pinkston Maraud is a pseudonymous transactional lawyer who in fact has for many years made a practice of business, nonprofit, and estate matters. He has served mostly middle-class, individual clients who own small businesses or are professionals in a variety of fields including medicine, nursing, accounting, education, publication, and engineering. He has referred worker's compensation, personal-injury, and other matters to other lawyers while accepting referrals within his own fields. While his own health remains good, he has known lawyers facing serious mental and physical health issues, including terminal illness, and has assisted some of those lawyers in transitioning out of their law practices. He has also supported lawyers in character-and-fitness matters.

Tipler McGee is a pseudonymous insurance defense lawyer whose practice has included defense of products makers, physicians, hospitals, transportation companies, landowners, and others alleged to have caused injury or property damage. He has tried cases to juries in the state and federal courts. He speaks and writes for his state's continuing-legal-education institute and occasionally publishes writings for practitioners, in insurance and defense journals. He likes making opening statements and closing arguments, and conducting direct and cross-examinations, but admits not caring much for jury voir dire, where, he says, one is less in control. He hates taking verdicts, despite having generally done well.

Nelson P. Miller is a professor and associate dean at Western Michigan University Thomas M. Cooley Law School. Before joining WMU-Cooley, Dean Miller practiced civil litigation for 16 years in a small-firm setting, representing individuals, corporations, agencies, and public and private universities. He has published thirty-seven books and dozens of book chapters and articles on law, law school, and law practice. The State Bar of Michigan recognized Dean Miller with the John W. Cummiskey Award for pro-bono service, while the law school recognized him with its Great Deeds award for similar service. He was also among about two dozen law professors recognized nationally in the Harvard University Press study and book *What the Best Law Teachers Do.*

Sarah Rae Miller is a third-year lawyer practicing mostly municipal and transactional law at a West Michigan-lakeshore mid-sized law firm that serves government, corporate, small-business, and individual clients. She also maintains a teacher's certification, teaches school part time, and has served her Western Michigan University Thomas M. Cooley Law School as an adjunct professor teaching Scholarly Writing. She is a winner of her law school's Great

284

Deeds Award for volunteer and pro bono service and is active in divorce care for children, at-risk-youth mentoring, and children's faith education, among other volunteer, community, and service activities.

Mona Moss-Keegan is a pseudonymous probate lawyer who has substantial experience in guardianship, conservatorship, and other family law and probate matters. She practices almost exclusively in the state courts on a range of individual and family matters, in part on planning matters but especially around crises in health, finances, and relationships. She has often been in hearings in the general trial, family, and probate divisions of her local court and handles occasional appeals from those courts. She also serves on the boards of nonprofit organizations advocating for the benefit of the elderly, underprivileged, and under-served, and for legal-services organizations serving the same populations. She writes frequently for law practitioner publications and occasionally includes fiction works.

Sam Preston is a pseudonymous civil-rights lawyer committed to achieving full recognition of the rights of all Michigan citizens through impact legislation, education, and public policy. His solo practice specializes in workplace rights and employment law. He is also a licensed private investigator under Michigan law. He believes that integrity, authenticity, and humility are the key ingredients to a successful law practice. He is active in the West Michigan nonprofit community, serving as a board member for several organizations. He has advocated tirelessly for diversification of these boards—with little success to date. His husband, a Major League Baseball player, made the All-Star team this year for the first time.

Lizz Robinson is a law student whose first formative memories are having her father read to her each night after dinner. She and her sisters would gather at his feet after cleaning up, to hear one chapter of stories starting with J.R.R. Tolkien, through C.S. Lewis, and ending with J.K. Rowling. Her family also often took long road trips, during which her mother would tell fantastic stories from her imagination, keeping Lizz both occupied and fascinated. With such creative parents, one could say that she was born to love storytelling. She anticipates putting her own storytelling expertise to the test in law practice.

Shelley Stein is a pseudonymous divorce lawyer who has decades of experience practicing in the family and probate divisions of state courts, including both trial and appellate work. She frequently publishes fiction and non-fiction works in book, article, and blog form, both law-related and unrelated to law. Her law publications include business development, professional ethics, and finances of law practice. She also gives frequent radio, television, print, and electronic-media interviews on current law issues in her field and on law practice and legal ethics, and speaks nationally at law conferences, while also serving on state- and local-bar boards and committees.

David Tarrien is a professor and auxiliary dean at Western Michigan University Thomas M. Cooley Law School, teaching writing and doctrinal courses, providing academic support, and helping to administer campus programs. He first practiced law handling matters involving educational and disability rights, before joining the law school about a decade and a half ago. Revered among students for his sensitivity to the academic challenges that law school presents, he organizes and sponsors a student chess club, advises student organizations, leads students in programs to teach parents educational rights for their children, and is the calm hand on the unsteady tiller of students at academic risk. He also instructs and mentors students who are considering law school.

Samuel J. Tosca is a pseudonymous personal-injury lawyer whose motion and trial practice has included a few police excessive-force cases. He has more-often handled motor-vehicle no-fault, medical-malpractice, products-liability, and other physical injury and wrongful-death cases mostly in the state courts, in solo and small-firm employment. When not practicing law, he enjoys exercising, walking dogs, reading, and writing for pleasure, and family and community life. He also serves local faith and charitable organizations both in law matters and through other volunteer activities. His lifelong ambition has been to write fiction, fulfilled in part here.

Priscilla Van Ost is a pseudonymous civil litigator who has taken business-breakup and other commercial-litigation cases on referral from transactional lawyers and former clients. Her skills include not only trial and pretrial-motion practice but also negotiation, mediation, arbitration, and related alternative dispute resolution, with which she has decades of practical experience. She has been a case evaluator in multiple counties and a state-certified mediator. She has based her practice in suburban and small-town locations, serving primarily a consumer, small-business, and homeowner client population. She does not generally take family law matters but agrees with the editor's introduction that business breakups can be just as difficult and emotional.

Graham Ward, a happily married veteran with adult sons of whom he is rightly proud, no longer practices civil litigation after a long and successful career at a major firm. He instead keeps an active hand teaching negotiation, mediation, and other dispute-resolution courses as an adjunct professor at Western Michigan University Thomas M. Cooley Law School. A council member of the State Bar of Michigan's Alternative Dispute Resolution Section, Professor Ward also speaks frequently on decision-making and dispute resolution in other undergraduate and graduate courses at Western Michigan University, while collaborating across disciplines on research and service projects, and in co-curricular activities.

CPSIA information can be obtained
at www.ICGtesting.com
Printed in the USA
BVHW041150250422
635251BV00006B/50